ELIF BATUMAN

The Possessed

ELIF BATUMAN was born in New York City and grew up in New Jersey. She now lives in San Francisco. She is the recipient of a Rona Jaffe Foundation Writers' Award. She teaches at Stanford University.

For more information about Elif Batuman and *The Possessed*, visit her website at www.elifbatuman.com.

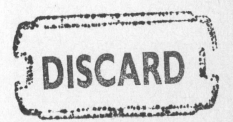

The Possessed

The Possessed

ADVENTURES WITH RUSSIAN BOOKS

AND THE PEOPLE WHO READ THEM

Elif Batuman

FARRAR, STRAUS AND GIROUX   NEW YORK

Farrar, Straus and Giroux
18 West 18th Street, New York 10011

Copyright © 2010 by Elif Batuman
All rights reserved
Distributed in Canada by D&M Publishers, Inc.
Printed in the United States of America
First edition, 2010

Some of these essays have appeared, in slightly different form, in *Harper's
Magazine*, *n+1*, and *The New Yorker*.

Library of Congress Cataloging-in-Publication Data
Batuman, Elif, 1977–
    The possessed : adventures with Russian books and the people who read
them / Elif Batuman.— 1st ed.
        p.   cm.
    ISBN 978-0-374-53218-5 (pbk. : alk. paper)
    1. Russian literature—Appreciation.   I. Title.

PG2986 .B33 2010
891.7'09—dc22

                                                            2009025416

Designed by Jonathan D. Lippincott

www.fsgbooks.com

3   5   7   9   10   8   6   4

Contents

The Possessed

Introduction

In Thomas Mann's *Magic Mountain*, a young man named Hans Castorp arrives at a Swiss sanatorium to visit his tubercular cousin for three weeks. Although Castorp himself does not have tuberculosis, he somehow ends up staying in that sanatorium for seven years. The plot of *The Magic Mountain* mirrors the history of its composition: Mann set out to write a short story, but ended up producing a 1,200-page novel. Despite the novel's complexity, its central question is very simple: How does someone who *doesn't actually have tuberculosis* end up spending seven years at a tuberculosis sanatorium? I often ask myself a similar question: How does someone with no real academic aspirations end up spending seven years in suburban California studying the form of the Russian novel?

In *The Magic Mountain*, it all happens because of love. While visiting his cousin, Castorp becomes infatuated with another patient: the estranged wife of a Russian officer. Her high cheekbones and her gray-blue "Kirghiz-shaped eyes" recall to him a childhood fascination with Slavicness—specifically, with an idolized older boy at school, from whom the hero once, in the happiest moment of his life, borrowed a pencil. The Russian lady's eyes, in particular, "amazingly and frighteningly resemble" those of this schoolboy; indeed, Mann emends, " 'resembled' was not the right word—they were the same eyes." Under their mesmerizing influence, Castorp is seized by a passion to learn about samovars, Cossacks, and the Russian language, colorfully characterized by Mann as "the muddy, barbaric, boneless tongue from the East." One afternoon, Castorp attends a lecture titled "Love as a Pathogenic Force," in which the sanatorium psychoanalyst diagnoses his entire audience as so many victims of love: "Symptoms of disease are nothing but a disguised manifestation of the power of love; and all disease is only love transformed." Castorp recognizes the truth of this lecture. He ends up so terribly in love with the married Russian woman that he develops a fever and appears to have a damp spot on one of his lungs. This real or imagined damp spot, combined with the hope of glimpsing his beloved at mealtimes, is what keeps him on the Magic Mountain.

Of course, there are many differences between my story and that of Hans Castorp. But there are also similarities. The seven years I ended up spending in the Stanford comparative literature department were also a matter of love, and fascination with Russianness. This love was also prefigured during my schooldays by a chance encounter with a Russian person, and developed in an institutional setting.

The first Russian person I ever met was my teacher at the Manhattan School of Music, where I studied the violin on Saturdays. Maxim wore black turtlenecks, played a mellow-toned, orange-colored violin, and produced an impression of being deeply absorbed by considerations and calculations beyond the normal range of human cognition. Toward the end of one lesson, for example, he told me that he had to leave ten minutes early—and then proceeded to spend the *entire ten minutes* unraveling the tortuous logic of how his early departure wasn't actually depriving me of any violin instruction. "Tell me, Elif," he shouted, having worked himself up to an almost amazing degree. "When you buy a dress, do you buy the dress that is the most beautiful . . . or the dress that is made with the most cloth?"

Another time, Maxim instructed me to listen to a particular Soviet recording of the Mozart violin concerti. Sitting in a wooden library carrel, I listened to all five concerti in a row: a fluid, elegant performance, with passages of singing intensity through which one seemed to glimpse the whole cosmic pathos of Mozart's life on earth. But as I listened, I found myself distracted by the CD case, by the slightly blurred three-quarters photograph of the soloist, who looked *literally indistinguishable* from my violin teacher. The stiff posture, the downturned mouth, the intent and melancholy eyebrows—everything was the same. His name was even Maxim, although he had a different surname.

The following week, Maxim specifically asked whether I had noticed anything unusual about the violinist.

"Like what?" I asked.

"Well, let's say, his appearance. In Moscow, at the conservatory, people used to say that he and I looked alike . . . very much alike. More than the brothers."

"Actually, yeah—I did sort of notice that from the photograph."

At this innocuous remark, an expression of gloom descended upon him, as abruptly as if someone had dropped a black cloth over his head. "It's nothing, nothing," he said, sounding almost angry.

Probably the strangest episode with Maxim involved the yearly juried examinations at the music school. In the weeks before the exams, Maxim was constantly changing his mind about which études and scales I should prepare, even telephoning me once in the middle of the night to announce a change in plan. "We have to be very well prepared because we do not know who is on this jury," he kept saying. "We do not know what they will ask you to play. We can guess, of course, but we cannot know."

When the day of the juries came, I was called into the examination room, with its grand piano and long table, at the head of which, presiding over two more junior faculty members, sat not some unknown judge, but *Maxim himself.*

"Hello, Elif," he said pleasantly.

Such mystifications can have a very strong effect on young people, and this one was compounded by the circumstance that I had just read *Eugene Onegin,* and had been particularly moved by Tatyana's dream: the famous sequence in which Pushkin's heroine finds herself crossing a snowy plain, "surrounded by sad murk," and pursued by a bear. The bear scoops her up and Tatyana loses consciousness, waking up as the bear deposits her at the end of a hallway where she hears cries and the clink of glasses, "as if at some big funeral." Through a crack in the door she sees a long table surrounded by reveling monsters—a dancing windmill, a half crane, a half cat— presided over, as she realizes with inexplicable horror, by none other than Eugene Onegin.

Tatyana's dream is fulfilled in waking life at her name-day party: an ill-fated event during which Onegin, motivated apparently by nothing but boredom, breaks Tatyana's heart and fatally quarrels with his young friend Lensky. (By the time Onegin falls in love with Tatyana, years later in Moscow, it's too late. She still loves him but is married to an old general.) I read *Onegin* in Nabokov's English edition, and was greatly struck by his note that the language of the dream not only contains "echoes of rhythms and terms" from Tatyana's experiences earlier in the book, but also foreshadows the future: "a certain dreamlike quality is carried on to the name-day party and later to the duel." The guests at Tatyana's party and at the balls in Moscow, Nabokov writes, "are benightmared and foreshadowed by the fairy-tale ghouls and hybrid monsters in her dream."

To me it seemed that the violin jury had also been benightmared and foreshadowed by Tatyana's dream, and that some hidden portent was borne by Maxim's apparition at their head.

If this incident didn't immediately send me looking to Maxim's national literature for answers, it was nonetheless at the back of my mind that summer when I discovered a 1970s Penguin edition of *Anna Karenina* in my grandmother's apartment in Ankara. I had run out of English books, and was especially happy to find one that was so long. Think of the time it must have taken for Tolstoy to write it! He hadn't been ashamed to spend his time that way, rather than relaxing by playing Frisbee or attending a barbecue. Nobody in *Anna Karenina* was oppressed, as I was, by the tyranny of leisure. The leisure activities in Tolstoy's novel—ice skating, balls, horse races—were beautiful, dignified, and meaningful in terms of plot.

I spent the next two weeks flopped on my grandmother's super-bourgeois rose-colored velvet sofa, consuming massive quantities of grapes, reading obsessively. *Anna Karenina* seemed to pick up exactly where *Onegin* left off, in the same world, as if the people in the opera house were also benightmared by Tatyana's dream, whose atmosphere had already seeped into Anna's experiences at the horse races and on the snowbound train. It was the same world, the same air, only everything was bigger—as if a minutely detailed dollhouse had been transformed into a real house with long hallways, shining fixtures, a rambling garden. Elements from *Onegin* reappeared: a snowy dream, a fatal ball, a revolver, a bear. It was as if all of *Onegin* had been dreamed by Anna, who in her own life fulfilled Tatyana's unresolved fate.[*]

Anna Karenina was a perfect book, with an otherworldly perfection: unthinkable, monolithic, occupying a supercharged gray zone between nature and culture. How had any human being ever managed to write something simultaneously so big and so small—so serious and so light—so strange and so natural? The heroine didn't turn up until chapter 18, and the book went on for nineteen more chapters after her death, and Anna's lover and her husband had the same first name (Alexei). Anna's maid and daughter were both called Anna, and Anna's son and Levin's half brother were both Sergei. The repetition of names struck me as remarkable, surprising, and true to life.

My mother was happy to see me reading what turned out to be her old copy of *Anna Karenina*. "Now you can tell me what it really means!" she said. My mother often asked me to tell her what things really meant: books, movies, things people said to her at work. (She worked at the SUNY Downstate Medical Center, where people seemed to make particularly inscrutable remarks.) The pretext for these questions was that I am a native English speaker and she isn't. Actually, my mother studied from early childhood at an American school in Ankara and speaks beautiful English, and I remember only one time that her question was to any extent resolved by my telling her

---

[*]The Formalist critic Boris Eikhenbaum expresses this idea in *Tolstoy in the Seventies*, characterizing *Anna Karenina* as "a continuation of *Eugene Onegin*," and Anna as "a kind of reincarnation of Tatyana."

the literal meaning of an English phrase. (The phrase was "Knock yourself out.") In all other instances—and, in fact, also in that instance—"What does that really mean?" itself really meant something like: "What underlying attitude toward me, or toward people like me, is represented by these words?" My mother believed that people harbored essential stances of like or dislike toward others, and betrayed these stances in their words and actions. If you came out looking terrible in a photograph, it was a sign that the person who took it didn't really like you.

"So what did it all mean?" my mother asked, when I had finished *Anna Karenina*. "What was Tolstoy trying to say? Did Vronsky just not really love Anna?"

We were in the kitchen in Ankara, a city with an anagrammatic relationship to *Anna Karenina*, drinking what Turkish people call "Turkish tea": very strong, sugary Lipton, served in little tulip-shaped glasses.

I said that I thought Vronsky had really loved Anna.

"He couldn't have loved her enough, or she wouldn't have killed herself. It just wouldn't have happened." My mother's theory was that the double plot in *Anna Karenina* represents the two kinds of men in the world: those who really like women, and those who don't. Vronsky, a man who really liked women, overwhelmed Anna and was overwhelmed by her—but some part of him was never committed to her in the way that Levin, a man who essentially did not like women, was committed to Kitty.

"That kind of makes sense," I admitted.

"Is Tolstoy saying that it's better for women to be with men like Levin? Kitty made the right choice, and Anna made the wrong choice, right?"

"I don't know," I said. I really didn't know. Looking back, by that point I had already acquired certain ideas about literature. I believed that it "really meant" something, and that this meaning was dependent on linguistic competence, on the Chomskians' iron law: "The intuitions of a native speaker." ("*You* really speak English," my mother would say admiringly, in our conversations about books.) That's probably why I decided to study linguistics when I got to college; it didn't even occur to me to study literature. I remember believing firmly that the best novels drew their material and inspiration exclusively from life, and not from other novels, and that, as an aspiring novelist, I should therefore try not to read too many novels.

I was also uninterested by what I knew of literary theory and history. It was a received idea in those days that "theory" was bad for writers, infecting them with a hostility toward language and making them turn out postmodern; and what did it have to offer, anyway, besides the reduction of a novel to a set of unpleasant facts about power structures, or the superficial thrill of juxtaposing *Pride and Prejudice* with the uncertainty principle? As for history, it struck me as pedantic, unambitious. Why all that trouble to prove things that nobody would ever dispute in the first place, like that an earlier author had influenced a later author?

In fact I had no historical consciousness in those days, and no interest in acquiring one. It struck me as narrow-minded to privilege historical events, simply because things happened to have worked out that way. Why be a slave to the arbitrary truth? I didn't care about truth; I cared about beauty. It took me many years—it took the experience of lived time—to realize that they really are the same thing.

In the meantime I became a linguistics major. I wanted to learn the raw mechanism of language, the pure form itself. For the foreign language requirement, I enrolled in beginning Russian: maybe someday I could tell my mother what Tolstoy really meant.

The nail in the coffin of my brief career as a linguist was probably a seminar I took that winter about the philosophy of language. The aim of this seminar was to formulate a theory that would explain to a Martian "what it is that we know when we know a language." I could not imagine a more objectless, melancholy project. The solution turned out to consist of a series of propositions having the form " 'Snow is white' is true iff snow is white." The professor, a gaunt logician with a wild mane of red hair and a deep concern about Martians, wrote this sentence on the board during nearly every class, and we would discuss why it wasn't trivial. Outside the window, snow piled deeper and deeper. *You Martians who so love form and logic—what are you doing here, so far from home?*

By contrast with the philosophy of language and my other classes in psycholinguistics, syntax, and phonetics, beginning Russian struck me as profoundly human. I had expected linguistics (the general study of language) to resemble a story, and Russian (the study of a particular language) to resemble a set of rules, but the reality was just the opposite. For the first several months of Russian class, we studied an ingenious text called "The Story of Vera." It opened with Vera, a physics graduate student, going to visit her boyfriend and classmate, Ivan. Ivan wasn't home—he had left a note saying, "Forget me." "Why did we never understand him?" Ivan's father sighed, and slammed the door in Vera's face. These initial installments used an amazingly small vocabulary and grammar. As the story progressed, details of the plot were filled in, along with the missing cases and tenses, so that knowledge was accompanied by the means of its expression. In this way, introductory Russian manifested itself to me as a perfect language, in which form was an ideal reflection of content.

As it turned out, Ivan had fled to Siberia to work in the lab of his estranged uncle, and somehow got married there.

Vera followed him, and fell in love with another physicist, whom she met in a taxi at the Novosibirsk airport. In the last chapter, Vera went to a physics conference and presented a paper, which was received as "the very latest word in physics." Ivan, who was also at the conference, congratulated her and seemed ready to offer some explanation of his actions, but Vera didn't care anymore.

Tatyana and Onegin, Anna and Vronsky, Ivan and Vera: at every step, the riddle of human behavior and the nature of love appeared bound up with Russian. This association was further strengthened when I myself fell in love with one of my classmates from Russian class, a math major who had briefly studied Russian as a child behind the Iron Curtain. His Russian name was Valya, which was close to his Hungarian name. He was a senior, and was going to spend the summer in Budapest before heading to Berkeley for graduate school. I was only a freshman, so clearly, after June, we were never going to see each other again—except that then he somehow got me a summer job with a philanthropic organization that sent American college students to teach English in Hungarian villages.

There was something mysterious and absent about Valya, and in fact it turned out that, like Ivan in the story from Russian class, he also had a girlfriend about whom I knew nothing, and whom he eventually married. By the time this mystery was revealed to me, it was too late not to go to the Hungarian village, so I went. But, like Tatyana reading the manual of dream interpretation, I was already aware of something somewhere portending "a multitude of sad adventures."

In the village of Kál, I was hosted by an extremely kind family who drove me to see all the local historic sites, most of which commemorated victories over the Ottoman invaders. I taught English for seven hours a day, which proved to be interesting but exhausting work. I didn't call Valya at all for the first two weeks. In the third week the village sent me to a children's camp at a beautiful historic town on the Danube. All the female staff slept in a single cabin: me, a young English teacher, and five gym teachers. Unknown parties had strongly impressed upon the camp organizers that I, as an American, ate nothing but corn and watermelon. Every day they brought me cans and cans of corn, and nearly a whole watermelon, which I ate alone in the cabin. In the absence of any formal duties I was pursued in their every free minute by a group of tiny, indefatigable Hungarian girls, who gently demanded that I play badminton with them and braid their hair.

I was surviving this all OK until Saturday evening, when the gym teachers organized a special entertainment: a boys' leg contest.

"The American girl will judge the leg contest!" they announced. I was still hoping that I had misunderstood them, even as German techno music was turned on and all the boys in the camp, ages eight to fourteen, were paraded out behind a screen that hid their bodies from the waist up; identifying numbers had been pinned to their shorts. I was given a clipboard with a form on which to rate their legs on a scale from one to ten. Gripped by panic, I stared at the clipboard. Nothing in either my life experience or my studies had prepared me to judge an adolescent boys' leg contest. Finally the English teacher, who appeared to understand my predicament, whispered to me some scores of her own devising, and I wrote them on the form as if I had thought of them myself.

The next day, Sunday, I was alone in the cabin reading when someone came crashing through the door. It was the winner of the boys' leg contest, a fourteen-year-old daredevil named Gábor, his prizewinning left leg covered in blood.

"Can you help me?" he asked, handing me a first aid kit. Closer inspection revealed a long, jagged gash on his knee. I had opened the first aid kit and successfully identified a bottle of iodine when we were joined by two of the gym teachers.

"Lukács Gábor, you leave the American alone!" they shouted and, steering the boy away, disinfected and bandaged his knee in a visibly efficient fashion. The English teacher appeared at my side: "He wants something from you," she said darkly.

During the lunch hour, as soon as they had brought me my watermelon, I slipped away to the commuter rail station, bought a phone card, and called Valya's parents' house in Budapest. Valya asked where I was. Two hours later, he and his mother drove up in his mother's Opel, with a canoe tied to the roof. His mother thought it would be fun for us to go canoeing on the Danube. She drove back in the car, and we actually paddled that canoe all the way back to Budapest, which took more than seven hours. All around us, towering sixteen-wheel trucks glided by on barges. Apparently it was illegal for the trucks to drive on the streets on Sundays.

In Budapest, having missed the docking place, we ended up moored in a swamp. Valya dragged the canoe aground, helped me out, and then went to find a pay phone. I was supposed to stay with the canoe.

"I should be back in fifteen or twenty minutes," he said.

The sun sank behind some prehistoric-looking vegetation, and a liquid blueness descended upon the world. Valya was gone for two hours, which I spent guarding the canoe—from whom? By what means? Noticing a willow nearby, I entertained and dismissed the idea of concealing the canoe with willow branches. As it happened, the only sentient beings I saw in the whole two hours were a man with four goats, none of whom evinced any interest in either me or the canoe, and two policemen. The policemen stopped their mopeds when they saw me, and tried to question me in Hungarian. The only question I understood was whether I was homeless. "Do you have a *house*?" they said loudly, and one of them put his hands over his head in the shape of a pointed roof.

"My friend went to the telephone," I said. To my surprise, this explanation seemed to satisfy the policemen. "Good, good," they said, then got back on their mopeds and rode away.

I had just taken a pen and notebook out of my bag and was trying in the dark to write a note explaining that I was incapable of guarding the canoe anymore when I heard the approach of pounding footsteps. They grew louder and louder and then Valya flopped down to the ground beside me, out of breath, his shirt torn and muddy. He had been chased several kilometers cross-country by a wild dog. He must be the kind of man who likes women, I remember thinking.

The next afternoon, Valya drove me back to the camp, stopping at the Thai embassy to pick up his visa—he was leaving the next day for a math conference. After we said goodbye, I spent some hours wandering around the historic town, its Serbian graveyards and churches. Eventually I had to return to the campground. I was greeted at the gate by the English teacher, closely followed by the bandaged boy leg champion.

"You have been . . . *loafing*," said the English teacher accusingly.

"Your hair looks cool," Gábor said.

"No it doesn't!" snapped the English teacher.

Today this all strikes me as somehow typical of the way things happen, when you try to follow life. Events and places succeed one another like items on a shopping list. There may be interesting and moving experiences, but one thing is guaranteed: they won't naturally assume the shape of a wonderful book.

When I got back to school that fall, I couldn't face linguistics again—it had let me down, failed to reveal anything about language and what it meant. But I kept studying Russian. It seemed like the only possible place to look for an explanation for the things that had happened to me. I even signed up for an accelerated class. Two years later—without, incidentally, having read more than seven or eight novels—I found myself about to receive a degree in literature: after folklore and mythology, the major with the fewest requirements.

Among the not very numerous theoretical texts I read as a literature major, one that made a strong impression on me was Foucault's short essay on *Don Quixote* in *The Order of Things*, the one that likens the tall, skinny, weird-looking hidalgo to "a sign, a long, thin graphism, a letter that has just escaped from the open pages of a book." I immediately identified with this description because *elif*, the Turkish word for *alif* or *aleph*—the first letter of the Arabic and Hebrew alphabets—is drawn as a straight line. My parents chose this name for me because I was an unusually long and skinny baby (I was born one month early).

I thought of Foucault's essay again when I recently came across a psychological study showing that Americans tend to choose careers whose labels resemble their names. Thus the name *Dennis* is statistically overrepresented among dentists, and the ranks of geoscientists contain disproportionately high numbers of Georges and Geoffreys. The study ascribed these phenomena to "implicit egotism": the "generally positive feelings" that people have about their own names. I wonder whether some of the Dennises in dentistry school ended up there by a different motivation: the secret wish to bring arbitrary language in tune with physical reality. Maybe that's why I was drawn in by *Don Quixote*: it gave me a way to fulfill the truth of my name in the world's terms. It would be fitting, since this is the point of Foucault's essay: Don Quixote decides to prove that he is a knight just like the knights in chivalric romances, and that the world he inhabits is likewise a forum for proving heroism, and so he sets out to find—or create—resemblances between the word and the world. "Flocks, serving girls, and inns become once more the language of books to the imperceptible degree to which they resemble castles, ladies, and armies," writes Foucault.

Don Quixote, I realized, had broken the binary of life and literature. He had lived life *and* read books; he lived life *through* books, generating an even better book. Foucault, meanwhile, broke my idea of literary theory: instead of reducing complexity and beauty, he had produced it. My interest in truth came only later, but beauty had already begun to draw me into the study of literature.

My plan for after graduation was still to write a novel—but writing novels takes time, and time is expensive. I took the precaution of applying to some PhD literature programs. I did not consider getting a creative writing MFA, because I knew they made you pay tuition, and go to workshops. Whatever reservations I had about the usefulness of reading and analyzing great novels went double for reading and analyzing the writings of a bunch of kids like me. I did, however, send an application to an artists' colony on Cape Cod. To my surprise, they offered me a fiction writing fellowship, on the basis of a seventy-five-page first-person narrative I had written from the perspective of a dog.

One extremely windy and rainy day that March, I rented

a car and drove to Cape Cod, to see just what kind of outfit these people were running. The colony was located on the grounds of a prerevolutionary lumber mill. I made my way over a muddy wooden footpath to a boatlike building, where a man was making a video recording of a machine apparently designed to pour concrete onto the floor out of a vat. When I asked him where the writers were, the artist waved his hand at the window, at the teeming rain.

I located the writers in a trailer, huddled around a space heater, wearing plaid shirts and plastic-rimmed glasses. The program director, a windswept, gray-eyed local writer of romantic appearance, treated me with remarkable kindness, especially considering my status as the twenty-one-year-old author of a first-person dog novella. Nonetheless, we weren't on the same page. Our priorities and our worldviews were not synchronized.

"What will you do if you *don't* come here?" he asked. I told him I had applied to some graduate schools. There was a long pause. "Well, if you want to be an academic, go to graduate school," he said. "If you want to be a writer, come here."

I wanted to be a writer, not an academic. But that afternoon, standing under a noisy tin awning in a parking lot facing the ocean, eating the peanut-butter sandwiches I had made in the cafeteria at breakfast, I reached some conclusive state of disillusionment with the transcendentalist New England culture of "creative writing." In this culture, to which the writing workshop belonged, the academic study of literature was understood to be bad for a writer's formation. By what mechanism, I found myself wondering, was it bad? Conversely, why was it automatically good for a writer to live in a barn, reading short stories by short-story writers who didn't seem to be read by anyone other than writing students?

. . .

I turned down the writing fellowship. The director of the writing colony sent me a postcard with a photograph of a sailboat on it, wishing me luck. My boyfriend at the time, Eric, had been offered a job designing intelligent radar detectors in Silicon Valley, and I had been offered five years of funding in the comparative literature department at Stanford. We moved to California, a place I had never been before. Under rolling green hills, positrons were speeding through the world's longest linear accelerator; in towers high above the palm trees lay the complete Paris files of the Russian Imperial secret police. Stanford was essentially the opposite of a colonial New England lumber mill.

For many years, I gave little thought to the choice I had made between creative writing and literary criticism. In 2006, *n+1* magazine asked me to write about the state of the American short story, using the *Best American Short Stories* anthologies of 2004 and 2005 as data. Only then, as I turned the pages in the name of science, did I find myself remembering the emptiness I had felt on that rainy day on Cape Cod.

I remembered then the puritanical culture of creative writing, embodied by colonies and workshops and the ideal of "craft." I realized that I would greatly prefer to think of literature as a profession, an art, a science, or pretty much anything else, rather than a craft. What did craft ever try to say about the world, the human condition, or the search for meaning? All it had were its negative dictates: "Show, don't tell"; "Murder your darlings"; "Omit needless words." As if writing were a matter of overcoming bad habits—of omitting needless words.

I thought it was the dictate of craft that had pared many of the *Best American* stories to a nearly unreadable core of brisk verbs and vivid nouns—like entries in a contest to identify as many concrete entities as possible, in the fewest possible words. The first sentences were crammed with so many specificities, exceptions, subverted expectations, and minor collisions that one half expected to learn they were acrostics, or had been written without using the letter *e*. They all began in medias res. Often, they answered the "five Ws and one H."*

The premium on conciseness and concreteness made proper names a great value—so they came flying at you as if out of a tennis ball machine: Julia, Juliet, Viola, Violet, Rusty, Lefty, Carl, Carla, Carleton, Mamie, Sharee, Sharon, Rose of Sharon (a Native American), Hassan.† Each name betrayed a secret calculation, a weighing of plausibility against precision: on the one hand, John Briggs and John Hillman . . . on the other, Sybil Mildred Clemm Legrand Pascal, who invites the reader to call her Miss Sibby. On the one hand, the cat called King Spanky; on the other, the cat called Cat. In either case, the result somehow seemed false, contrived—unlike Tolstoy's double Alexeis, and unlike Chekhov's characters, many of whom didn't have names at all. In "Lady with Lapdog," Gurov's wife, Anna's husband, Gurov's crony at the club, even the lapdog, are all nameless. *No contemporary American short-story writer would have had the stamina not to name that lapdog.* They were too caught up in trying to bootstrap from a proper name to a meaningful individual essence—like the "compassionate" TV doctor who informs her colleagues: "She has a *name*."

---

*For example: "The morning after her granddaughter's frantic phone call, Lorraine skipped her usual coffee session at the Limestone Diner and drove out to the accident scene instead"; "Graves had been sick for three days when, on the long, straight highway between Mazar and Kunduz, a dark blue truck coming toward them shed its rear wheel in a spray of orange-yellow sparks."

†The *Best American* anthologies of 2004 and 2005 each included one story involving the Islamic world, each with a character called Hassan.

But names don't work that way. As Derrida once wrote, the singularity of the proper name is inextricable from its generality: it always has to be possible for one thing to be *named after* any other named thing, and for different people, like the characters in *Anna Karenina*, to be called by the same name. The basic tension of the name is that it simultaneously does and does not designate the unique individual. As someone who likes to keep to a minimum her visits to Planet Derrida—that land where all seemingly secondary phenomena are actually primary, and anything you can think of doing is an act of violence, practically by virtue of your having thought about it using some words that were also known to Aristotle—I nonetheless felt that Derrida had been right about names. More important, he had really *thought* about names, about how special they are, so that, even if *Of Grammatology* was more painful to read than the *Best American Short Stories*, still it belonged to a discourse that tried to say something about what things mean.

Moreover, even if the literary criticism discourse is no less susceptible than the creative writing workshop to charges of self-sufficiency and hermeticism, it has one crucial advantage: its fundamentally collaborative premise. Each work of criticism is supposed to build upon the existing body of work, to increase the sum total of human understanding. It's not like filling your house with more and more beautiful wicker baskets. It's supposed to be cumulative—it believes in progress.

The creative writing workshop, by contrast, *seems* to have a collaborative premise, and does indeed involve a collaborative *process*—but the signs of that process are systematically effaced from the finished product. Contemporary short stories contain virtually no reference to any interesting work being done in the field over the past twenty, fifty, or hundred years; instead, middle-class women keep struggling with kleptomania, deviant siblings keep going in and out of institutions, people continue to be upset by power outages and natural disasters, and rueful writerly types go on hesitating about things.

I don't know if I ended up siding with the academics just because I happened to end up in graduate school, or if I ended up in graduate school because I already secretly sided with the academics. In any case, I stopped believing that "theory" had the power to ruin literature for anyone, or that it was possible to compromise something you loved by studying it. Was love really such a tenuous thing? Wasn't the point of love that it made you want to learn more, to immerse yourself, to become possessed?

This isn't to say that graduate school was one long walk in the park, especially not at first. I did have the good fortune to strike an immediate friendship with one of my classmates, Luba, a Russian émigré who had grown up in Tashkent. I feel very lucky to have met such a wonderful person at that delicate point in my career. In between sessions of a seminar on an obscure school of 1920s Russian filmmakers, known for their "eccentric" use of circus paraphernalia and human-size rubber mannequins, we would take long walks around the graduate-student housing complex, invariably getting lost, and once even falling into some kind of a ditch. Like Mann's hero in his first weeks on the Magic Mountain, I thought: This can't last much longer.

In fact, between classes, conferences, teaching, and endless lunches, it became clear to me that I wasn't going to get anything but term papers written at Stanford. At the end of the year, I filed for a leave of absence and moved to San Francisco where, between odd jobs, I wrote a great deal. Nonetheless, the result somehow wasn't a novel. It didn't have a beginning or an end. It didn't seem to be telling any particular story. This was surprising and difficult for me to understand. It had occurred to me to worry in advance about writer's block, but the production of a huge non-novel just wasn't a possibility I had anticipated.

I was thinking over the problem on the evening of September 13, 2001, while running to the Golden Gate Bridge, when I tripped over some kind of plastic barrier, erected, I later learned, with the intention of protecting the bridge from terrorists. Some other joggers helped me to my feet. My arm felt very strange. I walked to the nearest hospital and spent some hours in the waiting room, where a ceiling-mounted television showed endless footage of bodies being excavated from the World Trade Center. Eventually I was admitted to the emergency room, where doctors removed the gravel from my knees, x-rayed my arm, informed me that my elbow was broken, and outfitted me with a cast and sling. The bill came to $1,700. This experience caused me to take a cold, hard look at the direction my life was headed. What was I doing, running around this world—a place about which I clearly understood nothing—with no health insurance and no real job, writing an endless novel about God knows what? A week later, the department head called and asked if I wanted to return to Stanford. I said yes.

That's when I was sucked in, deeper than I ever expected. The title of this book is borrowed from Dostoevsky's weirdest novel, *The Demons*, formerly translated as *The Possessed*, which narrates the descent into madness of a circle of intellectuals in a remote Russian province: a situation analogous, in certain ways, to my own experiences in graduate school.

When I reemerged into the real world, I thought differently about lots of things. I no longer believed that novels should or could be inspired only by life, and not by other novels. I knew now that this belief was itself a novelistic device—that it was precisely the European novel tradition, after *Don Quixote*, that gave rise to the idea of the falseness and sterility of literature, its disconnect with real life and real education.

In fact, this idea wasn't unambiguously present in *Don Quixote*. Consider the famous "book inquisition" episode, in which the priest and barber attempt to cure the knight's madness by purging his library. The received version of this episode is that Quixote's friends burn most of his books, mirroring the received message of *Don Quixote* that romances are stupid and dangerous. But if you actually keep count, you see that, of thirty books mentioned during the inquisition, only fourteen are consigned to the flames, while another fourteen are officially pardoned. This equivalence reflects the balance between life and literature in the plot—which, as Foucault observed, consists of "a diligent search over the entire surface of the earth for forms that will prove that what the books say is true." Quixote's adventures in the world, his friendship with Sancho Panza, his reconciling of sundered lovers, the entertainment he affords to countless bored Spaniards—all this, no less than the damage he causes, comes from his determination to experience life in terms of his favorite books, to bring books into the field. *Don Quixote* could only have been written by someone who really loved chivalric romances, really wanted his life to resemble them more closely, and understood just what it would cost.

Thinking about *Don Quixote*, I began to wonder about other possible methods for bringing one's life closer to one's favorite books. From Cervantes onward, the method of the novel has typically been imitation: the characters try to resemble the characters in the books they find meaningful. But what if you tried something different—what if you tried study instead of imitation, and metonymy instead of metaphor? What if, instead of going out into your neighborhood pretending to be the hero of *Amadís of Gaul*, you instead devoted your life to the mystery of its original author, learned Spanish and Portuguese, tracked down all the scholarly experts, figured out where Gaul is (most scholars think Wales or Brittany)—what if you did it all yourself, instead of inventing a fictional character? What if you wrote a book and it was all true?

What if you read *Lost Illusions* and, instead of moving to New York, living in a garret, self-publishing your poetry, writing book reviews, and having love affairs—instead of living your own version of *Lost Illusions*, in order to someday write the same novel for twenty-first-century America—what if instead you went to Balzac's house and Madame Hanska's estate, read every word he ever wrote, dug up every last thing you could about him—and *then* started writing?

That is the idea behind this book.

Babel in California

When the Russian Academy of Sciences puts together an author's *Collected Works*, they aren't aiming for something you can put in a suitcase and run away with. The "millennium" edition of Tolstoy fills a hundred volumes and weighs as much as a newborn beluga whale. (I brought my bathroom scale to the library and weighed it, ten volumes at a time.) Dostoevsky comes in thirty volumes, Turgenev in twenty-eight, Pushkin in seventeen. Even Lermontov, a lyric poet killed in a duel at age twenty-six, has four volumes. It's different in France, where definitive editions are printed on "Bible paper." The Bibliothèque de la Pléiade manages to fit Balzac's entire *Human Comedy* in twelve volumes, and his remaining writings in two volumes, for a combined total weight of eighteen pounds.

The Collected Works of Isaac Babel fills only two small volumes. Comparing Tolstoy's *Works* to Babel's is like comparing a long road to a pocket watch. Babel's best-loved works all fit in the first volume: the Odessa, Childhood, and Petersburg cycles; *Red Cavalry*; and the 1920 diary, on which *Red Cavalry* is based. The compactness makes itself felt all the more acutely, since Babel's oeuvre is known to be incomplete. When the NKVD came to his dacha in 1939, Babel's first words were, "They didn't let me finish." The secret police seized and confiscated nine folders from the dacha, and fifteen from Babel's Moscow apartment. They seized and confiscated Babel himself, on charges of spying for France and even Austria. Neither manuscripts nor writer were seen again.

In the next years, Babel's published works were removed from circulation. His name was erased from encyclopedias and film credits. Rumors circulated—Babel was in a special camp for writers, he was writing for the camp newspaper— but nobody knew for sure if he was dead or alive. In 1954, the year after Stalin's death, Babel was officially exonerated, and the dossier of his criminal case made public. Inside was just one page: a certificate attesting to his death, under unknown circumstances, on March 17, 1941. Like Sherlock Holmes in "The Adventure of the Final Problem," Babel had vanished, leaving behind a single sheet of paper.

Nobody really knows why Babel was arrested when he was. He had made powerful enemies early in his career with the publication of the *Red Cavalry* stories, which immortalize the botched Russo-Polish military campaign of 1920. In 1924, Commander Semyon Budyonny of the First Cavalry publicly accused Babel of "counterrevolutionary lies" and character assassination. In later years, as Budyonny rose in the Party system, from marshal of the Soviet Union to first deputy commissar for defense and Hero of the Soviet Union, Babel found himself on increasingly thin ice—especially after the death of his protector, Maxim Gorky, in 1936. Nonetheless, he survived the height of the Great Purge in 1937–38, and was arrested only in 1939, when World War II was just around the corner and Stalin presumably had bigger fish to fry. What tipped the scale?

The Nazi-Soviet pact might have played a role: because of Babel's close ties with the French Left, his continued existence was necessary to maintain Soviet-French diplomatic relations—

which became a moot point once Stalin sided with Hitler. Some evidence suggests that Babel was arrested in preparation for one last show trial that was to accuse the entire intellectual elite, from the film legend Sergei Eisenstein to the polar explorer Otto Schmidt, but which was called off in September when Hitler invaded Poland.

Some scholars attribute Babel's arrest to his bizarre relationship with the former people's commissar Nikolai Yezhov: Babel had had an affair in the 1920s with Evgeniya Gladun-Khayutina, Yezhov's future wife, and it was said that, even in the 1930s, Babel would visit the couple at home where they would all play ninepins and listen to Yezhov tell gruesome stories about the gulag. When Lavrenty ("Stalin's Butcher") Beria came to power in 1938, he made a point of exterminating anyone who had ever had anything to do with Yezhov.

Others insist that Babel was arrested "for no reason at all," and that to say otherwise is to commit the sin of attributing logic to the totalitarian machine.

When Babel's box in the KGB archives was declassified in the 1990s, it became known that the warrant for his arrest had been issued thirty-five days after the fact. Following seventy-two hours of continuous interrogation and probably torture, Babel had signed a confession testifying that he had been recruited into a spy network in 1927 by Ilya Ehrenburg and for years systematically supplied André Malraux with the secrets of Soviet aviation—the last detail apparently borrowed from Babel's late screenplay, *Number 4 Staraya Square* (1939), which chronicles the byzantine intrigues among scientists in a plant devoted to the construction of Soviet dirigibles.

"I am innocent. I have never been a spy," Babel says in the transcript of his twenty-minute "trial," which took place in Beria's chambers. "I accused myself falsely. I was forced to make false accusations against myself and others . . . I am asking for only one thing—let me finish my work." Babel was executed by firing squad in the basement of the Lubyanka on January 26, 1940, and his body was dumped in a communal grave. Nineteen forty, not 1941: even the death certificate had been a lie.

The first time I read Isaac Babel was in a college creative writing class. The instructor was a sympathetic Jewish novelist with a Jesus-like beard, an affinity for Russian literature, and a melancholy sense of humor, such that one afternoon he even "realized" the truth of human mortality, right there in the classroom. He pointed at each of us around the seminar table: "*You're* going to die. And *you're* going to die. And *you're* going to die." I still remember the expression on the face of one of my classmates, a genial scion of the Kennedy family who always wrote the same story, about a busy corporate lawyer who neglected his wife. The expression was confused.

In this class we were assigned to read "My First Goose," the story of a Jewish intellectual's first night at a new Red Army billet during the 1920 campaign. Immediately upon his arrival, his new comrades, illiterate Cossacks, greet him by throwing his suitcase in the street. The intellectual, noticing a goose waddling around the billet, steps on its neck, impales it on a saber, and orders the landlady to cook it for his dinner. The Cossacks then accept him as one of their own and make room for him at the fireside, where he reads them one of Lenin's speeches from a recent issue of *Pravda*.

When I first read this story in college, it made absolutely no sense to me. Why did he have to kill that goose? What was so great about sitting around a campfire, reading Lenin? Among the stories we read in that class, Chekhov's "Lady with

Lapdog" moved me much more deeply. I especially remember the passage about how everyone has two lives—one open and visible, full of work, convention, responsibilities, jokes, and the other "running its course in secret"—and how easy it is for circumstances to line up so that everything you hold most important, interesting, and meaningful is somehow in the second life, the secret one. In fact, this theme of a second, secret life is extremely important to Babel, but I didn't figure that out until later.

The second time I read Babel was in graduate school, for a seminar on literary biography. I read the 1920 diary and the entire *Red Cavalry* cycle in one sitting, on a rainy Saturday in February, while baking a Black Forest cake. As Babel immortalized for posterity the military embarrassment of the botched 1920 Russo-Polish campaign, so he immortalized for me the culinary embarrassment of this cake, which came out of the oven looking like an old hat and which, after I had optimistically treated it with half a two-dollar bottle of Kirschwasser, produced the final pansensory impression of an old hat soaked in cough syrup.

There are certain books that one remembers together with the material circumstances of reading: how long it took, the time of year, the color of the cover. Often, it's the material circumstances themselves that make you remember a book that way—but sometimes it's the other way around. I'm sure that my memory of that afternoon—the smell of rain and baking chocolate, the depressing apartment with its inflatable sofa, the sliding glass door that overlooked rainy palm trees and a Safeway parking lot—is due to the precious, almost-lost quality of Babel's 1920 diary.

The diary starts on page fifty-five—Babel lost the first

fifty-four pages. Three days later, another twenty-one pages go missing—a month's worth of entries. "Slept badly, thinking of the manuscripts," Babel writes. "Dejection, loss of energy, I know I will get over it, but when?" For the next couple of days, despite all his efforts, everything reminds him of the lost pages: "A peasant (Parfenty Melnik, the one who did his military service in Elisavetpol) complains that his horse is swollen with milk, they took away her foal, sadness, the manuscripts, the manuscripts . . ."

The diary isn't about war, but about a writer during a war—about a writer voraciously experiencing war as a source of material. Viktor Shklovsky, who invented the theory that literary subject material is always secondary to literary form, was a great admirer of Babel. "He wasn't alienated from life," Shklovsky wrote. "But it always seemed to me that Babel, when he went to bed every night, appended his signature to the day he had just lived, as if it were a story." Babel wasn't alienated from life—to the contrary, he sought it out—but he was incapable of living it otherwise than as the material for literature.

The epigraph to the 1920 diary could be the famous phrase from the beginning of *Don Quixote*: "since I'm always reading, even scraps of paper I find in the street . . ." In Brody, in the aftermath of a pogrom, while looking for oats to feed his horse, Babel stumbles upon a German bookstore: "marvelous uncut books, albums . . . a chrestomathy, the history of all the Boleslaws . . . Tetmajer, new translations, a pile of new Polish national literature, textbooks. I rummage like a madman, I run around." In a looted Polish estate, in a drawing room where horses are standing on the carpet, he discovers a chest of "extremely precious books": "the constitution approved by the Sejm at the beginning of the 18th century, old folios from the times of Nicholas I, the Polish code of laws, precious bindings, Polish manuscripts of the 16th century, writings of monks, old French novels . . . French novels on little tables, many French and Polish books about child care, smashed intimate feminine accessories, remnants of butter in a butter dish—newlyweds?" In an abandoned Polish castle, he finds "French letters dated 1820, *nôtre petit héros achève 7 semaines*. My God, who wrote it, when . . ."

These materials are assimilated and expanded upon in the *Red Cavalry* stories, for example in "Berestechko," whose narrator also finds a French letter in a Polish castle: *"Paul, mon bien aimé, on dit que l'empereur Napoléon est mort, est-ce vrai? Moi, je me sens bien, les couches ont été faciles . . ."* From the phrase *"nôtre petit héros achève 7 semaines,"* Babel conjures the full precariousness of time, a point as delicately positioned in human history as a seven-week-old child, or a false rumor of Napoleon's death.

Reading the whole *Red Cavalry* cycle after the diary, I understood "My First Goose." I understood how important it was that the suitcase thrown in the street by the Cossacks was full of manuscripts and newspapers. I understood what it meant for Babel to read Lenin aloud to the Cossacks. It was the first hostile encounter of writing with life itself. "My First Goose," like much of *Red Cavalry*, is about the price Babel paid for his literary material. Osip Mandelstam once asked Babel why he went out of his way to socialize with agents of the secret police, with people like Yezhov: "Was it a desire to see what it was like in the exclusive store where the merchandise was death? Did he just want to touch it with his fingers? 'No,' Babel replied, 'I don't want to touch it with my fingers—I just like to have a sniff and see what it smells like.'" But of course he had to touch it with his fingers. He had to shed blood with his own hands, if only that of a goose. Without that blood, *Red Cavalry* could never have been written. "It sometimes happens that I don't spare myself and spend an hour kicking the enemy, or sometimes more than an hour," observes one of Babel's narrators, a Cossack swineherd turned Red Army general. "I want to understand life, to learn what it really is."

The imperative to understand life and describe it provides an urgent, moving refrain in the 1920 diary.

"Describe the orderlies—the divisional chief of staff and the others—Cherkashin, Tarasov."

"Describe Matyazh, Misha. *Muzhiks*, I want to penetrate their souls."

Whenever Babel meets anyone, he has to fathom what he is. Always "what," not "who."

"What is Mikhail Karlovich?" "What is Zholnarkevich? A Pole? His feelings?"

"What are our soldiers?" "What are Cossacks?" "What is Bolshevism?"

"What is Kiperman? Describe his trousers."

"Describe the work of a war correspondent, what is a war correspondent?" (At the time he wrote this sentence, Babel himself was technically a war correspondent.)

Sometimes he seems to beg the question, asking, of somebody called Vinokurov: "What is this gluttonous, pitiful, tall youth, with his soft voice, droopy soul, and sharp mind?"

"What is Grishchuk? Submissiveness, endless silence, boundless indolence. Fifty *versts* from home, hasn't been home in six years, doesn't run."

"I go into the mill. What is a water mill? Describe."

"Describe the forest."

"Two emaciated horses, describe the horses."

"Describe the air, the soldiers."

"Describe the bazaar, baskets of cherries, the inside of the tavern."

"Describe this unendurable rain."

"Describe 'rapid fire.' "

"Describe the wounded."

"The intolerable desire to sleep—describe."

"Absolutely must describe limping Gubanov, scourge of the regiment."

"Describe Bakhturov, Ivan Ivanovich, and Petro."

"The castle of Count Raciborski. A seventy-year-old man and his ninety-year-old mother. People say it was always just the two of them, that they're crazy. Describe."

Babel's "describe" in his diaries shares a certain melancholy quality with Watson's mention of those of Sherlock Holmes's cases that do not appear in his annals: "the case of the Darlington substitution scandal," the "singular affair of the aluminum crutch," "the mystery of the Giant Rat of Sumatra . . . for which the world is not yet prepared." All the stories that will never be told—all the writers who were not allowed to finish! It's much more comforting to think that, in their way, the promises have already been executed—that perhaps Babel has already sufficiently described limping Gubanov, scourge of the regiment, and that the mystery of the Giant Rat of Sumatra is, after all, already the mystery of the Giant Rat of Sumatra. Babel does return to the Raciborskis in *Red Cavalry*: "A ninety-year-old countess and her son had lived in the castle. She had tormented him for not having given the dying clan any heirs, and—the *muzhiks* told me this—she used to beat him with the coachman's whip." But even with the Zolaesque note of hereditary vitiation, the Turgenevian kinkiness of the coachman's whip, and the hinted Soviet rhetoric of a knightly Poland "gone berserk" (a phrase from Babel's own propaganda work), the "description" is still just two sentences.

·   ·   ·

One of the most chilling relics to emerge from Babel's KGB dossier was the pair of mug shots taken upon his arrest in 1939.

Photographed in profile, Babel gazes into the distance, chin raised, with an expression of pained resoluteness. Photographed face-on, however, he seems to be looking at something quite close to him. He seems to be looking at someone who he knows to be on the verge of committing a terrible action. Of these images, a German historian once observed: "Both show the writer without his glasses and with one black eye, medically speaking a *monocle haematoma*, evidence of the violence used against him."

I felt sorry for the German historian. I understood that it was the inadequacy of "without his glasses and with one black eye" that drove him to use a phrase so absurd as "medically speaking a *monocle haematoma*." The absence of glasses is unspeakably violent. You need long words, Latin words, to describe it. Babel was never photographed without his glasses. He never wrote without them, either. His narrator always has, to quote a popular line from the Odessa stories, "spectacles on his nose and autumn in his heart." Another famous line, spoken by Babel's narrator to a nearsighted comrade at a beautiful Finnish winter resort: "I beg you, Alexander Fyodorovich, buy a pair of glasses!"

In "My First Goose," the Cossack divisional commander yells at the Jewish intellectual: "They send you over without asking—and here you'll get killed just for wearing glasses! So, you think you can live with us?" The glasses represent precisely Babel's determination to live with them, to watch their every move, with an attention bordering on love—to see everything and write it all down. "Everything about Babel gave an impression of all-consuming curiosity," Nadezhda Mandelstam once wrote: "the way he held his head, his mouth and chin, and particularly his eyes. It is not often that one sees such undisguised curiosity in the eyes of a grownup. I had the feeling that Babel's main driving force was the unbridled curiosity with which he scrutinized life and people." That's what they took away when they replaced his glasses with the *monocle haematoma*.

I had been persuaded to sign up for the biography seminar by one of my classmates, Matej, who knew the professor. "He's a textbook Jewish intellectual from New York," Matej said excitedly, as if describing some rare woodland creature. (Matej was a textbook Catholic intellectual from Zagreb.) "When he talks about Isaac Babel, he gets so excited that he starts to stutter. But it's not the annoying kind of stutter that obstructs understanding. It's an endearing stutter that makes you feel sympathy and affection."

At the end of the term, Matej and I had agreed to collaborate on a presentation about Babel. We met one cold, gray afternoon at a dirty metal table outside the library, where we compared notes, drank coffee, and went through nearly an entire pack of Matej's Winston Lights, which, I learned, he ordered in bulk from an Indian reservation. We settled on a general angle right away, but when it came to details, we didn't see eye to eye on anything. For nearly an hour we argued about a single sentence in "The Tachanka Theory": a story about the transformation of warfare by the *tachanka*, a wagon with a machine gun attached to the back. Once it is armed with *tachanki*, Babel writes, a Ukrainian village ceases to be a military target, because the guns can be buried under haystacks.

When it started to rain, Matej and I decided to go into the library to look up the Russian original of the sentence we disagreed about: "These hidden points—suggested, but not directly perceived—yield in their sum a construction of the new Ukrainian village: savage, rebellious, and self-seeking." Even once we had the Russian text, though, we still disagreed about the meaning of "hidden points." Rereading this story now, I can't see what we could have been debating for so long, but I remember Matej saying irritably, "You're making it sound as if he's just adding things up, like he's some kind of double-entry bookkeeper."

"That's exactly right," I snapped. "He *is* a double-entry bookkeeper!"

We concluded that we would never agree on anything because I was a materialist, whereas he had a fundamentally religious view of history. Finally we parted ways, Matej to write about Babel's replacement of old gods with a new mythology, and I to write about Babel as a bookkeeper.

"How good it is," writes Mandelstam, "that I managed to love not the priestly flame of the icon lamp but the little red flame of literary spite!" I don't know if Matej wrote his presentation in the priestly flame of the icon lamp, but I think it was literary spite that made me want to prove that Babel "was really" a bookkeeper. But, to my own surprise, it actually turned out to be true: not only did accountants and clerks keep turning up in Babel's stories, but Babel himself had been educated at the Kiev Commercial Institute, where he received top marks in general accounting. I was particularly struck by the story "Pan Apolek," in which the Polish protagonist calls the narrator "Mr. Clerk"—"*pan pisar'*" in the original. *Pan* is Polish for "sir" or "Mr.," and *pisar'* is a Russian word for "clerk." In Polish, however, *pisarz* means not "clerk," but "writer." Pan Apolek was trying to call the narrator "Mr. Writer," but the writer in the Red Cavalry turned into a clerk.

I ended up writing about the double-entry relationship in Babel's work between literature and lived experience, centering on "Pan Apolek" (the story of a village church painter who endows biblical figures with the faces of his fellow villagers: a double-entry of preexisting artistic form with observations from life). The seminar presentation went well, and I expanded upon it a few months later at a Slavic colloquium, where it caught the interest of the department Babel expert, Grisha Freidin. Freidin said he would help me revise the paper for publication—"Why would you study the gospel with anyone but St. Peter?" he demanded—and offered me a job doing research for his new critical biography of Babel.

The title of the book was fluctuating at that time between *A Jew on Horseback* and *The Other Babel*. I was fascinated by the idea of *The Other Babel*, namely, that Babel wasn't who we thought he was, or who said he was: he was some *other person*. His "Autobiography"—a document barely one and a half pages long—is full of untruths, such as his claim to have worked for the Cheka starting in October 1917, two months before the Cheka was founded, or to have fought on "the Romanian front." "Now you might think 'the Romanian front' is a joke," Freidin said. "Well, it's not, it seems it really did exist. But Babel was never there."

Babel's undocumented life was likewise full of mysteries—chief among them, why he had returned to Moscow from Paris in 1933, after having spent nearly all of 1932 struggling to get permission to go abroad. Stranger still, why, in 1935, just when the purges were starting, did Babel begin making plans to bring his mother, sister, wife, and daughter from Brussels and Paris back to the Soviet Union?

As my first research assignment, I went to the Herbert Hoover archive to look up the Russian émigré newspapers in Paris from 1934 and 1935, starting with the assassination

of Sergei Kirov, to see how much Babel's family would have
known about the purges. The newspapers hadn't been transferred to microfilm, and the originals, which had been bound
in enormous, tombstone-size books, couldn't be photocopied
because of the fragility of the paper. I sat in a corner with my
laptop, typing out the lists of people who had been shot or
sent to Siberia, typing the headlines about Kirov, and other
headlines like "Who Burned the Reichstag?" and "Bonnie
and Clyde Shot Dead." Hours slipped by and the next thing I
knew, all the lights went out. When I got up, I realized that the
entire library was not only dark but also deserted and locked.
I banged on the locked doors for a while with no result, then
felt my way through the dark to a hallway with administrative offices, where I was happy to discover a tiny Russian
woman reading a microfiche and eating lasagna from a tiny
plastic box. She seemed surprised to see me, and even more
surprised when I asked for directions on how to leave the
building.

"'Get out'?" she echoed, as if referring to the exotic custom of an unknown people. "Ah, I do not know."

"Oh," I said. "But how are *you* going to get out?"

"Me? Well, it is . . ." She glanced away, evasively. "But
I show you something." She got up from her desk, took a
flashlight from a drawer, and went back into the hallway,
motioning me to follow. We came to an emergency door with
a big sign: ALARM WILL SOUND.

"It is not locked," she said. "But behind you, it will
lock."

The alarm did not sound. I went down several flights of
steps and out another fire door, and found myself in the yellow late-afternoon sunlight, standing in a concrete well below
ground level. At the main entrance to Hoover Tower, just
around the corner, two Chinese women wearing enormous

straw hats were rapping on the door. I unlocked my bicycle and slowly rode home. I had no idea why Babel wanted his family to come back to the Soviet Union in 1935.

That month, Freidin began organizing an international Babel conference, to be held at Stanford, and I started working on an accompanying exhibit of literary materials from the Hoover archive.

The contents of the hundred-plus boxes on Babel turned out to be extremely diverse, a bit like one of those looted Polish manors: copies of *Red Cavalry* in Spanish and Hebrew; "original watercolors" of the Polish conflict, executed circa 1970; a *Big Book of Jewish Humor*, circa 1990; an issue of the avant-garde journal *LEF*, edited by Mayakovsky; *The Way They Were*, a book of childhood photographs of famous people, in alphabetical order, with a bookmark to the page where fourteen-year-old Babel in a sailor suit was facing a teenage Joan Baez. There was a book on the Cavalry Army designed by Alexander Rodchenko, with a photograph of Commander Budyonny's mother, Melaniya Nikitichna, standing outside a hut, squinting at the camera, bearing in her arms a baby goose. ("Budyonny's first goose," observed Freidin, "and Budyonny's trousers." The trousers were hanging on a clothesline in the background.)

I had also been instructed to choose two propaganda posters from 1920, one Polish and one Soviet. The exhibit coordinator took me into a labyrinthine basement, where a new collection was being indexed. On top of a bank of filing cabinets lay various posters from 1920 representing Russia as the Whore of Babylon, or as the four horsemen of the apocalypse, on horses with Lenin and Trotsky heads; one showed Christ's body lying in the postapocalyptic rubble—"This Is How All

of Poland Will Look, Once Conquered by the Bolsheviks"—
bringing to mind Babel's diary entry about "the looting of an
old church": "how many counts and serfs, magnificent Italian art, rosy Paters rocking the infant Jesus, Rembrandt . . .
It's very clear, the old gods are being destroyed."

"I'm sorry we don't have any Russian propaganda posters," the coordinator said. "I'm afraid it's a bit one-sided."

"But look," I said, noticing some Cyrillic script in the
stack. "Here is one in Russian." I drew out an enormous
poster showing a slavering bulldog wearing a king's crown:
"Majestic Poland: Last Dog of the Entente."

"Oh, sure," said the coordinator, "there are posters *in*
Russian, but they aren't pro-Bolshevik. These are all Polish
posters."

I stared at the poster, wondering why Polish people had
chosen that terrifying, wild-eyed dog as a representation of
"Majestic Poland." Then I spotted a second poster in Russian, with a picture of a round little capitalist with a mustache and a derby hat—like the Monopoly man, but holding
a whip.

" 'The Polish masters want to turn the Russian peasants
into slaves,' " I read aloud. I suggested it was difficult to interpret this as a pro-Polish poster.

The coordinator nodded enthusiastically: "Yes, these
posters are full of ambiguous imagery."

Back upstairs in the reading room, I put on my gloves—
everyone in the archive had to wear white cotton gloves, like
at Alice's mad tea party—and turned to a box of 1920 Polish
war memorabilia. My eye was caught by a single yellowed
sheet of paper with a printed Polish text signed by Commander in Chief Józef Piłsudski, July 3, 1920, beginning with
the phrase *"Obywatele Rzeczpospolitej!"* I recognized the
phrase from Babel's diary entry of July 15. He had found

a copy of this very proclamation on the ground in Belyov:
" 'We will remember you, everything will be for you, Soldiers
of the *Rzceczpospolita*!' Touching, sad, without the steel of
Bolshevik slogans . . . no words like *order*, *ideals*, and *living
in freedom*."

In *Red Cavalry*, the narrator discovers this same proclamation while accidentally urinating on a corpse in the dark:

> I switched on my flashlight . . . and saw lying on the
> ground the body of a Pole, drenched in my urine. A
> notebook and scraps of Piłsudski's proclamation lay
> next to the corpse. In the . . . notebook, his expenses,
> a list of performances at the Krakow Dramatic The-
> ater, and the birthday of a woman by the name of
> Maria-Louisa. I used the proclamation of Piłsudski,
> marshal and commander-in-chief, to wipe the stink-
> ing liquid from my unknown brother's skull, and then
> I walked on, bent under the weight of my saddle.

To think this was the very document I was holding in
my hands! I wondered whether it was really such an unlikely
coincidence. Probably thousands of copies had been printed,
so why shouldn't one of them have ended up in the archive—
it's not as if the Hoover had received the exact copy with
Babel's urine on it, although Freidin did start making jokes
to the effect that we should exhibit the proclamation "side
by side with a bottle of urine." The joke was directed at the
Hoover staff, who kept hinting that the exhibit would be
more accessible to the general community if all those books
and papers were offset by "more three-dimensional objects."
Somebody suggested we construct a diorama based on the
ending of "The Rabbi's Son," with pictures of Maimonides
and Lenin, and a phylactery. Freidin maintained that if we

included the phylactery, we would have to have "the withered genitalia of an aging Semite," which also appear at the end of the story. The diorama idea was abandoned.

Finding the Piłsudski proclamation made me realize that, even if the withered genitalia were lost to posterity, textual objects related to Babel's writings might still be uncovered. I decided to look for materials related to my favorite character in the 1920 diary, Frank Mosher, the captured American pilot whom Babel interrogates on July 14:

A shot-down American pilot, barefoot but elegant, neck like a column, dazzlingly white teeth, his uniform covered with oil and dirt. He asks me worriedly: Did I maybe commit a crime by fighting against Soviet Russia? Our position is strong. O the scent of Europe, coffee, civilization, strength, ancient culture, many thoughts. I watch him, can't let him go. A letter from Major Fauntleroy: things in Poland are bad, there's no constitution, the Bolsheviks are strong . . . An endless conversation with Mosher, I sink into the past, they'll shake you up, Mosher, ekh, Conan Doyle, letters to New York. Is Mosher fooling—he keeps asking frantically what Bolshevism is. A sad, heartwarming impression.

I loved this passage because of the mention of Conan Doyle, coffee, someone called Major Fauntleroy, and the "sad, heartwarming impression." Furthermore, "Frank Mosher" was the alias of Captain Merian Caldwell Cooper, future creator and producer of the motion picture *King Kong*. This really happened: in Galicia in July 1920, the future creator of *King Kong* was interrogated by the future creator of *Red Cavalry*. And when I looked up Merian Cooper in the library catalogue, it was like magic: Hoover turned out to hold the bulk of his papers.

Merian Cooper, I learned, was born in 1894, the same year as Babel. He served as a pilot in the First World War, commanded a squadron in the battle of St.-Mihiel, was shot down in flames in the Argonne, and spent the last months of the war in a German prison, where he "was thrown with Russians a good deal" and developed a lifelong aversion to Bolshevism. In 1918 he was awarded a Purple Heart. In 1919 he joined nine other American pilots in the Kosciuszko Air Squadron, an official unit of the Polish Air Force, to combat the Red menace under the command of Major Cedric Fauntleroy. Cooper took his pseudonym, Corporal Frank R. Mosher, from the waistband of the secondhand underwear he had received from the Red Cross.

On July 13, 1920, the Associated Press reported that Cooper had been "brought down by Cossacks" behind enemy lines in Galicia. According to local peasants, Cooper had been "rushed by horsemen of Budyonny's cavalry," and would have been killed on the spot, had not an *unnamed English-speaking Bolshevik* interfered on his behalf. The next day, July 14, the Frank Mosher entry appears in Babel's diary.

Although Cooper left a "sad, heartwarming impression" on Babel, Babel seems to have left no particular impression on Cooper, who recorded nothing of their "endless conversation." Of his time in the Red Cavalry, he has written only of his interrogation by Budyonny, who invited him "to join the Bolshevist army as an aviation instructor." (Babel was right, by the way; Mosher *was* fooling when he pretended to wonder whether he had committed "a crime by fighting against Soviet Russia.") Refusing to become a flight instructor, Cooper found himself "the 'guest' of a Bolshevist flying squadron for five days. I escaped, but was recaptured after two days, and taken under heavy guard to Moscow." He spent the winter shoveling snow from the Moscow railway line. In the spring, he escaped Vladykino Prison in the company of two Polish lieutenants, and hopped freight trains up to the Latvian frontier ("We adapted the American hobo methods to our circumstances"). At the border, they were obliged to bribe the guards. Cooper handed over his boots, and made another barefoot entrance in Riga.

One of Cooper's fellow pilots, Kenneth Shrewsbury, had kept a scrapbook—and, by a marvelous stroke of luck, it had also ended up at Stanford. Using a dry-plate camera, Shrewsbury had documented the entire Polish campaign, as well as an initial stopover in Paris. (There was a group portrait of the entire Kosciuszko squadron standing outside the Ritz; a long shot of the Champs-Élysées, eerily deserted except for a single horse-drawn carriage and two automobiles; and a close-up of a swan in what looked like the Tuileries.) For weeks I had been looking at 1920s photographs of Galicia and Volhynia, but these were the first that looked like the same place Babel was describing. Everything was there: a village clumped at the foot of a medieval castle, a church "destroyed by the Bolsheviks," airplanes, the handsome Major Fauntleroy, "Jews leveling a field," "Polish mechanics," mounted troops riding past a pharmacy in Podolia—and Cooper himself, looking just like Babel described him, big, American, with a neck like a column. In one photograph he was smiling slightly and holding a pipe, like Arthur Conan Doyle.

Cooper turned to filmmaking in 1923, in collaboration with fellow Russo-Polish veteran Captain Ernest B. Schoedsack. Looking for "danger, adventure, and natural beauty," they went to Turkey and filmed the annual migration of the Bakhtiari tribe to Persia (*Grass: A Nation's Battle for Life*); next, in Thailand, they filmed *Chang: A Drama of the Wilderness* (1927), about a resourceful Lao family who dig a pit outside their house to catch wild animals. All kinds of animals turn up in the pit: leopards, tigers, a white gibbon, and finally a mysterious creature called a *chang*, eventually revealed to be a baby elephant. Cooper claimed that, while filming *Chang*, he was able to predict the cast's behavior based on phases of the moon. A passionate aeronaut, Cooper often looked to the sky for answers: among his papers I found a letter from the 1950s outlining his plan to colonize the solar system, in order to both stymie the Soviets and solve California's impending crises of human and automobile overpopulation.

In 1931, the year Babel published "The Awakening," Cooper devised the premise for *King Kong*: on a remote island, a documentary filmmaker and his team discover the "highest representative of prehistoric animal life." The documentary filmmaker would be a composite of Cooper and Schoedsack: "Put us in it," Cooper instructed the scriptwriters. "Give it the spirit of a real Cooper-Schoedsack expedition." The team would bring the prehistoric monster to New York City to "confront our materialistic, mechanistic civilization."

I borrowed *King Kong* from the library that week. Watching the gigantic ape hanging off the Empire State Building, swiping at the biplanes, I realized that Babel had painted an analogous scene in "Squadron Commander Trunov." At the end of the story, Trunov stands on a hill with a machine gun to take on four bombers from the Kosciuszko Squadron— "machines from the air squadron of Major Fauntleroy, large, armored machines . . . The airplanes came flying over the station in tighter circles, rattled fussily high in the air, plunged, drew arcs . . ." Like King Kong, Trunov has no plane. Like King Kong, he goes down. From the DVD notes, I learned that the pilots in the close-up shots of the Empire State Building scene were none other than Schoedsack and Cooper themselves, acting on Cooper's suggestion that "We should kill the sonofabitch ourselves." In other words, King Kong and Commander Trunov were both shot down by members of the Kosciuszko Squadron.

The other fascinating detail of *King Kong*'s production is that the set for Skull Island was used at night to represent Ship-Trap Island in Cooper and Schoedsack's *The Most Dangerous Game*, an adaptation of Richard Connell's 1924 short story. *The Most Dangerous Game* finds the two stars of *King Kong*, Robert Armstrong and Fay Wray, again marooned on a tropical island, where they must again contend with a primitive monster: a mad Cossack cavalry general who hunts shipwrecked sailors for sport, attended by his mute sidekick, Ivan. ("A gigantic creature, solidly made and black bearded to the waist," Ivan "once had the honor of serving as official knouter to the Great White Tsar.")

I reported these findings to Grisha Freidin. "Well look, there he is! Squadron Commander Trunov!" he exclaimed, peering at the film still I had brought, showing King Kong and the navy planes. "The image must have been in the collective unconscious," he mused. "You know what we should do? We should go back to Hoover and look at all the anti-Bolshevik posters. I am certain that we will find one representing Bolshevism as a giant ape."

He telephoned the archive directly and asked them to run a search for *ape* and *propaganda* in the poster database. The eighteen-page printout was waiting for me when I got there. Unfortunately, it included not just the keyword *ape* but any word beginning with *ape-* in any language.

The actual apes, once isolated from items such as *"Apertura a sinistra"* and *"25 lat Apelu Sztokholmskiego,"* proved to be few in number. First was a German poster of an ape in a Prussian hat, grabbing a woman in one paw, and holding in the other a club labeled *"Kultur."* I had no idea how to interpret this image, but decided it wasn't related to Bolshevism. Next was a Hungarian poster whose central figure, described in the catalogue as an "ape man," looked more like an extremely ugly human, covered in blood, which he was attempting to wash off in the Danube at the foot of the Parliament.

Just as I was starting to wonder how I would break the news to Freidin, I happened upon an Italian World War II poster: *"La mostruosa minaccia torna a pesare sull'Europa."* The monstrous menace of Bolshevism was represented as a bright red, embarrassed-looking ape, standing on a map of Europe and brandishing a sickle and hammer. The artist, possibly concerned that the ape hadn't come out menacing enough, had taken the precaution of representing a masked figure of Death standing behind its shoulder.

One ape on a map of Europe, the other on the Empire State Building. I took off the white gloves; my work here was done.

Or so I thought. First, my copy was sent back to me with a note: "Please call ASAP regarding portrayal of Cossacks as primitive monsters." I tried to explain that I myself wasn't calling the Cossacks primitive monsters—I was only suggesting that others had felt that way. The exhibit coordinator disagreed. Others, she said, *didn't* consider Cossacks to be primitive monsters: "In fact, Cossacks have a rather romantic image."

I debated citing the entry for Cossack in Flaubert's *Diction-*

ary of Received Ideas—"Eats tallow candles"—but instead I simply observed the likelihood of any Cossacks actually attending the exhibit was very slim.

"Well, that's really not the point. Anyway, you never know in California."

A few days later, I began to receive phone calls about the "three-dimensional objects." "Elif, glad I caught you! How would you feel if we put a fur hat in your Red Cavalry display case?"

I considered this. "What kind of fur hat?"

"Well, that's the thing, I'm afraid it's not quite authentic. Someone picked it up at a flea market in Moscow. But it looks, you know, like a Russian fur hat."

"Thanks so much for asking me," I said, "but I really think it should be up to Professor Freidin."

"Oh," she said. "Professor Freidin is not going to want that hat in the display case."

"No," I acknowledged.

The next day, the telephone rang again. "OK, Elif, tell me what you think: we'll put, sort of lying along the bottom of your display case—a Cossack national costume."

"A Cossack national costume?" I repeated.

"Well—well—OK, *the problem is* that it's child's size. It's sort of a children's Cossack costume. But that's not entirely a bad thing. I mean, because it's in a child's size, it will definitely fit in the case, which might not happen with an adult-size costume."

Nearly every day they thought of something new: a samovar, a Talmud, a three-foot rubber King Kong. Finally they settled on a giant Cossack saber, also, I suspect, acquired at the Moscow flea market. They put the saber in a case that had no semantic link to sabers, so people at the exhibit kept asking me what it meant. "Why didn't it go in the display about

'My First Goose'?" one visitor asked. "At least that story has a saber in it."

By that time, the conference had begun. Scholars arrived from around the world: Russia, Hungary, Uzbekistan. One professor came from Ben Gurion with a bibliography called "Babelobibliografiya" and a talk titled "Babel, Bialik, and Bereavement." But the star guests were Babel's children: Nathalie, the daughter from his wife Evgeniya; and Lidiya, the daughter from Antonina Pirozhkova, with whom Babel lived his last years.

When it turned out that Antonina Pirozhkova would be in attendance, my classmate Josh was ecstatic. Josh's parents were *Star Wars* fans and his full name is Joshua Sky Walker; to differentiate him from other Joshes, he was often called Skywalker. Skywalker was also working on the exhibit and, based on photographs from the 1930s, had developed a crush on Pirozhkova.

"Man, do I hope I get to pick *her* up from the airport," he said.

"You do realize she must be more than ninety years old?"

"I don't care—she is so hot. You don't understand."

I did understand, actually. I had noticed some Cossacks in the Rodchenko book whom I would gladly have picked up from the airport, were it not that, in accordance with my prediction, none of them came to the conference.

Skywalker, however, got his wish: he and his friend Fishkin, a native Russian speaker, were appointed to pick up Pirozhkova and Lidiya, the Sunday before the conference. I was initially supposed to pick up Nathalie Babel, but Nathalie Babel had called the department to warn that she had a very heavy trunk: "You must send me a strong male graduate student. Otherwise, do not bother. I will take a bus." So a male graduate student had been sent, and I had the afternoon free. I was cramming for my university orals, trying to read all eighteen pounds of the *Human Comedy* in one month, and was desperately speed-reading *Louis Lambert* when the telephone rang. It was Skywalker, who had apparently broken his foot the previous night at the Euromed 13 dance party, and wanted me to go pick up Pirozhkova and Lidiya. "You can't miss them," he said. "It'll be, like, a ninety-year-old woman who is gorgeous and a fifty-year-old woman who looks exactly like Isaac Babel."

"But—but what happened to Fishkin?"

"Fishkin went to Tahoe."

"How do you mean, he went to Tahoe?"

"Well, it's kind of a funny story, but the thing is that their plane lands in half an hour . . ."

I hung up the phone and rushed outside to dump all the garbage that had accumulated in my car. Realizing that I didn't remember Antonina Pirozhkova's patronymic, I ran back inside and Googled her. I was halfway out the door again when I also realized I had forgotten how to say "He broke his foot" in Russian. I looked that up, too. I wrote BABEL in big letters on a sheet of paper, stuffed it in my bag, and ran out the door, repeating "Antonina Nikolayevna, *slomal nogu.*"

I got to SFO ten minutes after their plane had landed. For half an hour I wandered around the terminal holding my BABEL sign, looking for a gorgeous ninety-year-old woman and a fifty-year-old woman who looked like Isaac Babel. Of the many people at the airport that day, none came close to matching this description.

In despair, I called Freidin and explained the situation.

There was a long silence. "They won't be looking for you," he said finally. "They're expecting a boy."

"That's the thing," I said. "What if they didn't see a boy and, you know, they took a bus."

"Well, my gut feeling is that they're still there, in the airport." He had been right about the Bolshevik ape, so I decided to keep looking. Sure enough, ten minutes later I spotted her sitting in a corner, wearing a white headband and surrounded by suitcases: a tiny elderly woman, nonetheless recognizable as the beauty from the archive photographs.

"Antonina Nikolayevna!" I exclaimed, beaming.

She glanced at me and turned slightly away, as if hoping I would disappear.

I tried again. "Excuse me, hello, are you here for the Babel conference?" She quickly turned toward me. "Babel," she said, sitting up. "Babel, yes."

"I'm so glad—I'm sorry you were waiting. A boy was going to get you, but he broke his foot."

She gave me a look. "You are glad," she observed, "you are smiling, but Lidiya is suffering and nervous. She went to look for a telephone."

"Oh no!" I said, looking around. There were no telephones in sight. "I'll go, I'll look for her."

"Why should you go, too? Then you'll both be lost. Better you should sit here and wait."

I sat, trying to look appropriately somber, and dialed Freidin again.

"Thank goodness," he said. "I knew they would still be there. How is Pirozhkova? Is she very angry?"

I looked at Pirozhkova. She did look a bit angry. "I don't know," I said.

"They told me they would send a Russian boy," she said loudly. "A boy who knows Russian."

. . .

The atmosphere in the car was somehow tense. Lidiya, who did indeed look very much like her father, sat in the front seat, reading aloud from every billboard. " 'Nokia Wireless,' " she said. " 'Johnnie Walker.' "

Pirozhkova sat in the back and spoke only once the whole trip: "Ask her," she told Lidiya, "what is that thing on her mirror."

The thing on my mirror was a McDonald's Happy Meal toy, a tiny stuffed Eeyore wearing a tiger suit. "It's a toy," I said.

"A toy," Lidiya said loudly, half turning. "It's an animal."

"Yes, but what kind of animal?"

"It's a donkey," I said. "A donkey in a tiger suit."

"You see, Mama?" said Lidiya loudly. "It's a donkey in a tiger suit."

"I don't understand. Is there a story behind this?"

The story, to my knowledge, was that Tigger had developed a neurosis about being adopted and having no heritage, so Eeyore put on a tiger suit and pretended to be his relative. As I was thinking of how to explain this, another patch of orange caught my eye. I glanced at the dashboard: it was the low fuel warning light.

"It's not my donkey," I said, switching off the fan. "It's my friend's donkey."

"What did she say?" Pirozhkova asked Lidiya.

"She said that it's her friend's donkey. So she doesn't know why he's wearing a tiger suit."

"What?" said Pirozhkova.

Lidiya rolled her eyes. "She said that the donkey put on the tiger suit in order to look stronger in front of the other donkeys."

There was a silence.

"I don't think she said that," said Pirozhkova.

We drove by another billboard: " 'Ted Lempert for State Senate.' "

"Ted Lempert," Lidiya mused, then turned to me. "Who is this Ted Lempert?"

"I don't know," I said. "I think he wants to be senator."

"Hmm," she said. "Lempert. I knew a Lempert once—an artist. His name was Vladimir. Vladimir Lempert."

"Oh," I said, trying to think of something to say. "I'm reading a novel by Balzac now about somebody called Louis Lambert." I tried to pronounce "Lambert" to sound like "Lempert."

We drove the rest of the way to the hotel in silence.

Babel's first daughter, Nathalie, looked younger than her age (seventy-four), but her voice was fathomless, sepulchral, with heavy French r's.

"YOUR HAND IS VERY COLD," she told me when we were introduced. It was later that same evening, and all the conference participants were heading to the Hoover Pavilion for an opening reception.

"We have black squirrels here at Stanford," another graduate student told Nathalie Babel, pointing at a squirrel. "Have you ever seen a black squirrel?"

Nathalie glanced vaguely in the direction of the squirrel. "I CANNOT SEE ANYTHING ANYMORE," she said. "I cannot hear, I cannot see, I cannot walk. For this reason," she continued, eyeing the steep cement stairway to the pavilion, "everyone thinks I am always drunk."

At the top of the stairs, two Chinese men were taking turns photographing each other with Viktor Zhivov, a Berkeley professor with a kind expression and a tobacco-stained Old Believer beard.

"Lots of Chinese," I overheard someone say in Russian.
"True. It's not clear why."
"They're taking pictures with Zhivov."
"They want to prove that they've been to California. Ha! Ha!"

The two Chinese were in fact filmmakers, whose adaptation of the *Red Cavalry* cycle, *Qi Bing Jun*, was supposed to premiere in Shanghai the following year. (I believe the project was eventually canceled.) The screenwriter was tall, round-faced, smiled a lot, and spoke very good English; the director was short, slight, serious, and didn't seem to speak at all. Both wore large cameras around their necks.

In the Chinese *Red Cavalry*, the screenwriter told us, Cossacks would be transformed into "barbarians from the north of China"; the Jewish narrator would be represented by a Chinese intellectual. "There are not so many differences between Jews and Chinese," he explained. "They give their children violin lessons, and they worry about money. Lyutov will be a Chinese, but he will still have 'spectacles on his nose and autumn in his heart.'" At *nose*, he touched his nose, and at *heart*, he struck his chest. The director nodded.

Looking at the Chinese filmmakers, I remembered Viktor Shklovsky's account of how Babel spent the whole year 1919 writing and rewriting "a story about two Chinese." "They grew young, they aged, broke windows, beat up a woman, organized this or that"; Babel hadn't finished with them when he joined the Red Cavalry. In the 1920 diary, "the story about the Chinese" becomes part of the propaganda that Babel relays in the pillaged shtetls: "I tell fairy tales about Bolshevism, its blossoming, the express trains, the Moscow textile mills, the universities, the free food, the

Revel Delegation, and, to crown it off, my tale about the Chinese, and I enthrall all these poor tortured people." At Stanford, we had it all: a university, free food, and, to crown it off, the Chinese.

Not all of the Russians were as delighted by the Chinese as I was. "We don't mess with your *I Ching . . . ,*" I overheard one audience member saying.

Some Russian people are skeptical or even offended when foreigners claim an interest in Russian literature. I still remember the passport control officer who stamped my first student visa. He suggested to me that there might be some American writers, "Jack London for example," whom I could study in America: "the language would be easier and you wouldn't need a visa." The resistance can be especially high when it comes to Babel, who wrote in an idiosyncratic Russian-Jewish Odessa vernacular—a language and humor that Russian-Jewish Odessans earned the hard way. While it's true that, as Tolstoy observed, every unhappy family is unhappy in its own way, and everyone on planet Earth, vale of tears that it is, is certainly entitled to the specificity of his or her suffering, one nonetheless likes to think that literature has the power to render comprehensible different kinds of unhappiness. If it can't do that, what's it good for? On these grounds I once became impatient with a colleague at a conference, who was trying to convince me that the *Red Cavalry* cycle would never be totally accessible to me because of Lyutov's "specifically Jewish alienation."

"Right," I finally said. "As a six-foot-tall first-generation Turkish woman growing up in New Jersey, I cannot possibly know as much about alienation as you, a short American Jew."

He nodded: "So you see the problem."

. . .

The reception was followed by a dinner, which began with toasts. A professor from Moscow was proposing a toast to Pirozhkova. "In Russian we have an expression, a little-known but good expression, that we say when someone dies: 'He ordered us to live a long time.' Now I look at Antonina Nikolayevna and I think of Babel who died before his time, and I think, 'Babel ordered her to live a long time.' We are so lucky for this, because she can tell us all the things that only she knows. A long life to Antonina Nikolayevna!"

This toast struck me as both bizarre and depressing. I downed nearly a whole glass of wine and became light-headed to the extent that I almost told a dirty joke to Freidin's eighteen-year-old daughter, Anna. Anna, who was applying to colleges, had asked about undergraduate advising at Harvard. I told her about my freshman adviser, a middle-aged British woman who held advisee meetings in a pub—once I missed our meeting because they were checking IDs at the door—and who worked in the telecommunications office.

"The telecommunications office?"

"Uh-huh. I would see her there when I went to pay my phone bill."

"Did she have any other connection to Harvard, other than working in the telecommunications office? Was she an alumna?"

"Yeah, she got an MA in the seventies, in Old Norse literature."

Anna stared at me. "Old Norse literature? What good is an MA in Old Norse literature?"

"I think it's useful in telecommunications work," I said.

"Old Norse literature," Anna repeated. "Hmm. Well, it must be a *fecund* area of study. Aren't the Norse the ones who invented Thor, god of thunder?"

"Oh—I know a joke about Thor!" The joke involves the

comic exchange between Thor and a farmer's daughter: "I AM THOR!" says Thor, to which the farmer's daughter replies: "I'm thor, too, but I had tho much fun!"

"So Thor comes down to earth for a day," I began, when I suddenly became conscious that Joseph Frank—the Stanford emeritus famous for his magisterial five-volume biography of Dostoevsky—had abandoned the lively discussion he had been having with a Berkeley professor about Louis XIII. Both were regarding me from across the table with unblinking interest.

"You know," I said to Anna, "I just remembered it's kind of an inappropriate joke. Maybe I'll tell you another time."

By now, every single person at the table was staring at me. Frank leaned over the arm of his wheelchair toward Freidin's wife, a professor at Berkeley who was also in a wheelchair. "Who is that?" he asked loudly.

"That is Elif, a graduate student who has been very helpful to Grisha," she replied.

"Ah." Joseph Frank nodded and turned his attention to his pasta.

These events took a toll on me, and I overslept the next morning, missing the nine a.m. panel on biography. I got to the conference center as everyone was leaving for lunch, and immediately spotted Luba, who is my height, with huge, sad, gray eyes, and an enormous quantity of extremely curly hair.

"Elishka!" she exclaimed. "Did you just wake up? Don't worry, I wrote everything down for you, in case you want to use it in a novel." We went to the student union for lunch, and Luba told me about the panel.

Three different people were writing biographies about Babel. The first, Freidin, presented on the Other Babel. The second, an American journalist, talked about her experiences researching Babel's life in 1962 Moscow. She had interviewed Babel's old acquaintance, the French chargé d'affaires, Jacques de Beaumarchais (descendant of the author of *Figaro*), and was followed by the KGB, whom Beaumarchais gallantly instructed *"Fichez le camp!"* but the KGB took her in for questioning anyway. The third, Werner Platt, a German who taught Russian history in Tashkent, read a paper called "Writing a Biography of Isaac Babel: A Detective's Task," largely about getting kicked out of various Russian archives and not managing to find out anything about Babel. On the premise that "good detective work means returning to the scene of the crime," the historian had made pilgrimages to Babel's old house in Odessa, the Moscow apartment, the dacha in Peredelkino—only to find that all had been torn down. Undiscouraged, Platt got on a bus to Lemberg. In his diary Babel had mentioned Budyonny's decision not to attack Lemberg in 1920: "Why not? Craziness, or the impossibility of taking a city by cavalry?" Looking around Lemberg, Platt concluded that, as Babel had implied by calling Budyonny's withdrawal "crazy," Lemberg was indeed a beautiful city.

His talk was poorly received. Someone had muttered: "For an incompetent scholar, everything is 'a detective's task.'" It seemed that some of the documents that Platt had been unable to access in the archives had been published years ago. "You can buy this in the Barnes & Noble," someone said.

Platt had also made some provocative claims about the lost manuscripts, which led to a free-for-all about the location and contents of the missing folders.

"Empty!" an unknown Russian had shouted. "The folders were empty!"

Nathalie Babel had stood up and taken the microphone— "The best part," Luba said, sitting up straighter and reading from her notebook in a deep, sepulchral voice.

"WHEN I WAS A LITTLE GIRL, I WAS TOLD THAT MY PUPPY WAS A WRITER." Pause. "LATER I HEARD PEOPLE TALKING ABOUT ISAAC BABEL, SAYING THAT HE WAS A GREAT WRITER." Pause. "TO ME, HE WAS MY PUPPY."

Long pause.

"I AM CONFUSED."

Another pause.

"I AM *CONFUSED*."

One minute, two minutes passed, in total silence. Finally, somebody asked Nathalie whether it was true that she was "still sitting on some unpublished letters."

Nathalie Babel sighed. "LET ME TELL YOU A STORY ABOUT LETTERS." The story was that Nathalie Babel had come into possession of a trunk of her father's letters. ("Her puppy's letters," Luba explained.) "I KNEW THE BIOGRA-PHER WOULD COME," she said, "BUT HE ANNOYED ME. SO I GAVE THE LETTERS TO MY AUNT. WHEN THE BIOGRAPHER CAME, I SAID, 'I HAVE NOTH-ING.'" And where were the letters now? Nathalie Babel didn't know. "MAYBE THEY ARE UNDER MY BED, I DON'T REMEMBER." The panel ended in pandemonium.

Later that afternoon, after the panel on Babel and World Literature, I rode my bike back to the graduate-student hous-ing complex and nearly ran over Fishkin, who was standing outside wearing pajamas and smoking a cigarette. I welcomed him back from Tahoe, and asked how he was enjoying the conference. Fishkin, I learned, was not enjoying the conference. Not only was he in trouble about Tahoe, but Boris Zalevsky, a well-known twentieth-centuryist, had given him the finger in the parking lot.

"Is that a joke?" I asked.

"N-n-no!" said Fishkin, who stuttered at emotional moments. "He really did it, I swear!"

I had been baffled by Zalevsky's character ever since the question-answer session after that afternoon's panel. A famous professor of comparative literature had just read what struck me as an incredibly lame paper comparing a passage in *Madame Bovary*, in which flies are dying in the bottom of a glass of cider, to Babel's description of the death of Squadron Commander Trunov. (The similarity was supposedly that both Babel and Flaubert were aestheticizing the banal.) The moderator—my adviser, Monika Greenleaf—returning to the subject of those flies in the cider, had compared them to the inkwell full of dead flies at the miser's estate in *Dead Souls*, and also to Captain Lebyadkin's lyric about cannibalistic flies in a jar in Dostoevsky's *Demons*. I thought this was a much more promising line of comparison—in fact, Babel, too, had a passage about "flies dying in a jar filled with milky liquid" in a Tiflis hotel. A beautiful passage: "Each fly was dying in its own way." But before my adviser could get to her point about dead flies, Zalevsky had interrupted: "The Flaubert example was pertinent, but your example is not pertinent."

This had confused me, because I had actually liked Zalevsky's paper. It had been far more interesting than the one about "aestheticizing the banal" and the "rapture of perception." But if he was such a smart guy, why was he (a) praising a mediocre paper and (b) being rude to Monika, who had at her fingertips every fly that had ever drowned in the whole Russian canon?

"He must be bipolar," I told Fishkin. "So how did it happen?"

Fishkin had had his turn signal on and was about to pull into a parking spot when suddenly a car came around the corner from the opposite direction and slipped in before him. The driver of this car proceeded to give Fishkin the finger—and, as if that weren't enough, he had gone and turned out to be Zalevsky!

"What did you do?" I asked.

"I-I-I turned my head, like this"—Fishkin turned his head to the left—"so that he wouldn't see my face. Then I drove away."

Back in my apartment, I made some tea and settled down to get through some more Balzac. But there was no escaping from Babel. In one of the critical forewords I found the following anecdote, which Balzac used to tell about his father's early career as a clerk to the public prosecutor in Paris, and which might justly be titled "My First Partridge":

> According to the custom of the time [Balzac's father] took his meals with the other clerks at his employer's table . . . The Prosecutor's wife, who was eyeing up the new clerk, asked him, "Monsieur Balzac, do you know how to carve?" "Yes, Madame," the young man replied, blushing to the roots of his hair. He plucked up his courage and grabbed the knife and fork. Being entirely ignorant of culinary anatomy, he divided the partridge into four, but with such vigor that he smashed the plate, ripped the tablecloth and carved right through to the wood of the table. The Prosecutor's wife smiled, and from that day on the young clerk was treated with great respect in the house.

As in "My First Goose," a young man starts a new job, goes to live among people from a potentially unwelcoming culture, and attains respect and acceptance through the mutilation of poultry.

The anecdote appears in Théophile Gautier's 1859 biography of Balzac. I wondered if it could be shown that Babel

had read Gautier. Then I wondered whether there was anything to eat at home. There wasn't. I got in my car and was
driving down El Camino Real when my cell phone started
ringing. The phone played a cheerful melody, but the letters
on the screen spelled "FREIDIN."

"Professor Freidin! What a pleasant surprise!"

"Elif, hello. I don't know if it is pleasant or a surprise,
but, yes, this is Grisha."

Freidin was at a dinner for the conference participants.
He was experiencing confusion due to the lack at this dinner
of any graduate-student presence. "You are not here. Fishkin
isn't here. Josh isn't here. Nobody is here. It looks—well, it
looks strange. It's a bit embarrassing."

"But we weren't invited to the dinner," I pointed out.

Silence.

"I see. You were waiting to be *invited*."

I made the next U-turn and headed to the faculty club.

Of the four tables in the private room, three were completely full, and one completely empty. As I was considering
whether to sit at the empty table by myself, Freidin noticed
me and made a space between him and Janet Lind, a professor who had edited the first English translation of the
1920 diary. The others at the table were Nathalie Babel;
the American journalist; Werner Platt; a literature professor
from Budapest; and a translator who had recently published
the first English edition of Babel's collected works.

Freidin introduced me to Janet Lind, and suggested that
we might like to talk about *King Kong*. It rapidly emerged
that she and I had very little to say to one another about *King
Kong*. What little spark there had been in this conversation
was soon extinguished by Nathalie Babel, who was staring at
Lind with a fixed, unbenevolent expression. A chilly silence
descended upon the table.

"JANET," Nathalie said finally, in her fathomless voice. "IS IT TRUE THAT YOU DESPISE ME?"

Janet Lind turned to her calmly. "I beg your pardon?"

"IS IT TRUE THAT YOU DESPISE ME?"

"I can't imagine what makes you say that."

"I say it because I would like to know if it is TRUE THAT YOU DESPISE ME."

"That is an extremely odd question. What gives you an idea like that?"

"I just think you were told that I'm a NASTY OLD WITCH."

"This is really extremely odd. Did someone say something to you?" Lind frowned slightly. "You and I have barely had any interactions."

"Even so, I had the impression—that you DESPISE ME."

This conversation continued for longer than one would have thought possible, given how clear it was that Janet Lind, for whatever reason, was just not going to tell Nathalie Babel that she did not despise her. Looking from Lind to Babel, I was struck by the nontrivial truth behind the Smiths song: "Some girls are bigger than others." It wasn't just that Nathalie Babel's face was physically larger—it was somehow visibly clear that she came from a different place and time, where the human scale was different, and bigger.

"Come, Nathalie," Freidin interceded.

She fixed him with her deep, watery eyes. "SOME PEOPLE DO DESPISE ME, YOU KNOW . . ." She sighed, and pointed at two wineglasses: "Which of these is my glass?"

"They're both yours."

"Oh? I can't see anything. Which is water?"

"It looks to me like they're both white wine."

Nathalie stared at him. "AND WHY DO I HAVE TWO GLASSES OF WINE?"

"Why do you say it like it's a bad thing? If it were me, I would think, 'This must mean that I've done something very good.' *Here*, however, is your water glass."

"Ah." Nathalie Babel took a drink of water.

There was a long silence.

"So," Platt said to Freidin, as the waiters were bringing out the entrées. "I hear that Slavic department enrollments are declining in the United States."

"Oh, do you? Well, you're probably right."

"Do you notice a decline here at Stanford?"

"I'd say we've had a pretty fair enrollment the past few years."

"What about graduate students—do you have many graduate students? I have somehow not seen your students."

"Here is Elif," said Freidin. "She is one of our graduate students."

Platt peered at me over the rims of his glasses for several seconds, then turned back to Freidin. "Yes—so. I see you have one specimen. Are there many others?"

By this point we had all been served some cutlets swimming in a sea of butter. These cutlets appeared to depress everyone. The Hungarian scholar even sent hers back, with detailed instructions. It reappeared a few minutes later, with no modification visible to the naked eye.

Toward the end of the meal, Lidiya Babel came over from her table, stood behind Nathalie's chair, put her arms around her shoulders, and patted her head. "My darling," she said, "how I love you! How *good* it is that we are all together!"

Nathalie glanced over her shoulder, with the expression of a cat who does not want to be picked up.

Freidin looked from Nathalie to Lidiya. "Thank you!" he exclaimed. "Thank you, Lidiya!"

Lidiya stared at him. "What for?"

"For coming! In your place maybe I would have hesitated."

"What do you mean to say—that you would find it difficult to travel with my mother?"

"No, of course not—but it's a long distance, an unknown place . . ."

"Speaking of your mother," Nathalie told Lidiya, "how old is she anyway? Some people say ninety-two, some people say ninety-six. Or is it a secret?"

"My mother is ninety-five."

"She doesn't look a day over ninety-three," said Freidin gallantly.

"It's true, she's in good health and looks well," Lidiya said. "However, not as well as she looked two years ago. But that isn't the main thing. The main thing is that everything is still all right *here*." She tapped her temple. "Her memory and her understanding."

When Lidiya went back to her table, Nathalie followed her with her eyes.

"THAT OLD WITCH WILL BURY US ALL," she remarked.

"Nathalie!" said Freidin.

She turned to stare at him. "YOU THINK I SHOULD KEEP MY MOUTH SHUT," she observed. "But—WHY? WHAT DO I HAVE TO LOSE? I HAVE NOTHING LEFT TO LOSE."

Freidin looked nonplussed. "Well, then, I guess you should risk everything," he said. And, making a visible effort to change the subject: "Nathalie, now that you're here, there is something I've been dying to ask you. What was your aunt's name? One sees it written so many ways. Meriam, Miriam, Mary, Maria—which was it?"

"Oh! Do tell us the correct spelling!" exclaimed Platt, his eyes lighting up.

Nathalie looked at him. "I don't understand what you mean by the correct spelling. Some called her Meriam, others Mary, others Maria. All three were used."

"How interesting," said Janet Lind, turning to Freidin. "I'm surprised you haven't already gone to Odessa and looked it up in the municipal register."

"I'm afraid there are many other surprises where that came from. I've always wanted to go to Odessa and look all these things up, but it somehow never happened."

"Why don't you go now?"

"For the same reason that the Babel conference is here, at Stanford: I don't really travel."

"Why not?" asked the American journalist.

Freidin explained that his wife's health kept him in the area, which I thought would end the discussion, but it didn't.

"Well, your daughter still lives with you, doesn't she?" someone asked. "Can't your daughter stay with her?"

"Anna is an enormous source of support and happiness, but she is eighteen years old, and she has a busy life of her own."

The journalist looked thoughtful. "You know what I think?" she said. "I think you should get her a dog."

Freidin stared at her. "Excuse me?"

"You should get your wife a dog," the journalist explained. "It will change her life."

"I really don't see what a dog has to do with any of this."

"The dog will change her life!"

"What makes you think that her life needs to be changed?" There was another silence. "There are various things that cannot be accomplished by a dog."

The journalist looked downcast. "I just thought that if she's sick, the dog can cuddle with her."

"Cuddling is not the problem," said Freidin firmly.

The journalist nodded. "I can see I've said something wrong," she said. "But I'm just crazy about dogs." She looked truly sorry.

"We did have a dog once, years ago," Freidin said, in a conciliatory tone, "called Kutya."

The Hungarian professor, a mournful-looking woman in gray, looked up with interest. "*Kutya* means 'dog' in Hungarian!" she said. She spoke in a head voice, a bit like a puppet.

"We think Kutya might have had some Hungarian blood. He had a complicated heritage—part German shepherd, part Labrador retriever, and part bass baritone."

"Your dog could *sing*? Did he also *speak*? We had a *cat* once who could speak."

Silence.

"What—," I ventured, and cleared my throat. "What did your cat say?"

The Hungarian professor stared at me. " '*I'm hungry*,' " she sang out.

The one person at the table who had remained completely silent during these exchanges was the English translator: a lithe, handsome man—a former dancer, I later learned—with high cheekbones, narrow eyes, and a faintly contemptuous expression. He spoke British English, with a hint of a foreign accent.

His translation was itself an enigma: there were passages of such brilliance that you would stare from the original to the English and wonder how anyone had arrived at anything so unlikely and yet dead-on, but there were also strange discrepancies. For example, at the end of "My First Fee," Babel writes, "I will not die before I wrest from the hands of love one more—*and this will be the last*—gold coin"; the translation reads: "I will not die until I snatch one more gold ruble (*and definitely not the last one!*) from love's hands." In "Guy de Maupassant," Babel writes: "Night *bolstered* my hungry youth with a bottle of '83 Muscatel." The translation says, "Night *obstructed* my youth with a bottle of Muscatel '83." The book was full of such odd changes. Babel says "at nine o'clock"; the translation says "shortly after eight." Babel says "at midnight"; the translation says "after eleven." Freidin didn't like the way "giving the fig" was rendered as "thumbing one's nose," or the passage in which the homeless poet during the Petrograd famine has "Siberian salmon caviar and a pound of bread in [his] pocket": on the grounds that "homeless people do not carry caviar in their pockets," Freidin considered the correct translation to be "salmon roe."

Because of these and other disagreements, we all ended up writing our own translations, with a note that "many translations were used in the preparation of this exhibit, including . . ."

Everything had seemed fine until the end of the dinner, when the handsome translator suddenly turned to Freidin.

"You know," he said, "I went to your exhibit yesterday, and I noticed something strange. Perhaps you can explain it to me." He had noticed his own book in a glass case, open to Babel's story "Odessa"—next to a caption quoting "Odessa," in a different translation.

"Copyediting," Freidin said promptly. "Hoover ran all our text through copyediting. You would not believe the changes they made." He told the story of the copy editor who had translated all the italicized Yiddish in such a way that *Luftmensch* (an impractical visionary) came out as "pilot"; *shamas* (the beadle of a synagogue) turned, via "shamus," into "private detective."

The translator looked completely unamused. "So you're saying that the Hoover copy editors changed my translation?"

"Well, I'm saying that these texts went through many different hands."

"But what am I supposed to think, as a translator? My book is put on display next to something I didn't write. Is it possible to take some sort of legal action?"

Freidin paused. "Michael," he said, "we all like your translation, and we are grateful to you. I want us to be friends. Let's not talk about legal action. It doesn't even make sense. We didn't charge admission for the exhibit."

"That isn't the point. The point is that there in the display case I see *my book*, and next to it I see a typed quotation *with mistakes*. And you're telling me nobody can be held accountable because you didn't charge admission?"

"Michael. I want us to be friends. Now let's be honest. Were there mistakes in the exhibit? Yes! There are mistakes everywhere. There are mistakes in the *Complete Works*, if it comes to that."

The translator, who had excellent posture, sat up even straighter. "What mistake? Do you mean in the notes? That was corrected in the paperback."

"No, I'm not talking about the notes."

"Well, frankly, I don't know what you *are* talking about."

"Michael, I want us to be friends. The *Complete Works* is very, very good. We all like it very much. But in translating Babel—in translating anyone—mistakes are unavoidable. *I* have found mistakes. *Elif* has found mistakes." The translator briefly turned his hooded eyes in my direction. "But *I want us to be friends*."

"Do you see what I'm up against?" Freidin demanded. We were standing outside the conference hall after dinner. The

Chinese were about to give their presentation. A junior professor of symbolism was standing nearby, smoking.

"What happened?" the symbolist asked.

"What didn't happen? It was a dinner from Dostoevsky, that's all."

"In what sense? 'The Two Families'?"

"Well, there was that."

"And what else?"

"Well—" Freidin broke off, glancing into the hall, where two professors and one Chinese filmmaker were crawling under a table, doing something with extension cords. "Excuse me." As Freidin hurried into the conference room, Lidiya Babel came up the stairs trailed by several International Babel Scholars, who were perhaps hoping to learn the things that *only she could tell us.* "Do you know," one of them said, "of those two Chinese, one is a Muslim?"

"Which one?"

"The short one."

"Are there many Chinese Muslims?" Lidiya asked.

"He is not Chinese!" shouted a depressed-looking historian.

Everyone turned and looked at him.

"I don't think he's really Chinese," the historian repeated.

"He does look—different," said Lidiya.

"Maybe he is a Uighur," Zalevsky suggested.

"Wha-a-at?"

"A Uighur, a Uighur, a Uighur."

"When I asked the other Chinese what his religion was," continued the first scholar, "he said to me, 'My religion is Isaac Babel.' "

"Very strange," said the historian.

Everyone turned to Lidiya Babel, as if awaiting some response. "It's an interesting thing," she said slowly. "I once knew a man who married a German woman, and they went to China and photographed Chinese children. Their pictures were put in a book, and published: a book of photographs of Chinese children. But the really interesting thing is that when they asked the man what kind of women he preferred, he would always say: 'Oh, ethereal—like a butterfly.' But when you saw the German woman—she was completely round."

There was a long pause.

"Ah, yes," said the symbolist finally. " 'The eternal disjuncture between reality and the dream.' "

"Completely round," repeated Lidiya Babel. "Whereas later, she ate nothing but cucumbers and black caviar, and now she's altogether thin. Of course, this was when black caviar in Russia sold for next to nothing."

I felt a strange feeling, close to panic. What if that was it, the thing that only she could tell us?

Inside the conference hall, the Chinese filmmakers sat at a long table in front of a flickering screen. The screenwriter smiled and made eye contact with everyone who came in. The director stared impassively into the back corner of the room. I wondered what he was thinking about, and whether he was really a Uighur.

"I used to be a student here at Stanford," the screenwriter began. "Right here. I used to study computer programming. I used to work all night in the computer cluster next door. Then I took a creative writing class to learn how to write stories. There, my teacher assigned Isaac Babel's story 'My First Goose.' This story changed my life."

I was amazed anew at the varieties of human experience: to think we had both read the same story under such similar circumstances, and it had had such different effects on us.

"Babel was like the father to me," continued the screen-writer. "I consider myself Babel's son. Therefore, Nathalie and Lidiya are my sisters." Something in the air suggested that not everyone in the audience had followed him in these logical steps. "Today I was able to shake hands with Nathalie, Lidiya, and Pirozhkova. I feel that I touched Babel's hand. I hope Babel is up there watching us right now!"

Next, the director gave a short address in Chinese, and the screenwriter translated. "I had the foundations of my existence rocked by Isaac Babel's *Red Cavalry*. His prose is so concise." The director gave a little nod when he heard the English word "concise." He went on to express his admiration of Babel's deep understanding of the relationship between men and horses. He himself was a horseman, and had filmed the movie known as the first Chinese Western. He had made films in all genres, including action, war, and family.

"I am so grateful because here I met Babel scholars from all over the world and the universe," the address concluded. "I saw so much passion! I can't show you my film of Isaac Babel's *Red Cavalry*, because I haven't made it yet. Instead I will show you some of my film, the first Chinese Western, *Swordsmen in Double Flag Town*. Then you will see how I feel about horses, and maybe you will understand how I feel about Isaac Babel."

The DVD was inserted into somebody's laptop and projected onto a big screen. The sound didn't work. Yellow dunes flashed silently by, a desert, the galloping legs of a horse, a row of Chinese characters. "*Swordsmen in Double Flag Town!*" cried the director, flinging out one arm. These were the first words he had spoken in English.

Later that night, Matej and I met at the picnic tables outside the housing complex. The world had changed two years' worth since the biography class. I had moved from the apartment across from the Safeway to a studio on campus. Matej now bought his Winston Lights from Australia, instead of from the American Indians. Matej had brought four bottles of beer—three for him and one for me—and I told him my story about the two Chinese, about their gratitude for having met scholars from all over the world, and the universe. "I think I saw one of them this afternoon," Matej said. "I saw one scholar, who was from the world, talking to another scholar, who was from elsewhere in the universe."

The subject of interplanetary visitors reminded me to tell Matej about Cooper's plan to simultaneously resolve the West Coast population boom and the Sputnik crisis by exporting Californians to the moon.

"What—like Nikolai Fyodorov?" Matej riposted.

I had forgotten all about Nikolai Fyodorov, the influential Russian philosopher who declared the future tasks of mankind to be the abolishment of death, the universal resurrection of all dead people, and the colonization of outer space (so the resurrected people would have somewhere to live).

Fyodorov published almost nothing in his lifetime. He worked as a librarian in Moscow, where his visitors included both the aging Lev Tolstoy and the teenage Konstantin Tsiolkovsky who, in 1903—the year of Fyodorov's death—mathematically proved the possibility of spaceflight. Tsiolkovsky went on to become the "grandfather of Soviet cosmonautics," and Soviet cosmonautics was Cooper's bête noire: "So there really is a path from Fyodorov to Cooper!" I concluded.

"If there wasn't, you would find one anyway," Matej replied. "You remind me of a Croatian proverb: the snow falls, not in order to cover the hill, but in order that the beast can leave its tracks."

"What's that supposed to mean?"

"Well, it's kind of an enigmatic proverb."

We talked then about Matej's current object of study: something called "the problem of the person." The problem, Matej explained, was that personhood is revealed and constituted by action, such that the whole person is always present in every action—and yet the person isn't "exhausted" by any single action, or even by the sum of all her actions. The action of writing "My First Goose," for example, expresses Babel's whole person (it isn't the case that only part of Babel wrote "My First Goose," while part of him remained uninvolved); nonetheless, neither "My First Goose," nor even the sum total of Babel's writings, express everything about him as a person.

"One way of putting it is like this," Matej said. "When you're in love with someone, what exactly is it you love?"

"I don't know," I said.

"That's just it, you see—you love . . . *the person*."

The person is never exhausted by his actions: there is always something left over. But what is that precious remainder—where do you find it?

Reflecting upon the problem of the person, I was brought to mind of a novel I had always liked, but never quite understood: Ivan Goncharov's *Oblomov* (1859), the story of a man so incapable of action or decision-making that he doesn't get off his sofa for the whole of part 1. In the first chapter, Oblomov receives various visitors who are active in different spheres of human activity. In all these forms of activity, Oblomov deplores the absence of "the person." A socialite rushes in, talks of balls, dinner parties, and *tableaux vivants*, and then rushes away, exclaiming that he has ten calls to make. "Ten visits in one day," Oblomov marvels. "Is this a life? Where is the person in all this?" And he rolls over, glad that he can stay put on his sofa, "safeguarding his peace and his human dignity."

The second visitor, a former colleague from the civil service, tells Oblomov about his recent promotion to department head, his new privileges and responsibilities. "In time he'll be a big shot and reach a high rank," Oblomov muses. "That's what we call a career! But how little of the person it requires: his mind, his will, his feelings aren't needed." Stretching out his limbs, Oblomov feels proud that he doesn't have any reports to write, and that here on the sofa there is "ample scope both for his feelings and his imagination."

I saw now that the problem of the person was the key to Oblomov's laziness. So loath is Oblomov to be reduced to the mere sum of his actions that he decides to systematically *not act*—thereby to reveal more fully his true person, and bask in it unadulterated.

Oblomov's third visitor, a critic, arrives in rapture over the invention of literary realism. "All the hidden wires are exposed, all the rungs of the social ladder are carefully examined," he gushes. "Every category of fallen woman is analyzed—French, German, Finnish, and all the others . . . it's all so true to life!" Oblomov not only refuses to read any realist works, but becomes almost impassioned. "Where is the person in all this? . . . They describe a thief or a prostitute, but forget the person, or are incapable of depicting him . . . The person, I demand the person!" he shouts.

Thinking over the problem of the person in the context of literary realism, I remembered a sentence from Babel's diary that I had initially taken as a joke: "What is this gluttonous, pitiful, tall youth, with his soft voice, droopy soul, and sharp mind?" It wasn't a joke—the question was where, in these characteristics, was the person? *What* was the person? In a speech in 1936, Babel described a change in his view of literary production: formerly, he had believed that the events of their time were so unusual and so surprising that all he had to do was write them down and "they would speak for themselves," but this literature of "objectivism" had turned out "uninteresting." "In my work there had been no person," Babel concluded. "The person had escaped himself." Three years later, the NKVD took him in, and didn't let him finish. The person had escaped for good.

The conversation with Matej turned to the way people are formed by their influences, by the fatal roles of others in their lives. I remember saying that I didn't believe Babel when he described Maupassant as the most significant of his literary influences.

"I suppose you have some other influence in mind?"

"Well . . . Cervantes." My latest theory was based on Babel's incorporation into one of his stories of various elements from the biography of Cervantes, who had worked for seven years as a bookkeeper for the Spanish Armada.

"My fear when I listen to you," Matej said finally, "is you remind me of this German philosopher." This German, Leo Strauss, had written a commentary to Western philosophy, arguing that all the greatest philosophers had felt it necessary to encrypt their real ideas. In the commentary, Strauss took it as his mission to reveal the Other Plato, the Other Hobbes, the Other Spinoza, all saying things that Plato and Hobbes and Spinoza had left unspoken.

"A lot of the ideas he attributes to Spinoza are interesting," Matej said, "but if Spinoza really thought those things, why didn't he say so?"

As he spoke these words, two figures approached through the darkness: Fishkin and Skywalker. •

"Elif!" said Skywalker. "Just the person we wanted to see. Isn't that right?"

"Yes," said Fishkin unhappily.

"Fishkin has something to tell you. Doesn't he?"

"Yes." Fishkin took a deep breath. "Remember how I said yesterday that Zalevsky gave me the finger? Well, actually it happened d-differently . . ." He trailed off.

"Ye-e-s?" Skywalker prompted.

"Actually," Fishkin said, "I gave *him* the finger. I had finally found a parking spot and was about to pull in—when all of a sudden this car came speeding from the opposite direction and stole my spot. Naturally, I gave the guy the finger. Then he gave me the finger, and I saw it was Zalevsky. Then I drove away. I meant to tell you the truth yesterday. But when I said Zalevsky gave me the finger, you were like, 'Oh my God, what a monster!'—I just couldn't tell you I did it first."

A straightforward relationship to factual truth never was one of Babel's top priorities. "I was a boy who told lies," begins one of the Childhood stories: "This came from reading." A later story about reading, "Guy de Maupassant," ends with a largely incorrect retelling of Édouard de Maynial's biography of Maupassant: "Having achieved fame, he cut his throat at the age of forty, bled profusely, but lived. They locked him in a madhouse. He crawled about on all fours and ate his own excrement . . ." Contemporary Babel scholarship has shown that "neither Maynial nor any other biographer has Maupassant walking on all fours or eating his excrement"; the image appears to be borrowed from either *Nana* (Count Muffat crawls at Nana's feet, thinking of saints who "eat their own excrement") or *Madame Bovary* (a reference to Voltaire on his deathbed, "devouring his own excrement"). In "Guy de Maupassant," Babel mentions neither Voltaire nor Zola nor Flaubert—except to claim that Maupassant's mother is Flaubert's cousin: a false rumor explicitly controverted by Maynial.

Was Babel trying to establish the independence of the person from his deeds—the independence of Maupassant, the person, from his factually accurate biography? Was it about the "premonition of truth" being more true than historical fact?

Walking back to my apartment, I passed the laundry room. Warm, detergent-scented air gusted from vents near the floor and a stereo in the open window was playing Leonard Cohen's "First We Take Manhattan": *I love your body and your spirit and your clothes.*

What is it you love, when you're in love? His clothes, his books, his toothbrush. All of the manufactured, formerly alienated commodities are magically rehabilitated as aspects of the person—as organic expressions of actions, of choice and use. After Eugene Onegin disappears in book 7, Tatyana starts visiting his abandoned estate. She looks at his pool cues, his library, his riding crop, "And everything seems priceless to her." "What is he?" she asks, poring over his books, examining the marks left by his thumbnail in the margins.

So, too, do scholars now pore over the articles that once belonged to Babel. One historian has annotated the inventory of belongings confiscated from Babel's Moscow apartment, his apartment in the Great Nikolo-Vorobinsky Lane. (In her memoirs, Pirozhkova writes about how impressed she was to learn about the existence of the Great Nikolo-Vorobinsky Lane, whose name literally means "Great Lane of Nikolai and the Sparrows"; Babel told her the street was named after the nearby Church of St. Nikolai-on-the-Sparrows, which had been built "with the help of sparrows, that is to say, in order to raise money for its construction, sparrows were caught, cooked and sold." This was totally untrue, as *Vorobinsky* actually came from an archaic word for "spindle," only coincidentally sharing the same adjectival form as "sparrow," but Babel could spin a story out of anything.) Can one glimpse the person, in the list of objects?

Binoculars—2 pr.
Manuscripts—15 folders
Drafts—43 it.
Schematic map of the motor transport network—1 it.
Foreign newspapers—4
Foreign magazines—9
Notebooks with notes—7 it.
Various letters—400 it.
Foreign letters and postcards—87 it.
Various telegrams—35 it.
Toothpaste—1 it.
Shaving cream
Suspenders—1 pr.
Old sandals
Duck for the bath
Soapdish—1

The fifteen folders of manuscripts vanished, along with the nine others seized from Babel's dacha. As for the personal items, they were held for three months before being surrendered to the state as "revenue." According to receipts, the binoculars eventually brought in 153 rubles and 39 kopeks, but there is no record of what happened to Babel's rubber duck.

Summer in Samarkand

When I try to remember how I ended up spending an entire summer in Samarkand, I am reminded of an anecdote about the folk hero Nasreddin Hoca. Walking along a deserted road one night, the story goes, Nasreddin Hoca noticed a troop of horsemen riding toward him. Filled with terror that they might rob him or conscript him into the army, Nasreddin leaped over a nearby wall and found himself in a graveyard. The horsemen, who were in fact ordinary travelers, were interested by this behavior, so they rode up to the wall and looked over to see Hoca lying motionless on the ground.

"Can we help you?" the travelers asked. "What are you doing here?"

"Well," Nasreddin Hoca replied, "it's more complicated than you think. You see, *I'm* here because of *you*; and *you're* here because of *me*."

The scene immediately conjures itself: the road at nightfall, a dog doubtless barking somewhere, the smell of damp soil, the sound of approaching horsemen, and finally the faces peering over the wall, concerned and mildly astonished. This story encapsulates the riddle of free will in human history: a realm where, as Friedrich Engels observed, free wills are constantly obstructing one another so that, inevitably, "what emerges is something that no one willed." Nobody, least of all Nasreddin Hoca, willed for Nasreddin Hoca to end up lying in the graveyard that night. Nobody forced him there, either—yet there he was.

The chain of events that eventually deposited me in Samarkand was set into motion by my decision to study Russian literature: in itself an impulsive decision, not unlike jumping over a wall and ending up in a graveyard, although things on the whole worked out for me. Still, learning Russian takes a long time, and time passes so slowly in college. After two years of what felt like endless study, I still couldn't pick up a Russian book and read it. I couldn't understand a Russian movie without subtitles. If I tried to talk to Russian people, they stared at me like I was retarded. I decided that the only solution was to actually go to Russia.

In the spring of my sophomore year, I applied for a grant for a study abroad program in Moscow, and for two jobs: one as a personal secretary to a frozen-foods exporter from Peru who was negotiating with a Moscow-based supermarket chain, and the other as a researcher for the *Let's Go* travel guides in Russia. The outcome of these applications wasn't exactly bad, but it wasn't anything I had willed, either. I got a travel grant—for half the amount I asked, not enough for the program tuition. The Peruvian entrepreneur said I could be his secretary—pending submission of a "recent full-body photograph." *Let's Go* offered me a job—in Turkey, because they said my Russian wasn't good enough for travel in Russia. My Turkish, by contrast, was good enough for travel in Turkey. The previous year, *Let's Go* had sent a young man who spoke no Turkish at all and who had consequently, as the result of a never fully explained "misunderstanding," gotten beaten up by a pimp in Konya, after which he had a nervous breakdown, which was minutely documented in *Rolling Stone* magazine as part of an exposé.

I tried to make the best of things. I wrote a polite refusal to the Peruvian, I used the grant money to arrange a two-week stay in Moscow with some destitute academics, and for the rest of the summer I took the job in Turkey.

The poshest of the Turkish itineraries—Istanbul and the Aegean coast—was assigned to a Turkish-born archaeology graduate student called Erhan, who got himself kidnapped somewhere near Ephesus, only it then turned out that he hadn't been kidnapped at all but had gotten married; nonetheless, he never came back to Boston, and never sent in any copy, either. My family was in an uproar—not about Erhan, because we didn't know about that at the time, but because I had been given such a dodgy itinerary: the disputed territory of Northern Cyprus; the Mediterranean coast, where the Eurotrash discos ended only as you approached the Syrian border and had to start looking out for the terrorist PKK; and the backwaters of Central Anatolia. My mother claimed never to have heard of half the cities on the list.

One city was called Tokat, which literally means "a slap in the face." This is also the title of a famous manifesto by the Russian futurists: "A Slap in the Face of Public Taste"—or, as it is known in Turkish, *"Toplumsal zevke bir tokat."* The "Ottoman slap"—a technique developed in the Ottoman army, where punching was considered bad form—is known as *Osmanli tokat* (or, more grammatically, *Osmanlı tokadı*), and if you enter this term in YouTube you will see hundreds of videos of Turkish people getting slapped in the face, mostly by other Turkish people, although also, in one case, by a monkey. My mother had particularly bad feelings about my going to Tokat.

When I got to Ankara, where I stayed at my grandmother's apartment, I gradually realized that my mother had taken steps to ensure my safety. She somehow convinced my aunt Arzu, an officer in the Turkish National Intelligence Organization, to have me followed after sundown: not by an actual intelligence officer, but by one of their chauffeurs. I met my pursuer one night in Gaziosmanpaşa, where all the foreign embassies and five-star hotels are. I was wandering around an enormous, depressing nightclub called No Parking, trying to determine the price of an Efes Pilsner, when a man in a suit tapped my shoulder and informed me that my car had arrived.

"But I didn't call a car," I said.

Nonetheless, explained the man in the suit, the car was there. It had perhaps been sent by a distinguished lady, possibly some kind of a relative.

"She gave a very detailed description of you." And, giving me a once-over, he repeated: "A very detailed description."

I followed him outside. Another man in a suit was standing beside a parked car. When I understood who he was, and why he was there, I felt so beleaguered that I burst into tears.

"Please don't upset yourself, miss," the driver said, opening the door to the backseat.

I climbed in. We drove back through Gaziosmanpaşa, past the bulletproof glass cubicles in which soldiers were reading newspapers and smoking cigarettes, back to Kavaklıdere, where my grandmother lived. The driver addressed me only once, at the big intersection outside Swan Park. In Swan Park, vendors sell bags of almond crackers, which you can eat yourself or feed to the swans. As a child I was fascinated by these crackers, which do not contain almonds, but are shaped like almonds. This was my first lesson in metaphor versus metonymy. Here, stopped at a red light, the driver half turned to face me.

"Would you like an apple?" he asked.

"No thanks," I said.

"I picked these apples myself," he said. "With my own hands, from my own garden."

From a plastic bag on the passenger seat, he produced a small apple.

The apple was hard, green, and misshapen, like the answer to some pointless riddle.

I left Ankara early in the morning, before my grandmother woke up. I left a note telling her not to worry, that I would call her soon. I did not specify my destination. Nonetheless, when I got off the bus in Tokat, I was personally greeted by the municipal water inspector. A melancholy bureaucrat with a mustache, he spoke of my aunt Arzu with great respect, and took me to visit the waterworks.

As I discovered over the next weeks, my aunt Arzu had mobilized a diverse group of contacts to look out for my welfare. One evening in Kayseri, the Turkish pastrami capital, I was collected from my hostel by a sergeant in the army. The sergeant drove me to a military kebab restaurant on top of an extinct volcano called Mount Erciyes. Skiing Turks, who I believe are not numerous, go there in the winter. At this time of year there was no snow on Erciyes. Outside the windows of the military restaurant, the sun was setting on some grazing sheep, dyeing them pink, like big dense clouds of cotton candy. It was strange to eat lamb while watching these pink fluffy sheep.

The sergeant asked about my studies. When I said that I studied literature, he asked whether I was reading the works of Yaşar Kemal (a famous Turkish novelist who wrote his first short story during his military service in Kayseri). I was not reading the works of Yaşar Kemal.

"What author are you reading? What author are you concentrating on?" he asked.

"I don't know yet," I said. "Maybe Pushkin."

"Pushkin? Who is that, an American?"

"Well, more of a Russian, actually."

This information clearly made no sense at all to the sergeant. He blinked once or twice and told me how lucky I was to study at such a famous American university, how many Turkish boys and girls—and not only boys and girls—would give their ears to have such an opportunity.

"An opportunity for what?" he demanded rhetorically, leaning toward me over the table.

"An opportunity for what?" I echoed.

"An opportunity for having their voices heard! For telling people the truth about Turkey, and not the nonsense propagated by Europeans!"

It was dark when we drove down to the city, past Kayseri's third claim to fame, after pastrami and skiing: a hulking fifteen-hundred-year-old citadel, hewn from black volcanic rock. Lit by spotlights, it resembled a diabolical cauldron.

Looking back, I am surprised by how much I took to heart the words of people like this sergeant. If I didn't actually believe in my responsibility to tell Americans the truth about Turkey, nevertheless I did feel it was somehow wasteful of me to study Russian literature instead of Turkish literature. I had repeatedly been told in linguistics classes that all languages were universally complex, to a biologically determined degree. Didn't that mean all languages were, objectively speaking, equally interesting? And I already *knew* Turkish; it had happened without any work, like a gift, and here I was tossing it away to break my head on a bunch of declensions that came effortlessly to anyone who happened to grow up in Russia.

Today, this strikes me as terrible reasoning. I now understand that love is a rare and valuable thing, and you don't get to choose its object. You just go around getting hung up on all the least convenient things—and if the only obstacle in your way is a little extra work, then *that's* the wonderful gift right there.

But I was younger and dumber then, and demoralized by the state of the Turkish novel. The thing that immediately struck one about the Turkish novel was that nobody read it, not even Turkish people. I often noticed this when I was in Turkey. Most people just weren't into novels at all. They liked funny short stories, funny fables, serious fables, essays, letters, short poems, long poems, newspapers, crossword puzzles—they liked practically any kind of printed matter better than novels. Even in 1997, of course, there was already Orhan Pamuk, already writing novels . . . and you could see how miserable he was about it. I bought *The Black Book* that summer. It was about a man who had lost a woman called "Dream." This guy was walking around the streets of Istanbul calling: "Dream! Dream!" I remember reading this on a bus in Turkey and feeling deeply, viscerally bored. I spent the rest of the bus ride looking out the window. I was interested by the names of towns. I remember the sign for a town called Şereflikoçhisar, literally, Fortress of the Honorable Ram.

As a less strenuous concession to the idea of "local color," I started reading Pushkin's Turkish travelogue, *Journey to Arzrum*. I found it much more entertaining than *The Black Book*. I was already entertained by the very premise that Pushkin had ever set foot in Turkey. It was fully as entertaining to me as the premise of Jesus Christ having set foot in England is to English people—for example, to William Blake: "And did those feet in ancient time / Walk upon England's mountains green?" Interestingly, one of Pushkin's most famous lyrics is an elegy to feet: "Ah, little feet, little feet! where are you now? . . . Cosseted in Oriental languor, you left no tracks on the sad northern snow." Pushkin is not here referring, of course, to his own feet. Nonetheless, I saw a pair of Pushkin's boots once in a museum, and they were very small.

As the summer rushed on, I took night buses from one unknown city to another, visiting caves where Christians had hidden from Romans, and Greek amphitheaters that had been converted into caravanserais by the Seljuks; drifting in and out of sleep, I looked out the bus windows for Pushkin's tracks. They could be anywhere! Indeed, Pushkin's cartoonish omnipresence is one of the wonderful things about Russian literary culture. Daniil Kharms wrote a play about it, called *Pushkin and Gogol*, in which Pushkin and Gogol keep tripping over each other:

> GOGOL, *getting up*: This is mockery, through and through! (*walks, trips on Pushkin and falls*) Pushkin again!

That's how it is: Pushkin is everywhere. To this day, "Pushkin" is used interchangeably with the phrase "someone's uncle" in Russian expressions such as: "And who will foot the bill—Pushkin?"

My favorite part of *Journey to Arzrum* is that Pushkin himself keeps stumbling over a nobleman called . . . Count Pushkin. Pushkin and Count Pushkin decide to travel together, but argue and part company. Pushkin will have no part in Count Pushkin's plan to cross a snowy mountain pass in a britska pulled by eighteen emaciated Ossetian bulls. Their courses diverge . . . but they meet again in Tiflis. They can't escape each other. In Turkey, I was reminded of Count Pushkin every time my path crossed that of another Elif, a thing I wasn't used to, growing up in the States. I went into all the stores called "Elif Clothing." I bought something from every "Elif Grocery." Once I gave some money to a Gypsy woman, who asked my name and offered to tell my fortune. "My daughter's name is Elif!" she exclaimed. "Isn't that right?" I was startled to realize that the daughter was actually standing beside her: a skinny child, five or six years old. The Gypsy looked at my palm and told me to beware of a woman called Mary.

The further I read in Pushkin's *Journey*, the more parallels I found with my own experience. As Pushkin was in hiding from the secret police, so was I hiding from my aunt Arzu. As Pushkin was mistaken in his travels for a Frenchman and a dervish, so was I mistaken for a Spaniard and a pilgrim. As Pushkin happened in his travels upon a soiled copy of his own earlier Caucasian poem, "Prisoner of the Caucasus"—the very text he was supposed to be updating with his new Eastern impressions—so was I constantly stumbling, in teahouses and gardens, upon earlier editions of *Let's Go*. Finally, as Pushkin, a Russian, was ambiguously positioned between the "Orient" and the seventeenth-century Anglo-French tradition of travelogue, so was I ambiguously positioned between Turkey and the exasperating twentieth-century discourse of "shoestring travel": the quest for an idyll where, for three U.S. dollars, Mustafa would serve you a home-cooked meal and tell you about his hair collection. The worst part of this discourse was its specious left-wing rhetoric, as if it were a form of "sticking it to the man" to reject a chain motel in favor of a cold-water pension completely filled with owls.

I stayed in all the novelty hotels—tree house hotels perched on stilts, troglodyte hotels carved from dolomites— and everywhere I found the same atmosphere of distrust. The travelers lived in terror of getting ripped off, or missing an "authentic" experience. The locals were terrified lest they miss some "opportunity" afforded by their foreign visitors.

Of course I met many kind and reasonable people among both groups, but by definition it's the importune ones who sought one out: the tourists cadging insider tips, the locals demanding that I lure rich foreigners to their establishments. A Turkish schoolteacher turned hotelier gave me a typed report he had written debunking the Armenian genocide, for me to give to the American government. A tour-bus operator wanted me to help his uncle get a kidney transplant "in Houston." "And who will pay for that," I reflected gloomily. "Pushkin?"

I spent the last two weeks of the summer living in Moscow with two very kind but depressed Russian academics: a mathematician from the Academy of Sciences, and his wife, a biologist who had recently been fired from the Academy of Sciences and who spent all night in the kitchen playing Super Mario Brothers on a Nintendo Game Boy. They were renting me the bedroom usually occupied by their daughter, who had been banished to a grandmother's dacha.

Back at school that year I managed to get a somewhat larger grant, and to enroll for the spring semester in a study-abroad program. This program was operated by two Russian entrepreneurs, both named Igor, and had a distant affiliation with a liberal arts college in Kansas.

Moscow in 1998 was like Paris during the Restoration. The Caspian oil pipeline had drawn the largest foreign investment in Russian history. The city was overrun by speculators. Mayor Luzhkov resurrected Peter the Great's Table of Ranks, and plotted the construction of an underground city in the suburbs. The state had stopped funding the maintenance of Lenin's corpse in Red Square, and the vast reserves of unemployed master embalmers were hired to restore the victims of

Mafia car bombings, and to mummify the nouveau riche in marble mausoleums.

In Moscow, for the first and last time in my life, I dated bankers. Things didn't work out with the first banker, but I still remember the second banker fondly. His name was Rustem, he had remarkable yellowish brown eyes, and he had until recently been an engineer at an explosives factory in Yekaterinburg, designing bombs that were named after flowers. Now he was working for Bank Menatep, which the oligarch Mikhail Khodorkovsky used to manage the state funds for Chernobyl victims, and also to commit alleged embezzlement and tax fraud for which he is, at the time of this writing, serving a prison sentence. Rustem was saving up money to pay for parachuting lessons.

Rustem regularly traveled to Uzbekistan: his sister had married an Uzbek businessman and now lived in Tashkent, which Rustem said resembled the American West of cowboy movies. He could count to ten in Uzbek, and I was amazed to learn that the numbers were almost the same as in Turkish. I had been told, but had not believed, that Uzbek was related to Turkish. The fact hadn't been presented in a convincing way. A distant uncle of mine had married an Uzbek beauty called Lola, who never talked to anyone or even opened her mouth (although she smiled often, showing beautiful dimples). Only two years after their marriage did it become generally known that Lola had three gold teeth. Everyone would always ask my uncle: "How do you live with someone you can't communicate with?" And my uncle always shouted: "Uzbek Turkish is very close to our Turkish language!"

I hadn't believed my uncle, partly because he was crazy—hadn't he spent his later years in a gardening shed in New Jersey, writing a book about string theory and spiders?— and partly because, in my experience, Turkish people thought that *every* language was close to our Turkish language. Many times I had been told that Hungarian was related to Turkish, that the Hungarians and Turks descended from the same Altaic peoples, that Attila the Hun was Turkish, and so on. When I went to Hungary, however, I discovered that Hungarians do not share these beliefs at all. "Of course we have some Turkish words in our language," they would say. "For example, *handcuffs*. But that's because you occupied our country for four hundred years."

But Rustem had some Uzbek money in his apartment, brilliantly colored bills on which the familiar Turkish words were set in Cyrillic type, above portraits of stern, almond-eyed Central Asian bards and geographers. It was like play money, the currency of a fantastic land where Turkish and Russian overlapped and generated some *other thing*.

Several years later, while writing my dissertation (about European novels), I formulated a theory of the novel: the novel form is "about" the protagonist's struggle to transform his arbitrary, fragmented, given experience into a narrative as meaningful as his favorite books. Looking back, this is how I understand my interest in Central Asia: there was an actual place you could visit, with a language you could learn, that linked my favorite books with one of the more arbitrary and "given" aspects of my life: being Turkish.

Once I learned about the existence of Tashkent, it, too, kept turning up. Anna Akhmatova was evacuated to Tashkent from Leningrad during the siege. So was Bulgakov's widow: that's where she hid the manuscript of *Master and Margarita*. Solzhenitsyn's stomach tumor was miraculously cured at a Tashkent hospital, which became the setting of *Cancer Ward*. In *Anna Karenina*, Vronsky ruins his brilliant military career by refusing a "flattering and dangerous assignment in Tashkent," instead running away to Italy with Anna.

I decided to visit Tashkent over spring break. Rustem wanted to come with me, but he couldn't leave the bank. The nation's bankers were working long hours in those days. I wasn't following the escalating financial malaise, which Rustem rarely mentioned; as for Raisa, the elderly pensioner with whom I was living, she only turned on the news when it was about the Lewinsky scandal. "I don't watch our news—it's so dark. It leaves you feeling bad."

"Monica Lewinsky leaves me feeling bad, too," I said.

Raisa shrugged. "For you in America, it's a big drama, but for us, it's just funny. Your Clinton is a young, healthy, good-looking man! Where's the misfortune? Look at our half-dead Yeltsin . . . if we found out Boris Nikolaevich was sleeping with a young girl, we would declare a national holiday."

Meanwhile, at the university, the smaller of the two Igors turned out to be a friend of Anatoly Chubais, the privatization czar who was at that point in charge of the entire, collapsing economy, and even got him to come and give a speech to the advanced Russian class. "You know who must have a lot of free time," I remarked to Rustem later, "is this guy Chubais. He's going around to universities, talking to foreign students." It took several minutes to convince Rustem that I wasn't joking. "She's seen Chubais!" he marveled. "And what did he say?"

Unfortunately I couldn't remember anything he had said, except that he had used a lot of participles.

I ended up going to Central Asia in the company of one of my classmates from the university, a Taiwanese mathematician called Alex. We got to Tashkent in the pouring rain and started to walk from the bus station to our hostel, making our way through a maze of courtyards, ignoring all the dogs that were barking at us from behind chain-link fences, crossing a huge puddle on a bridge made from a rotting plank.

"Tashkent is the Venice of the East," Alex announced, in his peculiar monotonic voice.

My recollections from this trip are scattered but vivid. We lived on some kind of chocolate spread, which we ate from a jar using a souvenir Uzbek scimitar. We constantly had to bribe people. At one point we spent twenty minutes wandering through a pool hall near a bus station, trying to identify the guy we were supposed to bribe. I had to do all the talking because nobody could understand anything Alex said. To my dismay, I also had to do all the financial calculations.

"Aren't you the math major?" I asked Alex once, in the middle of trying to sort out who owed what for a Kirghiz visa.

"I only deal with numbers on a theoretical level," Alex intoned.

We spent three days each in Uzbekistan, Kyrgyzstan, and Kazakhstan. We spent a lot of time in bus stations, where Alex made us do calisthenics, "like the Germans." "We are wasting minutes!" he would shout, attempting a German accent. Sometimes, the buses turned out to have been requisitioned by soldiers—there was a war in Kyrgyzstan—and then, even if there were empty seats left, we had to wait for the next bus.

"Couldn't we take this bus, too?" I asked once.

"What—with the soldiers?" exclaimed the station attendant. "Ha! Ha! Ha!"

In Bukhara we visited the emir's palace, which was overrun by peacocks. Some of the rooms had been filled with cement. "That used to be the conservatory but the Soviets objected to grand pianos." In the Kirghiz mountains, we visited a thermal bath, where we sat in wooden cubicles, immersed in sulfurous water. The sulfur blended with the sickly sweet smell of horsemeat, which someone was boiling outside over an open fire. In Bishkek we rode a Ferris wheel that marked the place where Tamerlane had allegedly once expressed the wish to be buried. He hadn't been buried there. The Ferris wheel stood in an otherwise empty plaza, where a little boy with several gold teeth was riding a bicycle in circles; another boy, dressed in a gray suit, was shooting at a lone shrub with a toy machine gun.

But the city that left the strongest impression on me was Samarkand, with its abandoned Soviet department store, and the astronomical observatory where, in the fifteenth century, Ulughbek had mapped the coordinates of 1,018 stars, and the deserted medieval university. The Lion Medrese's mosaic lions—half tiger, half clock—were clearly the work of someone who had never seen a lion. Samarkand is where Tamerlane was actually buried, under a six-foot slab of jade taken from a temple in China. It crossed my mind that I might like to come back someday, when I was less tired, dirty, and confused.

Shortly after I returned to the United States that summer, the Russian ruble crashed. Many of the banks, including Menatep, collapsed overnight. Rustem liquidated his rubles by buying fax machines; he occasionally sent me faxes at my summer job, in the copyediting department of a big New York publishing house. Eventually the faxes stopped; the summer came to an end.

Back at school that fall, I started studying the "Russian Orient": I read Soviet realist stories by Uzbek and Kirghiz writers, Pan-Slavic treatises by Soviet linguists, Pan-Turkic treatises by Kemalist Turks, "Caucasian" poems by Russian poets. I signed up for a beginning Uzbek class, which was taught by a graduate student, a Samarkand native called Gulnora. I was fascinated by the language, which seemed to me like a harsher, more naïve, more Russian version of

Turkish. Where Kemalist Turks had borrowed French words (for things like trains and ham), the Soviet Uzbeks borrowed Russian ones. At that time I happened upon a book about Pushkin by Stanford professor Monika Greenleaf. According to Greenleaf, Pushkin's journey to Arzrum was actually a substitute for a journey to Paris: a city Pushkin had dreamed of all his life—"In a week I'll definitely be in Paris!" begins an unfinished play—but had never visited.

Pushkin's travels began at age twenty-one when, on the basis of some radical political verses, he was banished from Petersburg on a civil service assignment to present-day Dnepropetrovsk. There he made the acquaintance of the 1812 hero General Raevsky, with whom he traveled for three months through the Caucasus and Crimea, accumulating material for *Prisoner of the Caucasus* and *The Fountain of Bakhchisaray*. Pushkin was transferred next to Moldova, and then to Odessa, where he fell desperately in love with the governor-general's wife, fought several duels, and was obliged to leave the civil service. Meanwhile, the secret police had just intercepted a letter in which Pushkin mentioned "studying pure atheism" from a deaf Englishman in Odessa who had conclusively disproven the immortality of the soul. On the pretext of these heretical lines, Pushkin was exiled to Pskov.

In 1826, the new tsar, Nikolai I, allowed Pushkin to return to Moscow, and even undertook the duty of censoring his works. Unfortunately, the tsar turned out to be Pushkin's most annoying censor yet. Worse still, he made Pushkin directly accountable to Count Benckendorff, the head of the secret police, who had to approve all his travel requests. (By this point, Greenleaf observes, Pushkin's "loudly lamented exile in the early 1820s" had already begun to "represent the peripatetic freedom of his youth.") When Benckendorff denied Pushkin's request to travel to Paris, in 1829, Pushkin decided to slip across the border to Turkey. And so the Orient, which was supposed to represent "the open spaces of adventure and personal reminiscence," actually represented the opposite of freedom: banishment from Paris, the center of the world, to the most meaningless peripheries.

When I returned to Stanford as a second-year graduate student, I had to start taking a Russian-language pedagogy class, to prepare for my mandatory year of teaching Russian to undergraduates. The class was taught in Russian by a Soviet-trained linguist called Alla who advised us, among other things, to treat our more stupid students with sympathy, "as if they had cancer."

While I was in pedagogy training, a scandal erupted around one of my classmates, Janine, a non-native Russian speaker who was at that time teaching first-year Russian. Dropping in on one of Janine's classes, Alla had seen her write on the blackboard the phrase *vasha imia* ("your name")—which would have been fine if *imia* ("name") were feminine, but in fact it is an irregular neuter, so the correct form is *vashe imia*. Janine's class was immediately reassigned to another graduate student (who now had a double teaching load); for the rest of the year, all Janine was allowed to do was grade homework papers, using an answer key.

I thought a long time about Janine's situation. Granted, "name" is a pretty common word in first-year language classes, so the teacher should probably know what gender it is. On the other hand, what we were really talking about here was a one-letter spelling mistake on an irregular noun. Who among us was safe from such a misstep?

As I was having these thoughts, UC Berkeley announced a search for an Uzbek language instructor—a clear gesture from the "invisible hand." I had had only one year of Uzbek language instruction, but the professor conducting the search—author of a famous semiotic study of suicide—said that if I took an intensive all-summer course in Uzbekistan, I could have the job. The director of the Stanford special-languages program also said I might be able to teach Uzbek at Stanford: either the Berkeley or the Stanford Uzbek class would count for my language teaching requirement. This seemed like a great idea to me, because who was going to refute my spelling of Uzbek words on the board? Nobody.

The only U.S.-accredited intensive immersion program in the Uzbek language was run by the American Council of Teachers of Russian (ACTR) and cost seven thousand dollars. "I wonder why it's so expensive," I remember remarking to the Berkeley professor. "Airfare is a thousand dollars . . . and after that, you'd think the overhead in Uzbekistan would be pretty low."

The semiotician counted off on three fingers: "One thousand for instruction, one thousand for room and board, and four thousand for the body bag to send you home."

I got the seven thousand dollars, most of it from Stanford and the rest from the U.S. Department of State, but then came a new development. It suddenly turned out that the salary for the Berkeley job was paid by a government grant for which only native Uzbek speakers were eligible. Bizarrely, it also turned out that the director of the Stanford special-languages program had told the grant-awarding committee that I had *fabricated the entire conversation and e-mail exchange* in which she told me there was a possibility of my teaching Uzbek at Stanford. I still have the e-mail to this day. It says: "I would be delighted to have you teach Uzbek in the Special Languages Program." "I never told that woman anything," the special-languages director apparently told the grants committee.

I didn't take the news too badly. Maybe, I reasoned, it was all for the best that I wasn't being encouraged to run away to Uzbekistan with a four-thousand-dollar body bag, just because I was afraid of being caught by Alla in a spelling mistake. I made an appointment with the administrator in charge of Newly Independent States (NIS) region grants, to explain that I wanted to return the money. As I told her my story, the administrator's expression grew more and more distant.

"This doesn't look good," she said finally. "You're backing out of your research proposal just because you aren't eligible for this particular job at Berkeley, this particular year?" She shook her head. "It doesn't look good. I like you, Elif, and I want you to succeed. That's why I'm telling you that, if you back out of your proposal now, the likelihood of this committee ever awarding you a grant again will be very small."

Of all the circumstances that contributed to my ending up in Samarkand, this ultimatum was the most unexpected. Go to Uzbekistan now . . . or you will never get departmental funding ever again? My first instinct was to tell them exactly what they could do with their departmental funding. But three things changed my mind. First, departmental funding and departmental goodwill are really, in the cold light of reason, nothing to sneeze at. Second, I was at that time greatly under the sway of *The Portrait of a Lady*, a book in which one finds the following line: "Afterwards, however, she always remembered that one should never regret a generous error." As a result I was constantly rethinking all my conservative decisions and amending them in favor of "generous errors," a category which surely included going to Samarkand to learn the great Uzbek language. Third, I was unhappy in love and wanted to get some distance.

The plan backfired somewhat because one of the people I wanted to get some distance from, my college boyfriend Eric, insisted on coming with me, for his own set of reasons (concern for my safety; his belief—accurate, as it turned out—that it would give us things to talk about later; and some obscure geopolitical ambitions that entailed a quest for total world knowledge). Despite myself, I was moved. I said I would ask what it would entail for him to come with me. As it turned out, it entailed almost nothing at all. Just a couple of hundred dollars added your significant other to your homestay arrangement, and even to your accidental death and dismemberment policy, which I received in the mail a few weeks later:

LIFE: $25,000

TWO OR MORE MEMBERS: $25,000

ONE MEMBER: $25,000

THUMB AND INDEX FINGER: $6,250

COMBINED MAXIMUM OF $50,000 FOR EMERGENCY OR MEDICAL REPATRIATION, OR REPATRIATION OF REMAINS.

REPATRIATION OF REMAINS: COVERED SERVICES INCLUDE, BUT ARE NOT LIMITED TO, EXPENSES FOR EMBALMING, CREMATION, MINIMALLY NECESSARY CASKET FOR TRANSPORT AND TRANSPORTATION.

"Orientation" took place in Washington, D.C., at a midrange hotel decorated completely in mauve. There were thirty-five students in the Russian Language and Area Studies program, thirty-three of them going to Russia.

At dinner the first night—"spring vegetable pasta" served at mauve tables in a mauve ballroom—we listened to an address by a linguistics professor who had invented a system of rating second-language proficiency. The genius of this system rested on the concept of rating second-language proficiency on a scale from one to four.

It occurred to me that nobody was actually forcing me

to stay in this room. Surely it would be more constructive to go buy a sun hat. (I have black hair and Uzbekistan is very sunny: along with Liechtenstein, it is one of only two double-landlocked countries in the world.) The speaker either affected not to notice or did not notice my departure from the mauve ballroom. In the lobby I asked the concierge, whose name tag said ALBRECHT, where I could buy a sun hat. Albrecht suggested that I might like to look for a hat in nearby Georgetown. "So we're *here* . . . ," he said, poising his hotel pen over a map. But the pen just hovered there, like a helicopter. Albrecht couldn't locate our hotel on the map. "This is very embarrassing," he said. His sincerity left a strong impression on me.

In the humid evening, fireflies hovered at eye level over little brick streets. Somehow I ended up in an Urban Outfitters. All around me, girls were buying absolutely unwearable-looking clothes: sheer dresses with V-necks down to the navel; jeans measuring literally two inches from waist to crotch; rhinestone-encrusted G-strings with *no elasticity whatsoever*. I found a hideous white ill-fitting sun hat, bought it, and fled to Barnes & Noble.

There was one other student in the program going to Uzbekistan: Dan, a Tashkent-bound political science major who was indescribably average in both appearance and demeanor, like some kind of composite sketch. On the plane, Dan managed to befriend a group of twelve Uzbek and Ukrainian exchange students. During the layover in Frankfurt, we all sat in two rows of seats in a waiting area, looking at a photo album belonging to a young Uzbek called Muratbek. Muratbek was very tan, with bleached hair and a fixed grin. To his every utterance in every language, he appended the exclamation:

"Awesome!" "*Turkcha gapirasizmi?*" he asked me. "Do you speak Turkish? Awesome!"

Having extinguished two hours of my youth in this way, I went to meet Eric, who had skipped the orientation and was flying to Frankfurt directly from San Francisco. His plane arrived in another, larger terminal. A BMW sedan, the grand prize for something, was parked in the middle of a vast atrium. On the other side of a glass panel, an open cart piled high with suitcases glided along the runway, against the pale early-morning sky. A wall-size television screen was broadcasting a World Cup match: Turkey versus Japan. A small group of Turkish janitors was gathered in front of the screen. At tense moments, they would drop their mop handles and grip one another's arms, shouting at the players in German.

Eric came out of the plane wearing a white T-shirt and a backpack, looking, with his gentle blinking Chinese eyes, as philosophical and good-humored as Snoopy. Because Eric was an intelligence officer in the U.S. Naval Reserve (part of his geopolitical ambitions), we ended up in some kind of a military lounge. It had free Internet and bran muffins, and a tiny television broadcasting the Japan-Turkey game. Turkey won, 1–0. Even inside the military lounge, we could hear the janitors cheering.

It was late at night when we got to Tashkent. The baggage claim area felt like a room in a dream, a room in someone's house. A breeze was blowing through an open window. We passed through customs and filed into a parking lot, where Dan's Tashkent host family came to pick him up: three teenage boys with hangdog expressions, and their mother, Marjuda, an overweight woman with gold teeth and a bright red dress. Marjuda greeted us all warmly; she wrote her phone number on a piece of paper and told me and Eric to visit her in Tashkent. Then she gestured to Dan to come to their car. Dan turned to me. "So you're going to stay with us tonight, right?" he said urgently, as though I were his closest friend.

"Ah, no, in a hotel," I said. They were sending a driver to take us to Samarkand the next day.

"But she just invited you!"

In a haze of sleep, Eric and I got into the car of an ACTR officer, who was taking us to our hotel. Propaganda slogans were printed in enormous letters on walls and billboards— I could recognize HALQIM, "my people," and VATANIM, "my country"—signed by Islom Karimov, the president of Uzbekistan since the fall of the Iron Curtain. His last reelection had been in 2000, when he won 91.9 percent of the vote against his sole opponent: a professor of Marxist philosophy, who later admitted that he himself had voted for Karimov.

In the morning, a tiny Korean car, buzzing with the vibrations of a poor-quality stereo, picked us up at a street corner. The driver, an inscrutable Tajik, turned off the stereo when we got into the car. Once we reached the main road, the sun blazed down and it was unbearably hot. The driver periodically made tiny adjustments to the temperature. He turned the air conditioner between "lo" and "off"; opened and closed the vents; rolled down the window a crack, then closed it again. No matter what he did, it was unbearably hot.

After an hour of silence, the driver turned to me and said, in Russian:

"So you didn't bring any cassette tapes with you?"

We hadn't, I said, but maybe we could listen to some of his tapes.

The driver remained silent for a moment. "What if you don't like my music?" he asked finally.

"Oh, I'm sure we'll like it," I said.

The driver looked genuinely confused. "How can you say that?" he asked. "You don't even know what kind of music I have."

Thirty kilometers of the highway from Tashkent to Samarkand passes through Kazakhstan. The moment we cleared the police checkpoint, the landscape looked completely different. Patchy, grayish fields stretched as far as the eye could see. There were no trees at all, no human figures. Here and there stood a few melancholy, skeletal horses, with drooping prehistoric heads.

Twenty minutes later, trees reappeared, leafy trees with their trunks painted white, on either side of the road; Uzbek police were guarding a roadblock.

"So we're back in Uzbekistan?" I asked the driver.

"Yes, this is Uzbekistan. Trees, you see."

"They, um, don't have trees in Kazakhstan?"

He shook his head, frowning. "Don't like them."

"The Kazakhs don't like . . . trees?"

The driver shook his head more emphatically. "No way."

We pulled up in front of the house late that afternoon. Two massive wooden doors were set in a pink plaster wall; one of them swung out slowly and Gulchekhra, our "host mother"—they really called her that, as if we were tapeworms—came outside. Peculiarly familiar music drifted toward us. Gulchekhra smiled graciously at me and Eric, and less graciously at the driver, whom she addressed in Tajik: she was evidently trying to dismiss him, while he shuffled his feet and looked at the ground, with the appearance of somebody waiting to be paid. It was not, as we later learned, a deceptive appearance. The driver was a sort of relative, in the broadest sense, so one tried to be kind to him, Gulchekhra explained, but it was the Americans in Tashkent who had his money; they hadn't given it to her.

We walked through a covered passage, to a stone court-yard with a square pool, its water green and cloudy with veg-etable life. The hot, shimmering air throbbed with what I belatedly recognized as a ballad by Enrique Iglesias. Next to a large boom box, a boy with a weedy adolescent mustache was washing a Daewoo sedan with a garden hose.

Eric and I were given an entire wing of the house, con-sisting of three rooms: a bedroom, a little sitting room with a television, and a dining room with a long table that could seat twenty. (The malfunctioning toilet was in a different wing.) Gulchekhra told us to call her Gulya, and announced her intention to call me "Emma," because my real name was so complicated. A former Communist apparatchik, she now worked as a travel agent and had been to "every country in the world, except America, Africa, and Japan." She had two children: Inom, the teenager with the car, and Lila, a four-year-old girl. Inom and Lila's father had, Gulya explained, "become a yogi" and moved to California two years ago.

That afternoon Inom drove me to the university, where I met Vice-Rector Safarov, a personage whose refrigerator-like build, rubbery face, and heavy eyelids brought to mind some anthropomorphic piece of furniture in a Disney movie. Reclin-ing in a leather chair in his office, speaking in accented Russian, Vice-Rector Safarov gave me a speech about the importance of comparative literary and cultural study.

"We can study symbols and how they are used in differ-ent cultures," he announced, "or we can study systems of folklore, or we can study how different languages structure people's perceptions of the world." He leaned back in his chair with his arms folded. "What kind of language do you wish to study here, in the principal aspect?"

"The Uzbek language," I ventured cautiously. Did he already know that I was supposed to teach Russian next year?

Safarov took out a notebook and proceeded to sketch my program of study. I would have four hours of class every day: two hours of "spoken speech" and two hours of "written speech," aka, the great Uzbek literary language. I was the sole student in these classes. Rising from his desk, Safarov opened the office door with a flourish, revealing a lanky young man in a button-down shirt. "Here is your language teacher," Safarov said. "His name is Muzaffar." Muzaffar, a philosophy graduate student, had pale skin, pale almond-shaped eyes, high cheekbones, and a floppy, sad, puppetlike comportment. He bowed, lifting one hand to his chest. Despite his exotic appearance and foreign gestures, his general air of malaise was familiar to me from previous observations of philosophy graduate students.

Muzaffar had been instructed to accompany me back to Gulya's house. I found his presence oppressive. At one point during our walk, we passed some Russian girls smoking cigarettes. "I have to apologize to you, Elif," Muzaffar said in English, softly and in what seemed to me an insinuating tone. "Our girls, Uzbek girls, of course do not smoke in street, but Russian girls, they do this."

"That's fine," I said. I tried twice to invite him to go home and let me walk the rest of the way alone, but it was no use; man or God had instilled in him too strong a sense of responsibility for my welfare.

We turned onto Gulya's street. "I will see you tomorrow," Muzaffar said. "We will work very hard."

"Great," I said.

"At our age," he observed, "we must work and study a lot, while we still have the strength."

This remark for the first time began to dispose me kindly toward Muzaffar. I laughed, and a glint of amusement appeared in his pale eyes. "While we still have time," he clarified. "Already time is running out, but soon we won't have strength left, either."

By now we were a few yards away from the massive wooden doors; I could already hear Enrique Iglesias. Muzaffar said that it was time to say goodbye, and that he would now stand behind a tree until I was safely inside the house.

"Oh, OK," I said. "Goodbye."

"Goodbye. You go into the house now. Don't worry. I will be here." He pointed at an emaciated tree.

I knocked on the door, glancing over my shoulder where Muzaffar, faithfully stationed behind the tree, raised one limp arm. I returned this gesture. Inside the courtyard, the music was very loud. Inom was washing his car again.

"Was there a man hiding behind that tree?" Gulya asked, suspiciously.

"I didn't see anyone," I said.

Who Killed Tolstoy?

The International Tolstoy Conference lasts four days and is held on the grounds of Yasnaya Polyana: the estate where Tolstoy was born, lived most of his life, wrote *War and Peace* and *Anna Karenina*, and is buried.

In the summer after my fourth year at Stanford, I presented part of a dissertation chapter at this conference. At the time, the department awarded two kinds of international travel grants: $1,000 for presenting a conference paper or $2,500 for field research. My needs clearly fell into the first category, but with an extra $1,500 on the line, I decided to have a go at writing a field-research proposal. Surely there was some mystery that could only be solved at Tolstoy's house?

I rode my bicycle through blinding sunshine to the library and spent several hours shut up in my refrigerated, fluorescent-lit carrel, with a copy of Henri Troyat's seven-hundred-page *Tolstoy*. I read with particular interest the final chapters, "Last Will and Testament" and "Flight." Then I checked out a treatise on poisonous plants and skimmed through it outside at the coffee stand. Finally, I went back inside and plugged in my laptop.

"Tolstoy died in November 1910 at the provincial train station of Astapovo, under what can only be described as strange circumstances," I typed. "The strangeness of these circumstances was immediately assimilated into the broader context of Tolstoy's life and work. After all, had anyone really expected the author of *The Death of Ivan Ilyich* to drop dead quietly, in some dark corner? And so a death was taken for granted that in fact merited closer examination."

I was rather pleased by my proposal, which I titled "Did Tolstoy Die of Natural Causes or Was He Murdered? A Forensic Investigation," and which included a historical survey of individuals who had motive and opportunity to effect Tolstoy's death:

Arguably Russia's most controversial public figure, Tolstoy was not without powerful enemies. "More letters threatening my life," he noted in 1897, when his defense of the Dukhobor sect* drew loud protests from the Orthodox Church and Tsar Nikolai, who even had Tolstoy followed by the secret police.

As is often the case, Tolstoy's enemies were no more alarming than his so-called friends, for instance, the pilgrims who swarmed Yasnaya Polyana: a shifting mass of philosophers, drifters, and desperados, collectively referred to by the domestic staff as "the Dark Ones." These volatile characters included a morphine addict who had written a mathematical proof of Christianity; a barefoot Swedish septuagenarian who preached sartorial "simplicity" and who

---

*The Dukhobors—literally, "Spirit Wrestlers"—were a Russian peasant religious sect, whose tenets included egalitarianism, pacificism, worship through prayer meetings, and the rejection of all written scripture in favor of an oral body of knowledge called the "Living Book." When they were persecuted for their refusal to fight in the Russo-Turkish war, Tolstoy donated all the proceeds from his novel *Resurrection* to finance their immigration to Canada in 1899.

eventually had to be driven away "because he was beginning to be indecent"; and a blind Old Believer who pursued the sound of Tolstoy's footsteps, shouting, "Liar! Hypocrite!"

Meanwhile, within the family circle, Tolstoy's will was the subject of bitter contention . . .

"You are certainly my most entertaining student," said my adviser when I told her about my theory. "Tolstoy—murdered! Ha! Ha! Ha! The man was eighty-two years old, with a history of stroke!"

"That's exactly what would make it the perfect crime," I explained patiently.

The department was not convinced. They did, however, give me the $1,000 grant to present my paper.

On the day of my flight to Moscow, I was late to the airport. Check-in was already closed. Although I was eventually let onto the plane, my suitcase was not, and it subsequently vanished altogether from the Aeroflot informational system. Air travel is like death: everything is taken from you.

Because there are no clothing stores in Yasnaya Polyana, I was obliged to wear, for four days of the conference, the same clothes in which I had traveled: flip-flops, sweatpants, and a flannel shirt. I had hoped to sleep on the plane and had dressed accordingly. Some International Tolstoy Scholars assumed that I was a Tolstoyan—that like Tolstoy and his followers I had taken a vow to walk around in sandals and wear the same peasant shirt all day and all night.

They were some twenty-five in number, the International Tolstoy Scholars. Together, between talks on Tolstoy, we wandered through Tolstoy's house and Tolstoy's garden, sat on Tolstoy's favorite bench, admired Tolstoy's beehives, marveled at Tolstoy's favorite hut, and avoided the vitiated descendants of Tolstoy's favorite geese: one of these almost feral creatures had bitten a cultural semiotician.

Every morning I called Aeroflot to ask about my suitcase. "Oh, it's you," sighed the clerk. "Yes, I have your request right here. Address: Yasnaya Polyana, Tolstoy's house. When we find the suitcase we will send it to you. In the meantime, are you familiar with our Russian phrase *resignation of the soul*?"

On the first morning of talks, a Malevich scholar read a paper about Tolstoy's iconoclasm and Malevich's Red Rectangle. He said that Nikolai Rostov was the Red Rectangle. For the whole rest of the day he sat with his head buried in his hands in a posture of great suffering. Next, an enormous Russian textologist in an enormous gray dress expounded at great length upon a new study of early variants of *War and Peace*. Fixing her eyes in the middle distance, consulting no notes, she chanted in a half-pleading, half-declaratory tone, like somebody proposing an hour-long toast.

Just when she seemed about to sit down, she bounced back up and added: "We will hear more about these very interesting editions on Thursday! . . . if we are still alive." It was fashionable among International Tolstoy Scholars to punctuate all statements about the future with this disclaimer: an allusion to Tolstoy's later diaries. After his religious rebirth in 1881, Tolstoy changed his practice of ending each diary entry with a plan for the next day; now, he simply wrote the phrase: "if I am alive." It occurred to me that, ever since 1881, Tolstoy had *always known he would be murdered*.

It was at the time of this conversion that Tolstoy decided

to give away all his copyrights "to the people." This decision pitted him in "a struggle to the death" against his wife,
Sonya, who managed the household finances and who, over
the course of the years, bore Tolstoy a total of thirteen children. Tolstoy eventually ceded Sonya the copyrights for all his
pre-1881 works, but turned the rest over to one of the Dark
Ones, Vladimir Chertkov, an aristocrat-turned-Tolstoyan
whose name contains the Russian word for "devil" (*chert*).

A doctrinaire known for his "heartless indifference to
human contingencies," Chertkov made it his mission to bring
Tolstoy's entire life and work into accord with the principles of Tolstoyanism. He became Tolstoy's constant companion, and eventually gained editorial control over all his new
writings—including the diaries, which treated the Tolstoys'
conjugal life in great detail. Sonya never forgave her husband.
The Tolstoys began to fight constantly, long into the night.
Their shouting and sobbing would make the walls shake.
Tolstoy would bellow that he was fleeing to America; Sonya
would run screaming into the garden, threatening suicide.
According to Tolstoy's secretary, Chertkov was succeeding
in his plan: to achieve "the moral destruction of Tolstoy's
wife in order to get control of his manuscripts." During this
stormy period in his marriage, Tolstoy wrote *The Kreutzer
Sonata*—a novella in which a husband resembling Tolstoy
brutally murders a wife resembling Sonya. Anyone investi-
gating foul play in the death of Tolstoy would find much of
interest in *The Kreutzer Sonata*.

That evening at the academicians' dormitory, I went onto
my balcony and lit a cigarette. A few minutes later, the
door of the adjacent balcony opened. The balconies were
extremely close, the railings separated by some ten inches

of black space. An elderly woman stepped outside and stood very still, gazing sternly into the distance, apparently pursuing her own thoughts about Tolstoy. Then she turned to me, quite abruptly. "Would you be so kind as to give me a light?" she asked.

I fished a matchbook from my pocket, lit a match, and held it over her balcony. She leaned over, ignited a Kent Light, and began puffing away. I decided to take advantage of this moment of human contact to ask for some shampoo. (There wasn't any in the academicians' bathrooms, and mine was lost somewhere with my suitcase.) When I mentioned shampoo, some strong emotion flickered across the old woman's face. Fear? Annoyance? Hatred? I consoled myself that I was providing her an opportunity to practice resignation of the soul.

"Just a minute," said my neighbor resignedly, as if she had read my thoughts. She set down her cigarette in a glass ashtray. The thread of smoke climbed up into the windless night. I ducked into my room to find a shampoo receptacle, choosing a ceramic mug with a picture of the historic white gates of Yasnaya Polyana. Under the picture was a quotation from L. N. Tolstoy, about how he was unable to imagine a Russia with no Yasnaya Polyana.

I held this mug over the narrow chasm, and my neighbor poured in some sudsy water from a small plastic bottle. I realized then that she was sharing with me literally her last drops of shampoo, which she had mixed with water in order to make them last longer. I thanked her as warmly as I knew how. She responded with a dignified nod. We stood a moment in silence.

"Do you have any cats or dogs?" she asked finally.

"No," I said. "And you?"

"In Moscow, I have a marvelous cat."

• • •

"There are no cats at the Tolstoy estate at Yasnaya Polyana," begins Amy Mandelker's well-known study, *Framing Anna Karenina*:

> Curled, or rather, coiled in the sunny patches in the Tolstoy house, protecting it from pestilential infestations, instead of the expected feline emblems of domesticity . . . [are] snakes . . . The ancestors of these ophibian house pets were adopted by Tolstoy's ailurophobic wife, Sofia Andreyevna [Sonya], to rid the house of rodents.

I was contemplating these lines on the second morning of talks, when I counted a total of four cats actually inside the conference room. That said, in fairness to Amy Mandelker, you couldn't accuse Yasnaya Polyana of a shortage of snakes. At breakfast, one historian had described his experience researching the marginalia in Tolstoy's editions of Kant: he had seen a snake right there in the archive.

"Were there at least any good marginalia?" someone asked.

"No. He didn't write anything in the margins at all," the historian said. He paused, before adding triumphantly: "But the books fell open to certain pages!"

"Oh?"

"Yes! Clearly, those were Tolstoy's favorite pages!"

The morning panel was devoted to comparisons of Tolstoy and Rousseau. I tried to pay attention, but I couldn't stop thinking about snakes. Perhaps Tolstoy had been killed by some kind of venom?

"The French critic Roland Barthes has said that the least

productive subject in literary criticism is the dialogue between authors," began the second speaker. "Nonetheless, today I am going to talk about Tolstoy and Rousseau."

I remembered a Sherlock Holmes story in which an heiress in Surrey is found in the throes of a fatal conniption, gasping, "It was the band! The speckled band!" Dr. Watson assumes that she was killed by a *band* of Gypsies who were camping on the property, and who wore polka-dotted kerchiefs. But Watson is wrong. The heiress's words actually referred to the rare spotted Indian adder introduced into her bedroom through a ventilation shaft by her wicked stepfather.

The heiress's dying words, "the speckled band," represent one of the early instances of the "clue" in detective fiction. Often, a clue is a signifier with multiple significations: a band of Gypsies, a handkerchief, an adder. But if the "speckled band" is a clue, I wondered drowsily, what is the snake? There was a loud noise and I jerked upright. The Tolstoy scholars were applauding. The second speaker had finished her talk and was pushing the microphone along the conference table to her neighbor.

"The most important element of nature, for both Tolstoy and Rousseau, was—air."

I walked along the birch-lined alleys of Yasnaya Polyana, looking for clues. Snakes were swimming in the pond, making a rippling pattern. Everything here was a museum. *The snakes are the genetic snake museum. The flies buzz across generations; I know they know, but they won't tell me.* I walked along the winding path to Tolstoy's grave: a grassy lump, resembling a Christmas log. I stared at it for three minutes. I thought I saw it move. Later, near Tolstoy's apiary, I sat on a bench, not Tolstoy's favorite, and looked in the garbage can. It was full of cigarette butts and cucumber peels.

On a tree stump in these very woods in 1909, Tolstoy signed a secret will. He left all his copyrights in the control of Chertkov and of his own youngest daughter, Sasha, a fervent Tolstoyan. This had long been Sonya's worst fear—"You want to give all your rights to Chertkov and let your grandchildren starve to death!"—and she addressed it through a rigorous program of espionage and domestic sleuth-work. She once spent an entire afternoon lying in a ditch, watching the entrance to the estate with binoculars.

One afternoon in September 1910, Sonya marched into Tolstoy's study with a child's cap pistol and shot Chertkov's picture, which she then tore into pieces and flushed down the toilet. When Tolstoy came into the room, she fired the pistol again, just to frighten him. Another day, Sonya shrieked, "I shall kill Chertkov! I'll have him poisoned! It's either him or me!"

On the afternoon of October 3, Tolstoy fell into a fit. His jaws moved spasmodically and he uttered mooing noises, interspersed with words from an article he was writing about socialism: "Faith . . . reason . . . religion . . . state." He then flew into convulsions so violent that three grown men were unable to restrain him. After five convulsions, Tolstoy fell asleep. He woke up the next morning, seemingly recovered.

A few days later, Tolstoy received a letter from Chertkov and refused to let Sonya see it. Sonya flew into a rage and renewed her accusations about the secret will. "Not only does her behavior toward me fail to express her love," Tolstoy wrote of Sonya, "but its evident object is to kill me." Tolstoy fled to his study and tried to distract himself by reading *The Brothers Karamazov*: "Which of the two families, Karamazov or Tolstoy, was the more horrible?" he asked. In

Tolstoy's view, *The Brothers Karamazov* was "anti-artistic, superficial, attitudinizing, irrelevant to the great problems."

At three in the morning on October 28, Tolstoy woke to the sound of Sonya rifling through his desk drawers. His heart began pounding wildly. It was the last straw. The sun had not yet risen when the great writer, gripping an electric flashlight, left Yasnaya Polyana for good. He was accompanied by his doctor, a Tolstoyan called Makovitsky. After a strenuous twenty-six-hour journey, the two arrived in Shamardino, where Tolstoy's sister Marya was a nun. Tolstoy decided to spend the remainder of his life here, in a rented hut. But the very next day he was joined by Sasha who, together with Dr. Makovitsky, convinced the feverish writer that he really ought to run away to the Caucasus. The little party left on October 31, in a second-class train carriage, purchasing their tickets from station to station to avoid pursuit.

Tolstoy's fever mounted. He shook with chills. By the time they reached Astapovo, he was too sick to travel. A sickroom was made up for him in the stationmaster's house. Here Tolstoy suffered fever, delirium, convulsions, loss of consciousness, shooting head pains, ringing in the ears, delusions, difficulty breathing, hiccups, an irregular and elevated pulse, tormenting thirst, thickening of the tongue, disorientation, and memory loss.

During his last days, Tolstoy frequently announced that he had written something new, and wanted to give dictation. Then he would utter either nothing at all, or an inarticulate jumble of words. "Read to me what I have said," he would order Sasha. "What did I write?" Once he became so angry that he began to wrestle with her, shouting, "Let me go; how dare you hold me! Let me go!"

Dr. Makovitsky's diagnosis was catarrhic pneumonia.

Sonya arrived at Astapovo on November 2. She was not allowed to enter the stationmaster's house and took up residence in a nearby train car. If Tolstoy recovered and tried to flee abroad, she decided, she would pay five thousand rubles to have him followed by a private detective.

Tolstoy's condition worsened. He breathed with great difficulty, producing fearsome wheezing sounds. He forgot how to use his pocket watch. In a final period of lucidity on November 6, he said to his daughters, "I advise you to remember that there are many people in the world besides Lev Tolstoy." He died of respiratory failure on November 7.

On the third day of the Tolstoy conference, a professor from Yale read a paper on tennis. In *Anna Karenina*, he began, Tolstoy represents lawn tennis in a very negative light. Anna and Vronsky swat futilely at the tiny ball, poised on the edge of a vast spiritual and moral abyss. When he wrote that scene, Tolstoy himself had never played tennis, which he only knew of as an English fad. At the age of sixty-eight, Tolstoy was given a tennis racket and taught the rules of the game. He became an instant tennis addict.

"No other writer was as prone to great contradictions," explained the professor, whose mustache and mobile eyebrows gave him the air of a nineteenth-century philanderer. All summer long, Tolstoy played tennis for three hours every day. No opponent could rival Tolstoy's indefatigable thirst for the game of tennis; his guests and children would take turns playing against him.

The International Tolstoy Scholars wondered at Tolstoy's athleticism. He should have lived to see eighty-five—ninety—one hundred!

Tolstoy had also been in his sixties when he learned how to ride a bicycle. He took his first lesson exactly one month after the death of his and Sonya's beloved youngest son. Both the bicycle and an introductory lesson were a gift from the Moscow Society of Velocipede-Lovers. One can only guess how Sonya felt, in her mourning, to see her husband teetering along the garden paths. "Tolstoy has learned to ride a bicycle," Chertkov noted at that time. "Is this not inconsistent with Christian ideals?"

On the last day of talks, wearing my Tolstoyan costume and flip-flops, I took my place at the long table and read my paper about the double plot in *Anna Karenina*. It ended with a brief comparison of Tolstoy's novel to *Alice's Adventures in Wonderland*, which turned out to be somewhat controversial, since I was unable to prove that Tolstoy had read *Alice* by the time he wrote *Anna Karenina*.

"Well, *Alice in Wonderland* was published in 1865," I said, trying to ignore a romance that was being enacted, just outside the window, by two of the descendants of Tolstoy's horses. "It's well known that Tolstoy liked to receive all the latest English books by mail."

"Tolstoy had a copy of *Alice in Wonderland* in his personal library," said one of the archivists.

"But it's an 1893 edition," objected the conference organizer. "It's inscribed to his daughter Sasha, and Sasha wasn't born until 1884."

"So Tolstoy *hadn't* read *Alice* in 1873!" an old man called from the back of the room.

"Well, you never know," said the archivist. "He might have read it earlier, and then bought a new copy to give to Sasha."

"And there might be mushrooms growing in my mouth—but then it wouldn't be a mouth, but a whole garden!" retorted the old man.

One of the Rousseau experts raised her hand. "If Anna represents Alice, and Levin represents the White Rabbit," she said, "then who is Vronsky?"

I tried to explain that I wasn't suggesting a one-to-one correspondence between every character in *Alice's Adventures in Wonderland* and *Anna Karenina*. The Rousseau expert stared at me. "Anyway," I concluded, "it's Oblonsky whom I was comparing to the White Rabbit—not Levin."

She frowned. "So Vronsky is the White Rabbit?"

"Vronsky is the Mad Hatter!" someone shouted.

The conference organizer rose to her feet. "I think we can continue this interesting discussion over tea."

In the crush at the tea table, I was approached by the archivist, who patted my shoulder. "I'm sure Tolstoy read *Alice in Wonderland* before 1873," she said. "Also, we received a police report today. A certain suitcase has been received and is being held in security."

She directed me to the security holding area, which was inside one of the historic white gate-towers of Yasnaya Polyana—one of the very towers depicted on the mug that I had used to solicit shampoo. The mug had been a clue. As the Keebler Elf factory is hidden inside a hollow tree, so was an entire security office concealed within a gatepost. Next to one of the officers' steel desks, under a framed portrait of Tolstoy, sat my suitcase. It had arrived two days ago, but the officers hadn't known whose it was. I signed a form and dragged my suitcase over moss and tree roots, back toward the conference hall. It was a good opportunity to look at the ground.

I was looking for *Hyoscyamus niger*, a toxic plant known as henbane or stinking nightshade that is native to Eurasia.

Henbane contains the toxin atropine, which is associated with nearly all of Tolstoy's symptoms, including fever, intense thirst, delirium, delusions, disorientation, rapid pulse, convulsions, difficulty breathing, combativeness, incoherence, inability to speak, memory loss, disturbances of vision, respiratory failure, and cardiopulmonary arrest. A particularly distinctive feature of atropine poisoning is that it dilates the pupils and causes sensitivity to light. I had no information about Tolstoy's pupils, but Chertkov's diary does contain one suggestive observation: "Tolstoy—to the amazement of his doctors—continued to show signs of consciousness to the very end . . . by turning away from the light that was shining into his eyes."

Nearly anyone might have slipped henbane into Tolstoy's tea (of which he drank large quantities). Chertkov, for example, in concert with Dr. Makovitsky. They, the fervent Tolstoyans, had motive enough: What if Tolstoy repented and changed his will again? What if, in his dotage, by some new weakness, he contradicted the principles of Tolstoyanism?

Sonya had, in addition to motive, a known interest in poisons. "I have consulted Florinsky's book on medicine to see what the effects of opium poisoning would be," wrote Sonya in her diary in 1910. "First excitement, then lethargy. *No antidote.*" Then there were the Tolstoys' sons: though the daughters tended to side with Tolstoy, the sons, who were usually short on money, sided with their mother. In 1910, Sonya boasted that, even if Tolstoy *had* written a secret will, she and their sons would have it thrown out: "We shall prove that he had become feeble-minded toward the end and had a series of strokes . . . We will prove that he was forced into writing that will in a moment of mental incapacity."

Perhaps Sonya had used atropine to simulate the effects of a stroke. She might not have intended to kill her husband—just to provide grounds to invalidate his will. But, in his atropine-induced delirium, Tolstoy had embarked on his bizarre and fatal flight.

After Tolstoy's death, Sonya, supported by a pension from the tsar, tried to fight Sasha and Chertkov for the copyrights. History opposed her in the form of the Great War, followed by the 1917 revolution. Sonya and Sasha were finally reconciled during the famine of 1918–19. Of her mother at this time Sasha recalled: "She seemed strangely indifferent to money, luxury, things she liked so much before." On her deathbed, Sonya made a strange confession: " 'I want to tell you,' she said, breathing heavily and interrupted by spasms of coughing, 'I know that I was the cause of your father's death.' "

Of all the papers at the conference, the most mysterious was about Tolstoy's little-read play *The Living Corpse*. This paper was delivered by a Czech septuagenarian with large, watery gray eyes, well liked both for his bombastic sociability and for his generosity with the bottle of single-malt scotch he carried in his suitcase. Everyone called him Vanya, though I believe that wasn't his real name.

The hero of *The Living Corpse* is a man called Fyodor. Fyodor is married, but he keeps running off with the Gypsies. He is chastely in love with a Gypsy singer. Meanwhile, his wife, Liza, is chastely in love with his best friend, whose name is, oddly, Karenin. (Karenin's mother's name is actually Anna Karenina.) Although Karenin returns Liza's love, the two are unable to act on their feelings unless Fyodor grants Liza a divorce. Fyodor, for his part, cannot file for divorce without besmirching the honor of the Gypsy singer. In despair, Fyodor resolves to kill himself and even writes a suicide note, but is persuaded by the Gypsy girl to adopt a different course: he simply leaves his own clothes on a riverbank, with the note in one pocket. Everyone believes he has drowned, including Liza and Karenin, who get married. But just at the point when a new life should begin for Fyodor as well—nothing happens. Somehow Fyodor doesn't change his name. He and the Gypsy girl don't get married. They quarrel and drift apart. Fyodor spends all his time in the tavern. "I am a corpse!" he shouts, slamming his glass on the table. Eventually, Fyodor's identity comes to light, and Liza is arrested for bigamy. In despair, Fyodor shoots himself. The living corpse becomes just an ordinary corpse.

The Living Corpse was based on the true story of an alcoholic called Gimer who had faked his own suicide and been sentenced to Siberia. The Moscow Art Theater very much wanted to stage it, but Tolstoy kept demurring. "It has seventeen acts," he said. "It needs a revolving stage." The real reason for Tolstoy's refusal came to light only much later. Gimer, it seems, had somehow learned that there was a play written about him and, upon his return from Siberia, presented himself at Yasnaya Polyana. Tolstoy took the unhappy man in hand, persuaded him to give up drink, and even found him a job in the very court that had convicted him. In light of Gimer's real-life "resurrection," Tolstoy abandoned the staging of *The Living Corpse*.

The strange story has an even stranger epilogue. As Tolstoy lay in a fever, in 1908, a visitor brought him news of this Gimer's death. "The corpse is now really dead," quipped the visitor—but Tolstoy had completely forgotten not only his former protégé but also the existence of the play. Even when the plot was recounted, Tolstoy had no recollection of having written such a thing: "And I am very, very glad that it escaped my mind to give place to something else." The central question of Vanya's talk was "Who is the living corpse?"

The argument twisted and coiled, glinting in the sun. At one moment it seemed that Tolstoy's Fyodor was actually Fyodor Dostoevsky, who had lived through the firing squad and survived the House of the Dead. Then it turned out that Fyodor was really Fyodorov, the philosopher-librarian who believed that the universal task of mankind was to harness the forces of science in order to abolish death and resurrect all dead people. Still later, it seemed the living corpse was actually Anna Karenina, who had died an adulteress in *Anna Karenina* and returned a mother-in-law in *The Living Corpse*. Then there was Jesus Christ, whose tomb was found empty after three days and nights: what was Tolstoy's God, if not a living corpse? And what was Tolstoy?

The banquet that night lasted until ten or eleven. Entertainment was provided by students from the Lev Tolstoy Accordion Academy: boys aged six to fifteen, already able to play the accordion with all the mannerisms of genial, nostalgic old men.* Even the tiniest of the boys, playing on a doll-size accordion, smiled knowingly, nodded, and even winked at the audience.

I had stopped at the dormitory first, where I took a shower and put on a linen dress. Many of the International Tolstoy Scholars congratulated me on my change of costume. Some of them had really thought that I didn't own any other clothes. A White Russian from Paris shook my hand. "You

---

*There really was an accordion concert, although I have been unable to confirm the existence of a Lev Tolstoy Accordion Academy.

should change three times this evening," he said, "to make up for lost time."

At dinner, many toasts were proposed. An unknown man in a sports jacket recited a particularly long, pointless toast; later, I learned that he was Tolstoy's great-great-grandson.

We had to get up early the next morning for the last event of the International Tolstoy Conference, a field trip to Anton Chekhov's former estate. Melikhovo lay directly along the three-hour route from Yasnaya Polyana to Moscow. In this respect, the field trip made a certain amount of logistical sense. Nonetheless, after five days of total devotion to Tolstoy, master of the Russian novel, it felt strange to drop in so breezily on Chekhov—master of the Russian short story and an altogether different writer—simply because one happened to be passing through the neighborhood.

And so, after the banquet, when the participants went to their rooms to pack their suitcases—mine, of course, had never been unpacked to begin with—I went onto the balcony to think about Chekhov. The air smelled like plants and cigar smoke, bringing to mind the marvelous story that begins with a young man's arrival, late one spring night, at the country estate of his former tutor, a famous horticulturalist. There is the nip of frost in the air, and the horticulturalist and his daughter are in a panic that the orchards might freeze. The daughter has resolved to stay up all night, supervising the bonfires. All night long, the young man and the daughter pace, coughing and weeping, through the rows of trees, watching the workers who stoke the smoldering bonfires with manure and damp straw. I tried to remember how the story ends. It doesn't end well.

Chekhov was nine years old when *War and Peace* was

published. He admired Tolstoy tremendously and longed to meet him; at the same time, the prospect of this meeting filled him with such alarm that he once ran out of a bathhouse in Moscow when he learned that Tolstoy was also there. Chekhov did not want to meet Tolstoy in the bath, but this apparently was his inescapable destiny. When at last he worked up the nerve to go to Yasnaya Polyana, Chekhov arrived at the exact moment when Tolstoy was headed to the stream for his daily ablutions. Tolstoy insisted that Chekhov join him; Chekhov later recalled that, as he and Tolstoy sat naked in the chin-deep water, Tolstoy's beard floated majestically before him.

Despite his lifelong hostility toward the medical profession, Tolstoy took an instant liking to Chekhov. "He is full of talent and undoubtedly has a very good heart," he said. "However, he does not seem to have any very definite attitude toward life." Chekhov had only a poorly defined attitude toward life, this strange process that brought one eye-to-eye with the floating beard of the greatest crank in world literature. Today, the stream where they bathed is partly obstructed, and full of vegetable life. One of the International Tolstoy Scholars, who insisted on sitting in it, came out completely green.

Chekhov, grandson of a serf, never saw the point of Tolstoyanism. Why should educated people lower themselves to the level of peasants? The peasants should be raised to the level of educated people! Nonetheless, Chekhov remained in awe of Tolstoy to the end of his days. "He is almost a perfect man," Chekhov observed once. And, another time: "I am afraid of Tolstoy's death. It would leave a great void in my life." In fact, Tolstoy outlived Chekhov by six years.

Ever since he was a medical student, Chekhov had experienced episodes of coughing blood. He dismissed them as bronchitis or the flu, but everyone knew the real cause. One night in 1897, while dining with his editor in Moscow's best restaurant, Chekhov suffered a severe lung hemorrhage. Blood poured from his mouth onto the white tablecloth. He was rushed to a private clinic and diagnosed with advanced tuberculosis in both lungs. He survived the attack but was, for some days, extremely weak and unable to speak. Only family members were admitted to see him. Then Tolstoy turned up, wearing an enormous bearskin coat. Nobody had the nerve to tell him to leave, so he sat at Chekhov's bedside and talked for a long time about the "immortality of the soul." Chekhov listened silently. Although he did not believe in the immortality of the soul, he was nonetheless touched by Lev Nikolayevich's solicitude.

The last meetings between Tolstoy and Chekhov took place in Yalta, where Chekhov had gone to die. One day in Yalta, Tolstoy put his arm around Chekhov. "My dear friend, I beg of you," he said, "do stop writing plays!" Another time, when the two writers were gazing at the sea, Tolstoy demanded, "Were you very profligate in your youth?" Chekhov was speechless with embarrassment. Tolstoy, glaring out at the horizon, announced, "I was insatiable!"

How could Chekhov not have sought treatment? How could he not have recognized his symptoms—especially when he spent weeks nursing his own brother Nikolai, who died of tuberculosis in 1889? I was reminded of a production of *Uncle Vanya*, the first play I ever saw in Russian, put on some years ago in Moscow. The actor playing Dr. Astrov had been a television star, famous for playing Dr. Watson in the Sherlock Holmes series on Soviet TV. Watching Dr. Astrov smoke a pipe, pore over maps, and rail against deforestation—watching Dr. Astrov fail to notice the really important thing, that Sonya was in love with him—I had been struck by his similarity to Dr. Watson. Doctor, I thought, you

see but you do not observe! For all your scientific enlightenment, you always misread the signs.

At six o'clock the next morning, the twenty-five International Tolstoy Scholars boarded a chartered bus to Moscow.
Nobody seemed to know how far Melikhovo was from Yasnaya Polyana, how long it would take to get there, or whether
there would be any stops along the way. Leena, an intense,
auburn-haired young woman who was writing a dissertation
about Tolstoy and Schopenhauer, was particularly concerned
about the subject of bathroom breaks. "The bus will bump,"
she observed. "There is no toilet on this bumping bus."

Leena and I made an insurance pact: if either of us had to
go to the bathroom, we would march to the front of the bus
together and request a stop.

The bus raced along the highway to Moscow. Through
the birch forests that flickered past my window, I glimpsed
the same north-south railway line that had carried Tolstoy
from Shamardino toward Astapovo.

About an hour north of Tula, Leena slipped into the seat
beside me. "It is time," she said. "Remember your promise."

"I remember," I said, preparing to get up, but Leena
didn't move. "I just got my period," she said, staring straight
ahead. "It's ten days early. It's not the right time." I made
some expression of sympathy. "It is the wrong time," she said
firmly, and then stood up.

We walked to the front of the bus. The driver didn't
acknowledge our request in any way, but something about his
shiny, shaven head indicated that he heard us. A few minutes
later the bus lurched off the road and skidded to a stop in a
gas station.

The women's bathroom was located fifty yards behind

the gas pumps, in a little hut on the edge of the woods. The door appeared to have been boarded over, but the boards were decayed and hanging from their nails. The enormous textologist went in first. She reemerged almost immediately, preceded by a kind of muffled splintering sound.

"Into the woods, girls," the textologist announced. We dispersed into the scraggly woods behind the gas station. The woods were full of garbage. Why am I here? I thought, looking at a vodka bottle that lay on the ground. It's because of Chekhov, I answered myself.

Back on the bus, the driver was cleaning his nails with a pocketknife. Leena came back after a minute or two. She said that she had been bitten by one of God's creatures.

"He made a lot of them," I observed, of God and his creatures.

I don't know how long we had been waiting in our seats before it suddenly began to seem odd that the bus hadn't left yet. I became aware of some external commotion. Just outside my window, the conference organizer—a brisk Canadian, who had written a well-received book about Tolstoy's representation of peasant life—was opening the luggage compartment. Her round, bespectacled face was set in a resolute expression, as she dragged out a suitcase and began carrying it away.

Looking around, I suddenly noticed the absence of several International Tolstoy Scholars: a military historian and his wife, the tennis scholar from Yale, and the expert on *The Living Corpse*. Leena and I got off the bus to investigate.

"I told him to just throw them out," the conference organizer was saying. "He insists on taking them with him. I'm at least going to find double bags." She strode off in the direction of the gas station, carrying a big plastic bag that appeared to contain some heavy object.

"It's going to be so awful when he opens the suitcase," said the military historian's wife.

It emerged that Vanya had had an accident, and was refusing to throw out his pants. He wanted them to be put into his suitcase, in a plastic bag. The military historian and the tennis scholar were in the men's toilet, trying to reason with him. Leena had turned completely pale. "It's the tyranny of the body," she said.

The conference organizer came back, with her double bags.

"We must not go to Melikhovo," Leena told her. "It is not the right time."

The conference organizer looked Leena in the eye. "We planned to go, so we are going to go."

Back on the bus, the driver was complaining about how he was going to be late. Instead of dropping us off in Moscow he was going to leave us at the outermost metro stop of the outermost suburbs.

"He is a bandit!" someone shouted, of the bus driver. There were murmurs of agreement. One by one, the remaining passengers returned to the bus. Last was Vanya, whose pale eyes roamed over the two aisles of International Tolstoy Scholars. "Ladies and gentlemen," he announced, clinging to the handrail as if climbing out of a swimming pool. "Ladies and gentlemen, I must apologize for the delay. I am an old man, you see. A very old man."

When the bus started again, a wave of sleepiness passed over me. I had stayed up late the previous night, reading a biography of Chekhov. I learned that, no matter how hard you tried to think about Chekhov here, you kept falling over Tolstoy. There was no way around it, and in fact the thing seemed to have been fated before they were born. In 1841, Chekhov's serf grandfather purchased his family's freedom from their master, a nobleman called Chertkov—who was none other than the future father of *Vladimir* Chertkov, the Dark One, the beneficiary of Tolstoy's secret will! (Chekhov's grandfather paid Chertkov's father 220 rubles per soul; Chertkov père, apparently not a bad guy, threw in one of Chekhov's aunts for free.) No wonder Chekhov didn't believe in the immortality of the soul. In the moment the money changed hands, his own grandfather had been a Gogolian "dead soul": a serf who had been paid for even as, *qua* serf, he ceased to exist.

I also learned that Tolstoy had seen *Uncle Vanya* during its first run in Moscow, when the role of Astrov was played by Stanislavsky himself. The only positive impression retained by Tolstoy from this production was of the sound of a cricket chirping in the final act. A well-known actor had spent an entire month acquiring precisely this skill, from a cricket in the Sandunov public baths. Nevertheless, his masterful chirping was not enough to counterbalance the overall terrible impression left on Tolstoy by *Uncle Vanya*. "Where is the drama?" Tolstoy once shouted, when the play was mentioned. He even harangued the actors, telling them that Astrov and Vanya had best marry peasant girls and leave the professor's wife in peace.

Tolstoy's diary entry for January 14, 1900, reads, "I went to see *Uncle Vanya* and was outraged. I wanted to write my play, *The Corpse*." Tolstoy started work on *The Living Corpse* that month.

I dreamed I was playing tennis against Tolstoy. As Alice in Wonderland plays croquet with a flamingo for a mallet, I was playing tennis with a goose for a racket. Lev Nikolayevich had a normal racket; only I had a goose. I served the ball, producing a flurry of fluffy gray down. Tolstoy's mighty backhand projected the ball far beyond the outermost limits of the tennis lawn, into the infinite dimension of total knowledge and human understanding. Match point.

I handed my goose over to Chekhov, who was next in the line of Tolstoy's opponents. Sitting on the edge of the lawn, watching the Tolstoy-Chekhov game, I suddenly realized, with a shiver, the identity of the living corpse. *It was Chekhov.* Tolstoy had written that play about Chekhov, whom he had always intended to outlive.

I woke to the crunching of gravel. We had reached Melikhovo, where we were offered the choice of a full or abridged tour. "We want the full tour," the conference organizer said grimly, pulling out her video camera. Our tour guide, a pensioner with hair dyed a strange tangerine color, took twenty minutes to guide us from the ticket booth to the front door. "Respected guests!" she shouted. "We are now located in the backyard of the neighbor of Anton Pavlovich Chekhov!"

Inside the house, I felt nothing. Yasnaya Polyana was Tolstoy's ancestral estate, and the center of his universe; it makes sense to visit Yasnaya Polyana. Chekhov had no ancestral estate. He bought Melikhovo, a house infested at that time by bedbugs and roaches, from a destitute artist; seven years later, when tuberculosis obliged him to seek a milder climate, he sold the land to a timber merchant and moved to Yalta. Melikhovo was just a stage for Chekhov—almost a stage *set*. The neighboring estates were owned by social outcasts: the body-building grandson of a Decembrist rebel; a fallen countess and her much younger lover.

No single room in Chekhov's house was large enough to

contain the entire body of International Tolstoy Scholars. We shuffled along a dark corridor. The guide gestured toward various rooms, too small to enter.

We passed to a tiny "*parloir*": "the scene of everlasting, interesting conversations."

"Did Chekhov play the piano?" someone asked.

"No!" the guide exclaimed, with great emphasis. "He absolutely did not play!"

I noticed a pocket of space around the *Living Corpse* scholar, who looked a bit forlorn. I approached him but inadvertently stepped back because of the smell.

Somewhere in the shadows that lay ahead, the guide was shouting, "Here is the beloved inkwell of the great writer!"

I extricated myself from the dark forest of shoulders, hurried down the narrow hallway, and exited into Chekhov's garden. The garden was empty but for the conference organizer, who was making a video recording of Chekhov's apple trees, and the Malevich scholar, who stooped to pick up an apple, stared at it, and took an enormous, yawning bite.

I walked quickly, trying to recapture the spark of mystery. Perhaps, I thought, Tolstoy had been killed by the "corpse"— by Gimer, who was supposedly dead two years at this time, but had anyone actually seen the body? "*Now* who's the corpse!" I imagined Gimer muttering, setting down the teaspoon—all I had to do was think of a motive. But somehow this time the motive wasn't forthcoming. My heart wasn't in it anymore. I found myself remembering "The Adventure of the Final Problem," the first and last story in which Watson has no trouble and no fun applying Holmes's method: "It was, alas, only too easy to do." Two sets of prints lead to the waterfall, and none lead back; nearby lies the alpenstock of the best and wisest man he has ever known.

Later, of course, Conan Doyle recants. Holmes's death and Watson's bereavement turn out to be a temporary illusion, and real life starts again: the late nights, the hansom rides, the peat bogs, the thrill of the chase. But can things ever really be the same between the doctor and the "living corpse"? Will there not come a time when Holmes has to tell his friend that all the murderers they apprehended were but the pawns of a far greater force, untouchable by human justice—a force even capable of acting independently, with no human agent?

Watson will be utterly confused. "A criminal act, without a criminal actor—my dear Holmes, surely you cannot have gone over to the supernaturalists!"

Holmes will smile sadly. "Nay, my old friend—I fear that, of all forces, it is the most natural."

Call it Professor Moriarty or Madame la Mort, call it the black monk, or use its Latin name: this killer has infinite means and unfathomable motives.

And still life goes on in Chekhov's garden, where it's always a fine day for hanging yourself, and somebody somewhere is playing the guitar. In a hotel in Kharkov, the old professor is deducing the identity of his future murderer: "I will be killed by . . . that abominable wallpaper!" Interior decoration is often the Final Problem; Ivan Ilyich was done in by some drapes. Now the samovar has almost gone cold, and frost has touched the cherry blossoms. Dr. Chekhov, loyal custodian of the human body, you who could look in the ear of an idle man and see an entire universe—where are you now?

Summer in Samarkand (continued)

If there is one thing I heard a thousand times in Samarkand, it's that they have the greatest bread in Uzbekistan because of their amazingly clean water and air. The famous bread of Samarkand comes in round, flat loaves, known in Russian as *lepyoshka*. As legend has it, the emir of Bukhara once summoned the best baker of Samarkand to bake him some Samarkand bread. The baker arrived in Bukhara bringing his own flour and water and firewood. But according to some kind of inter-emirate bread arbiter, the bread he baked didn't taste the same as real Samarkand bread. The emir decided to have the baker executed, pausing only to ask if he had anything to say in his own defense. "Well," the baker replied, "there isn't any Samarkand air here, to leaven the bread." The emir was so impressed by these words that he spared the baker's life.

This story was invariably deployed as evidence not of the baker's cleverness, but of some actual properties of the Samarkand air.

Instead of relying on one of the abstract or inedible representations of "bread" so popular in other parts of the world, the Samarkand bread sellers used, as signage, an actual *lepyoshka* hammered to a board with a large iron nail, like the body of Christ. Looking at those signs was like witnessing the first glimmerings of abstract thought. How does a loaf of bread nailed to a board differ from a loaf of bread in a store window at an unmarked bakery? Both indicate the sale of bread, but you can actually buy and eat the bread you see in a bakery window. In Samarkand, the bread had been sacrificed—rendered inedible by being nailed to a board and hung out all day, maybe multiple days, in the sun—in the name of signification.

My introduction to the *lepyoshka* of Samarkand took place on that first evening at Gulya's house. I had just returned from my first meeting at the university with Vice-Rector Safarov and my future language teacher, Muzaffar, and was so tired I could barely walk. I found Eric in the dining room of the guest wing of the house, sitting in a fake Louis XV chair at a long Louis XV table, solving chess problems. Bukhara carpets lay beneath his bare feet, and ghostly curtains floated in front of the windows. The sun was setting outside and orange light filled the room, bouncing off the mirrored walls and the crystal chandelier.

"You're awake!" I said.

"I waited for you," Eric said.

We stumbled into the bedroom. In my dream, the poor ward was trying to move Jane Fairfax's piano. "Emma! Emma!" shouted the ward, but the piano was still falling down the stairs, falling and continuing to fall, making a terrible racket. Gulya was rapping on the window. "Emma!" she called. "Em-*ma*!" I staggered out of bed and fumbled with the window latch. The sky outside was a deep, liquid blue. "Emma, dinner!" Gulya said. She was standing outside the window, just below eye level. Her features looked exaggerated, the heavily penciled eyes and eyebrows, the cartoonishly mouth-shaped mouth.

"Thank you very much," I said, "but I think we need to sleep some more. I think we need to sleep until the morning."

We had a long conversation then, about the dinner Gulya had cooked for us, and how angry my "husband" would be to wake up in the night and learn that I had kept it a secret from him. "Wake him up," Gulya suggested with steely playfulness. "Go on, Emma, wake him up."

Eric gazed at me with sleep-clouded eyes. "I think the easiest thing to do would be to just go eat dinner," he said.

Clutching each other's hands, we trudged across the courtyard to the annex kitchen where we were to eat all our meals: a narrow room with gas burners, a long table, a row of cabinets, and a refrigerator. The refrigerator was kept unplugged all night, to save electricity. Gulya handed us two enormous bowls of borscht, redolent of mutton, covered by a thin film of orange grease.

"This looks great," Eric said in a woolly, gentle voice. He was the kind of person who could eat anything at any time, and once ate one thousand dumplings in one week, just to make some kind of point.

I ate a piece of Samarkand bread and drank cup after cup of bitter green tea, while fielding Gulya's questions about our fictional wedding. We had been instructed to tell her that we were married. Conveniently, we already owned platinum wedding bands, purchased two years earlier as engagement rings, using the savings cleverly invested by Eric in Irish banks and especially in some Mexican corn-processing plants, whose stock had skyrocketed because of an unexpected U.S. subsidy for ethanol production. I had stopped wearing my ring after a few months, when it started giving me a rash. Having determined through online research that platinum was the world's most hypoallergenic metal, I interpreted this rash as a hysterical symptom, although it later turned out to have been caused by soap getting trapped under the ring, which was slightly too big. Meanwhile time had passed and although, in certain respects, nothing had changed—we never called off the engagement in so many words—things had, in other, almost imperceptible ways, changed a great deal, so that our old plans had gradually come to seem unreal, unrealizable, ill-advised.

We were wearing the rings again now. Eric had already finished his borscht, whereas I had managed only a few spoonfuls.

"You don't have to eat it, dear thing," he told me. When Gulya wasn't looking, we traded bowls and he ate all of my borscht, too.

Gulya wanted to know when and where the wedding had taken place, how many guests had attended, what kind of hat I had worn. I told her that we had had a small wedding, one and a half years ago, on a boat, in Canada.

"Where did you spend your honeymoon?" Gulya asked.

"On the boat," I said.

After dinner we rushed back to bed. Too jumpy to fall asleep, I started to read. Gradually I became aware of Eric rolling and kicking beside me. He suddenly opened his eyes and said, "Black king to e-seven." Closing his eyes, he added, "Black knight to j-four."

I put down my novel and picked up the book of chess problems that lay next to his pillow. "There is no j-four," I said, worried. "It only goes up to h."

"Oh, I'm really sorry," Eric said. Eyes still closed, he furrowed his brow and looked really sorry. "I thought it was one of those times when the knight goes outside, like to Kazakhstan."

I touched his forehead. It was cold and clammy. "Are you feeling OK?"

"Oh no, my friend," he said apologetically. "I'm really sick." A moment later he sat up, put on his sweatpants, and shuffled out the door and into the courtyard.

He came back a few minutes later and climbed into bed.

His skin was an indescribable color. My heart began to pound. Why had I let him eat that borscht? What if his mother found out? She already disliked me, Eric's mother. In my head I heard the voice of the professor from Berkeley: "Four thousand dollars for the body bag to send you home." Pulling on some shorts, I went out into the courtyard to look for Gulya.

Gulya said it was nothing to worry about. Foreigners always got sick. "Why aren't you sick?" she asked, looking suspicious.

She put some water to boil, brewed a pot of tea, and brought out a tin box, from which she produced mysterious items: a resinous amber log and a pink glassy rock. With a sharp knife, she shaved off pieces of these presumably medicinal objects and dissolved them in the tea.

Back in our room, Eric had fallen asleep. I struggled to lift him to a sitting position. His T-shirt was soaked through. It was like trying to pull a bear cub out of a river.

"If we ever have children," he announced, "they can say that their father was a methodical man."

"Oh—great," I said. I got him to take a sip of tea, and dragged off his wet T-shirt, a giveaway from a software company. Printed on the back was the slogan "No Whiners, No Crybabies, No Prima Donnas."

"What will they say about their mother?" I asked, pulling a fresh shirt over his head.

Eric fell back onto his pillow. "She was serious and lively."

I opened the screen door and stepped outside. The flagstones were cool under my feet. The moon had risen and a slight breeze rippled the greenish water in the pool. A phrase suddenly came to my mind: *the amber lozenge.* For the first time in many years, I found myself remembering a rainy afternoon in college when my friend Sanja appeared at my door, streaming wet, to notify me of the two simple keys that were necessary for a perfect understanding of the poet Osip Mandelstam.

"The first thing is 'as I come to you from the rubble of Petersburg, take a little honey from the palms of my hands.'" As she spoke these words, Sanja stared into my face with a deranged, wide-eyed expression, holding her cupped hands outstretched. "Second," she continued, "'Psyche is slow to hand Charon the amber lozenge.'" She looked at me meaningfully. "The *amber lozenge*," she repeated.

Later, when I happened myself to be reading Mandelstam, I discovered that the amber lozenge was actually a copper lozenge—literally, one of the coins Psyche carried in her mouth to pay Charon when she went to Hades to look for Persephone. Mandelstam's phrase was *mednaya lepyoshka*, the same word for the delicious bread of Samarkand.

I had seen it in Gulya's box, beside the glassy rock: the amber lozenge. I had given it to Eric myself; I had put it in his mouth with my own hands. Where had he gone? Whom was he seeing there?

I went back inside and fell into an uneasy sleep, troubled by distorted phrases and images from the past forty-eight hours. *In our nation's capital I partook of the deathly government salads. Handing Charon the amber lozenge, I passed to the other side. Dry laments surrounded me like a fine rain. I saw a white pawn become a queen, and the spirits of Sophocles and Euripides embattled in a fatal spelling bee.*

In the morning, Eric was completely recovered. He didn't remember anything at all.

All happy families are alike; all unhappy families are unhappy after their own fashion. The Uzbek Soviet Socialist Republic

(SSR) was established in 1925. Tajikistan became its own Soviet Socialist Republic in 1929. Samarkand, a predominantly Tajik city, remained in Uzbekistan.

I didn't know before I got there that the majority of the Samarkand population was still Tajik and spoke a form of Farsi, an Indo-European language grammatically unrelated to Turkish and Uzbek. Furthermore, our host family was actually Tajik. Gulya knew Uzbek from spending vacations with her aunt in the Fergana Valley, but at home with the children she spoke Tajik and Russian—mostly Russian. Four-year-old Lila, who was being groomed for the Russian school system, barely knew any Tajik at all. Not that I minded—my enthusiasm about learning Uzbek, already pretty lukewarm, was nonetheless a fiery furnace compared to my feelings about learning Tajik. Although I sometimes tried speaking Uzbek with Gulya, she would switch to Russian almost immediately, pointing out that we would understand each other better. Like most people, she was more interested in communicating her own thoughts and feelings than in helping to keep alight the flame of the Eastern Turkic languages.

At Gulya's request, I met a few times with Lila's nineteen-year-old brother, Inom, to help him with his English lessons.

"A book is at table," Inom said.

"Right, almost . . . The book is *on the* table."

"Uh-huh, OK . . . You know, Emma, it's hard for me to take English seriously, since I already speak three languages: Tajik, Russian, and Uzbek. English is much easier and simpler than these languages, so the little details of it aren't really important to me."

Discontinued by mutual agreement, these English lessons were rapidly incorporated into Gulya's ongoing invective against her son. "There's an American right here in our house, and you won't be bothered to talk English with her!

You care nothing about your future! All you care about is washing your car, you no-good *muzhik*!"

As soon as I had left for class, Gulya and Inom apparently began their day with a screaming argument. One morning, Gulya had actually picked up a brick from the ground and thrown it at her son, shrieking, *"Muzhik! Muzhik!"* I didn't believe Eric at first when he told me, but he showed me the broken brick in the courtyard, where it had shattered against a wall. After wearing themselves out, mother and son would get into Inom's car and drive to Gulya's travel agency—one of the few air-conditioned buildings I saw in Samarkand—where she processed visas and organized tours for foreigners.

I have never been so hungry in my life as I was that summer. I remember lying across the bed with Eric, fantasizing about buying *anything we wanted* from the twenty-four-hour Safeway across from our apartment in Mountain View.

"A whole catfish," I proposed.

"Birthday cake ice cream," Eric countered, alluding to a Safeway-brand flavor laced with blue frosting and pieces of cake.

When we first moved to Mountain View, I used to think it was depressing to look out the window and see a gigantic Safeway parking lot, but that was before I spent any time in the "Fourth Paradise."

Breakfast consisted of "soft-boiled" eggs, dipped briefly in warm (not boiling) water, with bread and orange jam. The jam came from a vat under the sink; when Gulya lifted its oilcloth cover, you could see a network of busy ants hurrying over the gemlike surface.

Our relationship with Gulya reached a new level of unspoken antagonism the day Eric discovered a second kitchen in the other wing of the house, where the jam container had a rubberized lid and no ants—we alone were given the jam with ants. In the absence of any visible jam shortage, this behavior was difficult for me to understand. Eric claimed that it was characteristic of the Tajik Communist elite. In a closet next to the secret kitchen, Eric had also discovered a secret, flushing toilet. The toilet in the main bathroom was broken, and Gulya said the man who fixed toilets was on vacation, so Eric and I had to use the "Uzbek-style" toilet: a hole in the ground. When you lifted the wooden cover over the Uzbek-style toilet, a dense black cloud of flies buzzed up in your face. Sometimes the Uzbek-style toilet clogged, and then you had to poke in it with a big pointed stick. Our feelings were very hurt when we learned that we were the only ones who had to use this toilet.

Every morning at seven thirty, I left Gulya's house for the university. Her street at that hour was quiet and deserted. A few times I saw a chicken walking around importantly, like some kind of a regional manager. There was a police station at the corner of the main road. Large numbers of police officers sprawled on benches in a yard, talking loudly. All along Sharof Rashidov Street, old men in skullcaps sat at card tables selling lottery tickets and single cigarettes. The proprietors of teahouses hosed down the sidewalks, waking up the stray dogs.

Despite these and other interesting sights offered by the city dubbed by Tamerlane "the Mirror of the World," I spent most of the walk staring at the ground, trying not to fall into the yawning chasms that appeared every few blocks. The people of Samarkand probably weren't thrilled to have all those yawning chasms in their sidewalks, but they made the most of things by using them to incinerate their household garbage. Newspapers, watermelon rinds, and other items smoldered obscurely in their depths. Often, the only way to traverse the yawning chasms of burning garbage was via wooden or metal planks. I was greatly impressed by the agility with which the Russian girls in particular trotted across these makeshift bridges, in their high-heeled sandals, with their somehow empty facial expressions—so unlike my own facial expression, which, I felt, probably conveyed a kind of deep literary trepidation.

The last part of the walk passed through a past or future construction site, a vast expanse of orange clayey soil and crumbly rocks. Walking on this terrain gave you the hopeless feeling of running in a dream, but afterward you knew it had been real because your shoes were orange. Eventually the orange clay gave way to sparse grass, and there was my destination: "the nine-story building," the biggest building in the university. A janitor at this building, with whom I later struck up a friendship, gave me his mailing address as "Samarkand State University, Nine-Story building, Janitor Habib." "That's how I get most of my mail," he explained.

In the morning, the lobby of the nine-story building was filled with serious young people. The girls wore bright red lipstick and brilliantly colored ankle-length dresses; the boys, light shirts, dark pants, and pointy-toed shoes. When they smiled, their gold teeth glinted in the sunlight. Uniformed guards at the door checked your pass and made you walk through a metal detector, which didn't appear to be plugged into anything.

The elevator was always broken, so I walked up to the fifth floor, where I met my language teacher, the philosophy graduate student Muzaffar. (His specialty, I later learned, was the Marburg school of neo-Kantians.) Muzaffar's teaching materials consisted of a 1973 Soviet textbook that presented the Uzbek language exclusively through the lens of cotton production: a valuable lesson in how monomania structures the world. The unit about the months and seasons was about the months and seasons in which cotton was sown or harvested. The unit about families was about the roles played by different family members in the production of cotton.

"Rustam works in a cotton mill all year round, but his younger sister, Nargiza, is still a student," I read. "She picks cotton only in the summer, with the other students."

"Did you understand?" Muzaffar asked.

"I did."

Muzaffar nodded. "I thought so."

We finished the textbook in two weeks. The basic grammar was nearly the same as in Turkish, as was much of the simple household vocabulary, though there were some differences in usage. The word *it*, for example, means "dog" in both Uzbek and Turkish—but in Uzbek it means a regular dog, whereas in Turkish it means a contemptible, low-down cur. As a Turkish person in Uzbekistan, one was always wondering why the Uzbeks spoke so insultingly about their dogs. Conversely, the standard Turkish future-tense verb ending exists in Uzbek, and is also a future-tense ending, but with a pompous or literary-heroic connotation. "You can use it to say, 'President Karimov will cover his nation in glory,' " Muzaffar explained, "but not to say that 'Muzaffar will drive to Tashkent to pick up Safarov's friend's visa.' " (Muzaffar worked part-time as Vice-Rector Safarov's secretary.)

After we finished the cotton production textbook, Muzaffar started making up his own grammatical texts, usually featuring one of these recurring characters: President Karimov and poor Muzaffar. I especially liked to hear about poor Muzaffar's troubles as a graduate student. One morning, for example, Muzaffar went to the library to get books for his dissertation. Samarkand State University had a closed-stack library which had never been fully catalogued, so you just had to write what kind of books you wanted on a request form and hope for the best. Muzaffar turned in his request at opening time. It hadn't been processed yet by lunch. The library was closed for an hour and a half, at which point the librarian disappeared altogether. Several hours later, he was discovered asleep in some corner, and was dispatched to the philosophy stacks in the basement, where he again vanished. The library closed for the day, and Muzaffar had to go home. Two days later, he rushed to the library in response to a phone call, and there was a big pile of books waiting for him . . . written in Arabic script, which had been discontinued in 1928. Muzaffar had to get his grandfather to read him the books. "But my grandfather isn't interested in philosophy. He would read to me only after I spent all Saturday pulling weeds from his cabbage garden. It was a particularly hot day . . ."

The Uzbek orthography had changed multiple times in the past seventy-five years, a reflection of the fact that, as of 1917, *there was no standard written or spoken language called Uzbek*. There was just a continuum of uncodified Turkic dialects, many of them mutually incomprehensible. The region's shared literary language, Chaghatay Turkish, was unknown to most "Uzbeks," whose rate of literacy was estimated by the Soviets at 2 or 3 percent.

Even more remarkably, the very concept of an Uzbek ethnicity dates only to the Soviet period. To quote a 1925 report by the All-Russian Academy of Sciences Commission for Studying the Tribal Makeup of the Population of Russia and Adjoining Countries: "Uzbeks could not conceive of the same sort of unified and distinct ethnic group for themselves

as the Kazakhs, Kirgiz, or Turkmens." Who were the Uzbeks?
Did they even exist?

The term *Uzbek* was used as early as the fourteenth
or fifteenth century, to designate a loose confederation of
nomadic Turkic-Mongolian tribes in Central Asia, a region
whose natives identified themselves primarily by their tribes
or clans, rather than by national or ethnic supergroups. In the
nineteenth century, Russians started colonizing Central Asia
to gain leverage against British India, initiating a century-
long strategic rivalry marked by proxy wars, puppet khans,
and double agents. The British called this conflict "The Great
Game," but no Russian people called it that. In 1867, Russia established the Russian Turkestan Governor-Generalship,
with its administrative capital in Tashkent. When approached
by skeptical Muslim envoys, the Russian governor-general
would show them an impressive document bound in gold:
an enumeration of his plenary powers. Uzbeks called him the
"semi-tsar."

After the 1917 Revolution, the people of Turkestan thought
they had seen the last of the Russians. They established an
autonomous government, which was, however, liquidated by
Red Army forces in 1918. In order to preempt further pan-
Turkic initiatives Lenin appointed a Commission for the
Regionalization of Central Asia, which, having collected maps,
ethnographic reports, economic inventories, and census data,
set about distributing the Turkestan natives among five "ethno-
genic" categories: Uzbek, Tajik, Turkmen, Kazakh, and Kyrgyz.
Most Central Asians were unable to identify themselves with
any one of these categories. Cartoons from the period show different tribesmen in regional dress having comical troubles filling out their national identity papers. By 1924, the designation
Turkestan had disappeared from common use. Under Stalin it
became a "forbidden political concept or name."

In 1921, a Language and Orthography Congress met to standardize the region's varying Arabic orthographies, and a Soviet commission was appointed to codify "the cleanest, most distinctive, most Uzbek" of the regional vernaculars. The commission settled upon the Iranized dialect of Tashkent, which was unusually high in Tajik-Persian words and unusually low in vowel harmony, a phonological rule in most Turkic languages.* In 1926, another commission replaced the Arabic orthography with a Latin alphabet. This All-Union Central Committee for the New Turkic Alphabet was fraught with discord between the Caucasian and Central Asian contingents, particularly over the inclusion of uppercase letters, which did not exist in Arabic. The Azeris felt that capital letters were universal and beautiful, as well as necessary for students of mathematics, chemistry, and foreign languages. The Uzbeks countered that the language reforms were targeted mainly at the illiterate masses, for whom an extra form of each letter was a "superfluous luxury." Though the Central Asians were eventually forced to accept the uppercase, a concession was won by the poet Fitrat: capital letters would look just like lowercase letters, only bigger. Fitrat and the other Turkic "nationalists" also succeeded in preserving vowel harmony in the new alphabet, which had nine different vowels (designated by diacritics).

In subsequent years, the Russian endings -*ov* and -*ova* were appended to Uzbek surnames. Khojand, Pishpek, and Dushanbe were renamed Leninabad, Frunze, and Stalinabad. (By the 1970s, there were no fewer than fifteen villages in the Samarkand district named Kalinin, after Lenin's and Stalin's

---

*In languages with vowel harmony, every word typically contains either "back vowels" (in Turkish, *a, ı, o, u*) or "front vowels" (*e, i, ö, ü*), but not both. There are multiple forms of every declension and verb tense to match the different kinds of vowels.

titular head of state.) "International" words were Russified: Uzbeks spoke of "Hamlet" as *Gamlet*, and "hectares" as *gektars*. Television and radio were broadcast in "Uzbek."

In the late thirties and early forties, each Central Asian SSR was outfitted with its own local Cyrillic alphabet. The Turkic languages were closer than ever to Russian . . . and further than ever from one another. The poet Fitrat was arrested and convicted of "bourgeois nationalism." He was shot during the Great Purges. Vowel harmony, upheld by Fitrat as the "iron law" of Turkic languages, was eliminated from Uzbek orthography. (To Turkish people, the near lack of vowel harmony makes Uzbek sound harsh and toneless.)

Throughout the Soviet era, the state universities, the post offices, and all other government agencies operated in Russian. During perestroika, the Soviets proposed a bill declaring Uzbek the "state language": a purported concession to Uzbek nationalists. The bill, which preserved Russian as the official "language of inter-ethnic communication," only served to infuriate the Uzbek Writers' Union. The poet Vahidov charged that, according to his textual analysis, the document itself had been translated into Uzbek from a Russian original; other writers demonstrated that the bill used the word *Russian* fifty-one times, and *Uzbek* only forty-seven times. The Uzbek Young Pioneers magazine, *Gulkhan*, received hundreds of angry letters. The editors wrote back, addressing their replies in Uzbek; the envelopes were all returned by the post office with a note in Russian: "Indicate address!" The bill was modified in 1995, specifying that by 2005, the state language was to be Uzbek, written with a new Latin alphabet. Everyone who had attained literacy after 1950 now needed to relearn the alphabet.

In the national mythology devised by the Soviets, Uzbek statehood was retroactively dated to the era of Timur (Tamerlane), whose grave was located in Samarkand. The Timurids were declared to be the Uzbeks' ancestors—even though, in real life, the people known as Uzbeks had been enemies of the Timurids. A statue of "Amir Timur" replaced the Karl Marx monument in the center of Tashkent; previously condemned by Marxists as a barbaric despot, Timur suddenly turned out to have understood all the forms of socioeconomic life: nomadic, agricultural, urban. He was declared to have been not only a military genius, but a great chess player, and even the inventor of a game called Perfect Chess, played on a 110-square board.

I was particularly intrigued by Perfect Chess, which reminded me both of Eric's delirious ravings and of *The Knight's Move*, a book by the Russian Formalist critic Viktor Shklovsky. In *The Knight's Move*, Shklovsky proposes that the history of literature proceeds not in a straight line, but in a bent one, like the L-shaped path of a chess knight. The authors who influence one another are not always the ones you would expect: "the legacy is transmitted not from father to son, but from uncle to nephew." Furthermore, literary forms themselves grow by assimilating foreign or extraliterary material, veering off in new angles.

Shklovsky would probably have liked Perfect Chess, in which each player has, in addition to the standard pieces, two giraffes, two camels, two siege engines, and a vizier. The camel moves in a "stretched" knight's move—one square diagonally and two squares forward—while a giraffe moves one square diagonally and at least three squares forward. The Soviet invention of an Uzbek national identity reminded me of the giraffe's move, a move two steps further than anyone would normally think of. They assimilated the Timurids, circumnavigated Genghis Khan: the legacy twists and turns, passing from the great-uncle to the great-nephew of the one who sacked his palace.

As Amir Timur was declared the father of Uzbek state-hood, so was the greatest Timurid poet, Mir Ali-Shir Navai (1441–1501), declared the father of Uzbek literature. Alisher Navoi, as he became known in Uzbek, was born and died in Herat, in present-day Afghanistan, and had previously been claimed as a shared patrimony by all of Chaghatay literary culture. The Soviets reclassified him, along with the Chaghatay language itself, as Old Uzbek. "Chaghataysm" was declared anti-Soviet. The term *Old Uzbek* gradually expanded to denote any human achievement that had ever taken place within the boundaries of the UzSSR, including the composition of Avicenna's medical textbook and Al-Khorazmi's treatise on algebra.

I learned many of these historical circumstances only later. They helped me understand the feeling I so often had, while studying Uzbek literature in Samarkand, of being a character in a Borges story, studying a literature invented by a secret cabal of academicians.

Every day for two hours, after my language class with Muzaffar, I studied "Old Uzbek" literature with Dilorom Salohiy, an assistant professor at Samarkand State University. Dilorom, who held doctoral degrees in both Russian and Uzbek literature, was a beautiful woman in her early forties, with high cheekbones, olive skin, and slightly Asiatic eyes outlined in kohl. She wore small gold hoop earrings and long silk dresses printed with tiny, amazingly variegated flowers. One dress had so many colors that I wrote them down in my notebook: brown, fuchsia, green, yellow, white, pink, purple, black, and orange-red. Unlike Muzaffar, Dilorom spoke perfect Russian, but she didn't know any English at all. Her voice was soft and regretful, as if she were gently breaking you some terrible news.

Dilorom spoke in Uzbek most of the time, very slowly, often addressing me as *qizim* ("my girl," "my daughter"). She didn't like to speak Russian, and used it only as a last resort. Nonetheless, to my surprise, I understood most of what she said—or at least I understood something, continuously, most of the time she was talking. The Chaghatay texts we read together in class, on the other hand, were almost completely impenetrable. I recognized about three words in ten, which, due to the metaphorical style of the writing, wasn't enough to get even the most basic gist. You would understand *man*, *snake*, and *evil*, and the poet could be talking about anything, from politics, to love, to snakes. At the end of each class, Dilorom loaned me a Russian or modern Uzbek translation to read at home. Sometimes the books seemed to confirm what she told me in class; other times, they seemed completely unrelated.

It was, furthermore, impossible to find any external confirmation of anything Dilorom told me simply by walking into a bookstore: *no Uzbek literature* was being printed in book form while I was there. The bookstores sold only romance and detective novels, Russian editions of *Windows for Dummies*, newspapers, and endless manuals about pregnancy and child-rearing. The state had recently declared the Uzbek birth rate to be in a crisis, and baby propaganda assailed you from all media outlets. One television commercial showed the spotlessly clean free maternity clinics open to all those who fulfilled their civic duty of procreation. Rosy babies lolled beatifically in individual glass basins. The resemblance of these basins to casserole dishes was accentuated by the maternity nurses' white aprons and tall white hats, which resembled chef's hats. This commercial always made me think of Swift's "A Modest Proposal."

. . .

As nineteenth-century British people considered Napoleon to be Satan incarnate, so did Dilorom consider Genghis Khan to be the superhuman nemesis of the Uzbek people, the wrecker of the "First Uzbek Renaissance" embodied by the achievements of Avicenna and Al-Biruni. Shaking her head sorrowfully, she told me that Genghis Khan not only rode a bull, but he didn't wear any pants. She said that God should forgive her for mentioning such things to me, "but he didn't wear any pants." Because the Mongols were too ignorant to make swords, they carried wooden sticks. In Samarkand, scholars were drinking tea from special porcelain teacups that rang different musical tones when you tapped them with a spoon. Genghis Khan destroyed every single one of these teacups, the secret of whose craftsmanship has been lost forever.

"In English we have an expression: 'like a bull in a china shop,'" I remarked.

"That's how Genghis Khan was—but even worse. He destroyed not a shop, but a whole civilization."

Timur was the opposite of Genghis Khan. The Mongols destroyed eleven centuries in 130 years; but Timur rebuilt it all in seventy years. This "Second Uzbek Renaissance" reached its fullest expression in the lifetime of Alisher Navoi. At the time of Navoi's birth, the people of Turkestan were already telling time using a chest from which a doll would emerge every hour. In Europe, people were still using the hourglass: a "sand clock." Only the Turks had clockwork, which they used to make an escalator that lifted the king onto his throne every morning.

Navoi lived for four years in Samarkand: a city so deeply imbued with poetry that even the doctors wrote their medical treatises in verse. But before Navoi himself transformed the Old Uzbek vernacular into a literary language, all of this poetry was written in Persian. In his *Muhakamat al-lughatayn*, or *Judgment of Two Languages* (1499), Navoi mathematically proved the superiority to Persian of Old Uzbek, a language so rich that it had words for seventy different species of duck. Persian just had *duck*. Impoverished Persian writers had no words with which to differentiate between a burr and a thorn; older and younger sisters; male, female, and infant boars; hunting and fowling; a beauty mark on a woman's face and a beauty mark somewhere else; deer and elands; being adorned and being *really* adorned; drinking something down all at once in a refined way, and drinking slowly while savoring each drop.

Persian, Dilorom told me, had only one word for crying, whereas Old Uzbek had one hundred. Old Uzbek had words for wanting to cry and not being able to, for being caused to sob by something, for loudly crying like thunder in the clouds, for crying in gasps, for weeping inwardly or secretly, for crying ceaselessly in a high voice, for crying in hiccups, and for crying while uttering the sound *hay hay*. Old Uzbek had special verbs for being unable to sleep, for speaking while feeding animals, for being a hypocrite, for gazing imploringly into a lover's face, for dispersing a crowd.

It was all just like a Borges story—except that Borges stories are always so short, whereas life in Samarkand kept dragging obscurely on and on. In Borges, the different peculiar languages yield up, in a matter of pages, some kind of interesting philosophical import: the languages of the northern hemisphere of Tlön have no nouns, a circumstance that immediately turns out to represent an extreme of Berkeleyan idealism whereby the world is perceived as a sequence of shifting shapes; the Chinese encyclopedia has different words for animals drawn with a fine camel's-hair brush and animals who have just broken a flower vase, which dramatizes the impossibility of devising any objective system of classifying knowledge.

By contrast, whatever it was that you learned about Uzbeks when you studied their language, it was something long and difficult to fathom. What did you know about Uzbekistan once you learned that Old Uzbek had a hundred different words for crying? I wasn't sure, but it didn't seem to bode well for my summer vacation.

The earliest texts composed in the Turkic vernacular, Dilorom said, were fables and didactic maxims. Of the fables, I particularly remember the tale of the deer and the hammam. One day, the story goes, the deer went to the hammam. Afterward he felt so clean and comfortable that he lay down for a nap in a cool, muddy spot under some trees. He woke up and went to visit his friends, not realizing that he was covered in mud.

"Where are you coming from?" his friends asked. "From the hammam," the deer replied.

"Can you guess the moral of this story?" Dilorom asked me.

I thought it over. "You can't tell where someone comes from just by looking at them?"

Dilorom shook her head, smiling sadly. "No, *qizim*, the moral is this: Don't resemble that deer!"

The greatest Old Uzbek didactic writer was the twelfth-century poet Adib Akhmad Yugnakiy. Yugnakiy, who suffered from congenital blindness, demonstrated in numerous ways his preternatural poetic vision—for instance, by molding a cooked bean into the shape of a ram, an animal he had never seen before. "A *ram*," Dilorom repeated, and drew in my notebook a picture of a bean, followed by a picture of a ram. The ram had a mild, sickly countenance and huge curved horns. Who was the true genius: Yugnakiy or the nameless one who first saw a bean mashed up by a blind poet and called it *ram*?

Dilorom told me, and I wrote in my notebook, that five copies of Yugnakiy's masterpiece, *The Gift of Reality*, had reached our era. They were discovered in 1915 by a Turkish scholar named Najib Osim. "Osim" didn't sound to me like a Turkish name—it violates vowel harmony—but I later found out that Turkish people call him Necip Asim "Yazıksız" ("the Merciless"). Turkish people refer to Adib Akhmad Yugnakiy as Edip Ahmet Yükneki; they call his book not *Xibatul Xaqoyiq*, but *Atabetü'l Hakayık*. Their name for the language it's written in isn't Old Uzbek, but Hakaniye Turkish, or "the King's Uighur." Despite these discrepancies, I was relieved to learn that "Yugnakiy" corresponded to something in the consensus view of reality.

"*Mana, qizim*—here is a precious, rare thing, a very old book," Dilorom said, reverently handing me a 1962 Soviet edition of the *Xibatul* in modern Uzbek translation. It was printed on newsprint and bound with yellowing glue. (Yugnakiy had been reprinted in a large edition under the Soviets, because he wrote about the dangers of wealth.) "This is a very precious, rare thing, but I will let you bring it home and read it tonight because I know you love books, and I know you will take good care of it." As homework that night, I translated some of Yugnakiy's maxims into Russian.

The world holds in one hand honey; in the other, poison. One hand feeds you honey, and the other— poisons you.

When you taste something sweet, consider it bitter. When the road seems easy, then come tens of difficulties. Hey, dreamer, so you want grief and ease: but when will hope achieve itself?

This world is like a snake: first it looks soft, but then it looks like a bitter draught. Even if the snake has a nice, soft appearance, nonetheless it has a bad character. Precisely when the snake appears to be very soft, that is when you should run away from it.

Dilorom, looking over my translations the next day, said that they were too literal. "You should think more about the meaning and less about the words," she advised me.

The most popular fourteenth-century literary genre, sometimes composed in Old Uzbek, was epistolary poetry. Poems during this period took the form of love letters between nightingales and sheep, between opium and wine, between red and green. One poet wrote to a girl that he had tried to drink a lake so he could swallow her reflection: this girl was cleaner than water. "Most people, like you and me, are dirtier than water," Dilorom explained. "That's why we take baths to get clean. But this girl is cleaner than water. If she puts her arm in the water, maybe the water will become cleaner."

Another poet compared his beloved's upper-lip hairs to the feathers of a parrot feeding a pistachio to the beloved's lips. To help me appreciate the richness of this poetic image, Dilorom drew a picture of it in my notebook. It was terrifying.

Most days, while I was at the university, Eric walked to the city to buy mineral water, which he hid under the bed or in our suitcases. We couldn't leave bottled water in plain sight because Gulya would grandly thank us for buying water and then she and Inom would drink it all. Every few days Eric changed dollars for sum. Without speaking any Uzbek or Russian, he somehow got a much better rate than at the exchange offices, and better, too, than the discount rate that Gulya offered us. When we walked around in the city, he frequently exchanged greetings with young money changers; they would tap their hearts and bow to each other. In his free time, Eric read and annotated the ACTR regional guide for Uzbekistan, underlining various interesting phrases: "several hostage-taking incidents in the Kyrgyz Republic"; "certificates verifying legal conversion of foreign currency"; "South Korea: 14%"; "purchasing power parity: $2,400"; "inflation rate (consumer prices): 40%"; "Islamic insurgents based in Tajikistan"; "generally valid for four years with multiple entries"; "only boiled water"; "only sporadically enforced."

Curiously, Eric also occupied his free time by writing poetry. I found several poems scribbled on the back of the regional guide, one about baseball, another about DNA. Apparently, I was the only one unaffected by Samarkand's preternaturally poetic atmosphere.

When I came back from class at noon, we ate lunch together in the annex kitchen: bread, raw tomatoes, and *kholodets*, a cold Ukrainian meat jelly, which Gulya prepared in unfathomable quantities. I'm not a huge *kholodets* fan, and this particular version came out not only lumpy but also full of tiny bones. Eric ate it anyway. After lunch, we took turns hosing each other's heads with the garden hose. Completely drenched (though we would be dry within two minutes), we walked to the city, stopping to purchase small permafrost-hard ice cream sandwiches of Russian manufacture from a tiny boy named Elbek, whose father owned the tobacco store. Elbek executed these transactions with touching professionalism, producing the ice cream from the big steel freezer with a flourish, scrupulously counting out the change. We wanted to give him a gift when we were leaving Samarkand, but couldn't find anything to buy him, and tried to give him a twenty-dollar bill. He looked crestfallen. He didn't want any money. His father came outside, and he also wouldn't take the twenty dollars.

"We like your son so much," I explained. "Can we at least buy him an ice cream?"

After some negotiation, Elbek's father let us buy him a small bottle of orange Fanta. Then he gave us each a small bottle of orange Fanta, for free. Our whole time in Samarkand, we were either trying not to give money to people who were trying to take it, or trying to give money to people who were trying to refuse it.

After devouring as much of the ice cream as possible before it completely melted, we rushed to the park to ride the Ferris wheel. This ancient, clattering apparatus was operated by a gloomy Turk from Trabzon, who let us ride around three times per ticket. When the wheel paused at the top, you could feel a faint, pleasant breeze that sometimes even rocked the seat, producing a loud braying.

From the Ferris wheel we often proceeded to the Internet salon in the Soviet part of the city: an infernal storefront jam-packed with teenagers who were possessedly manipulating avatars through gutted buildings and abandoned warehouses, shooting one another in the back with Uzis. Periodically, some young person, shot in the back one too many times, would leave in disgust, at which point the proprietor rushed to the abandoned station and sprayed the chair and keyboard from a can of Sure deodorant. Chemical clouds of shower-fresh deodorant hung in the sultry air, adding a certain *je ne sais quoi* to the ambience.

In the second week of class, Dilorom told me more about the life and works of Alisher Navoi. During his four years in

Samarkand, Navoi had tutored the king's children in history, and worked in the court. One day an old woman came to court and said that because the king had killed her son, she wanted to kill the king's son. The king was brought into court and placed in the defendant's seat—"precisely analogous to Clinton with Monica Lewinsky," Dilorom explained. Navoi offered the old woman a choice of the king's son's blood or some gold. She chose the gold. Everyone applauded Navoi's judgment, but he quit his job anyway. To be a good king, he said, you have to be blind and dumb—and also some kind of a paralytic. He was that, for seven years, and it was harder than life itself.

Dilorom gently pulled my notebook toward her and, with the apparent intention of illustrating Navoi's position in the court, drew an enormous serpent's head with a tiny man wearing a hat standing inside the serpent's mouth, staring into its throat: that was Alisher Navoi.

Navoi said that it is better to be a scholar than a king, because a scholar doesn't leave his learning at the door of the bathhouse. Being a king is no guarantee of happiness: Alexander the Great was not only the world's greatest king but also owned a magic mirror that showed him the whole empire, and even so, he died at age thirty-three in a terrible depression. Navoi expressed his views in an allegorical work about a dog's funeral in Khorezm. A row of dogs march single file to the graveyard; other dogs pace in a circle around the first dogs.

Navoi wrote an anatomy of human society, from the king to the beggar. A bad king is like a pig that roots around in the earth for no reason. A good king is like a farmer who roots around in the earth for orderly, beneficial reasons. The worst king in human history, Herod, had a plan for Pharaoh to fly to heaven in a basket powered by vultures in order to shoot God. The vultures kept flying because there was carrion on a stick over the basket. They saw the basket's shadow and thought it was God who had been shot down.

In addition to kings, humanity includes travelers, scholars, businessmen, farmers, gleaners, bakers, millers, orphans, and wives. Bad businessmen sell the same wares at different markets at different prices. "Be careful of that when you go to the market, *qizim*," Dilorom advised me. Farmers, she continued, are the highest people because they bring the garden of heaven to earth. There are good beggars, bad beggars, Sufis and Sufi teachers, called *shayx*. Good beggars are sick and have many children and are unable to work. A good *shayx* has such knowledge that he can blow and make the water part with his breath, or he can blow on a woman's belly and make her pregnant. A bad *shayx* tricks the people with false miracles: he produces a flame from a glass tube, but it turns out later that the tube contained a special kind of gas that combusts on contact with oxygen. That's no miracle!

"*Mana, qizim,*" Dilorom said: "Here, my daughter." She carefully removed from her handbag a folded piece of paper and smoothed it out on the table. It was a photocopy of a drawing of a man who looked just like a goat.

I inspected the drawing. "That's the bad *shayx*?"

"That's the bad *shayx*."

"He looks a bit like a goat."

Dilorom smiled. "Goats can lead sheep to the best place in the mountain," she said gently. "And if anyone steals anything from them, the goat knows."

Reaching into her bag again, she produced a flimsy paperback booklet: a trilingual Uzbek-German-English collection of Navoi's verses, titled *Pearls from the Ocean*.

> *Was it my heart—a bird—that was caught in your*
> *   locks that unfortunate night,*
> *Or was it bats of some kind?*

*Remember, the sultan dooms to death even his
    closest friend
If he learns the latter has secreted away money from
    the treasury.
Speak, Navoi, if love has not yet crippled your
    soul—
Why do you spew blood whenever you sob?*

Meanwhile in language class, Muzaffar started teaching me
about Uzbek conversational etiquette. Whenever Uzbeks meet,
he explained, they immediately begin bombarding each other
with questions: "How are you? How are the ones at home?
Are things peaceful? How is your wife? Is she in good health?
How is your work? Is your work good? Are you in good
health? Aren't you tired?" I initially tried to answer the questions, but it turned out that you were supposed to simply
shoot them back as fast as you could, while raising your right
hand to your heart and holding your left hand in the air.
"Look where my hands are," Muzaffar said, jerking his hand
to his chest in his puppetlike way. We practiced these nice-
ties for a long time, striking our hearts and shouting at one
another: "Are the ones at home good? Aren't you tired?"

Later we went to another floor of the nine-story building,
where I lurked in a hallway in order to assail total strangers
with these questions. Muzaffar stood half hidden in a doorway, making helpful gestures. By and large, once they had
gotten over their initial surprise, the strangers seemed to find
it perfectly pleasant and appropriate to be ambushed in this
manner. One diminutive woman in a housekeeper's uniform
pursued the exchange for ten minutes, firing off more and
more questions. "Do you like hot weather? Did you fly here
on an airplane? Are your ears pierced?" When I confirmed

that my ears were pierced, she stood on her toes to peer at my earlobe. "You should wear earrings!" she concluded.

Another day we learned about watermelons. Muzaffar taught me a folk expression: "The watermelon fell out of its armchair." "Can you guess what it means?" he asked.

I thought about it. "A usurper will always eventually be deposed?"

"Wha-a-at?"

It turned out that the Turkish word for armchair is the Uzbek word for armpit, so the expression actually meant "The watermelon fell out from under his arm," and was used to denote a great disillusionment. "Muzaffar is walking back from the market, proud of his watermelon," Muzaffar explained. "All of a sudden, something happens; he isn't proud anymore.

"In my family," he continued, moving from figurative to literal watermelons, "Muzaffar is famous for always buying the worst watermelon. 'Send Muzaffar to the market,' they say. 'He will bring us a big, round, beautiful melon and eating it will be like chewing on some old dry grass.'" Muzaffar's grandfather, by contrast, chose the best watermelons, which were often ugly in appearance, and which he identified by holding them up to his ear and listening to them "talk." Muzaffar had tried listening to the watermelons talk, but he never heard anything. He had tried deliberately buying ugly melons, but then he just ended up with a melon that united a pale and tasteless interior with an ugly exterior.

Muzaffar did his best to teach me how to buy a good watermelon. Some people, he said, maintained that a watermelon should be heavy and dense. Others said that the best melons were large and light. So that was no help. A good watermelon had to have an orange spot, to show where it had sat in the sun, and a dry belly button, to show that the vine had broken naturally. When you tapped it with your right hand, it had to resonate against your left hand. As to the rind, the important thing wasn't the color itself, but the contrast between the different colors.

Muzaffar and I kept trying to schedule an outing to the market, so he could watch me try to buy an Uzbek watermelon, but he was always prevented by either Vice-Rector Safarov or the Marburg neo-Kantians. Eventually he said I should go to the market without him. But he had impressed upon me so seriously that they would try to sell me the worst watermelon and overcharge me for it that I got demoralized and never bought any melons at all.

When Alisher Navoi was six years old, his favorite book was Farid al-Din Attar's didactic poem *Mantiq al-Tayr*, usually translated as *The Conference of Birds*, although Dilorom called it *The Logic of Birds*. He carried the volume with him everywhere and constantly recited from it until finally his parents confiscated the book and said they had given it to a sick orphan. It was too late; Alisher already knew the book by heart.

The Logic of Birds, Dilorom explained, is about a group of thirty birds, including a peacock, crane, duck, rooster, parrot, eagle, laughing crane, and hoopoe. The hoopoe says that he will lead the other birds to a great king, who is also a bird—specifically, a simurgh, the world's largest bird, who eats only delicious fruits and loves to sing, but only with its mate. Someone once captured a simurgh and put a mirror in its cage, but the simurgh was not deceived, did not sing, and died.

To reach the simurgh's bird paradise, the thirty birds fly for a long time over seas and mountains. Some of them get tired and want to turn back, but the hoopoe rallies their spirits by telling them didactic stories. Finally, after the birds have flown through seven realms, battling severe depression, without reaching the simurgh, the hoopoe announces: "You have already reached the simurgh—the simurgh is you. You forgot the bad things in your hearts and thought only of an ideal." This makes sense in Persian, a language in which the phrase *si murgh* means "thirty birds": the group of thirty birds striving for something beyond themselves is, thus, already the same thing as the transcendent bird paradise. That's the logic of birds.

All his life, Navoi wanted to write an answer to *The Logic of Birds*. Finally, at age fifty-eight, he wrote *The Language of Birds*, the central figure of which is an ugly, ash-colored bird called the qaqnus. The qaqnus bird has one thousand teeth in its beak, and each tooth sings a melody. Collecting thorns and twigs, it builds a tall nest, sits on top of it, and starts to sing. Its song is incredibly beautiful, but makes human listeners sick. (This song is called *navo*, the root of the name "Navoi.") As a function of singing, the qaqnus sets itself on fire, burns up, rises to heaven, and becomes a flower. A little bird comes from the ashes; that's its baby. The baby then spends its whole life collecting its own bonfire. "Such is the dialectic of the qaqnus," Dilorom explained. In *The Language of Birds*, Navoi compares Attar to the qaqnus, and himself to the baby bird that climbed out of the ashes.

According to the critic Vahid Abdullayev, who had been a friend of Dilorom's father, each writer in the history of literature is a qaqnus: he spends his whole life gathering firewood with which to burn up the previous generation of writers. This was Abdullayev's version of the "knight's move."

I thought a lot about the language of birds, and its relationship to the logic of birds. What were the birds—our strange uncles—trying to tell us? In various esoteric traditions, the "language of birds" is a code word for total knowledge. As Solomon exclaims in the Koran, "O mankind! Lo! We have been taught the language of the birds and have been given abundance of all things." Tiresias, endowed by Athena with the gift of prophecy, was suddenly able to understand birds. So was Siegfried, when he accidentally tasted dragon's blood. That was lucky for Siegfried because some nearby birds were just then discussing a plot to kill him. Among alchemists and Kabbalists, the perfect language that would unlock ultimate knowledge was known as either "the green language" or "the language of birds." The Russian futurist poet Velemir Khlebnikov is famous for inventing several "transrational" languages, among them "god language" and "bird language." Interestingly, Khlebnikov's father was an ornithologist.

Every day near sunset, when one could imagine that the temperature might be falling, Eric went to play soccer at a nearby stadium. (Like most Soviet-era stadiums, this one was called Dynamo.) I went with him a couple of times to use the track, which consisted of irregular rubberized panels laid on top of a bed of sand and gravel. Some of the panels overlapped, creating ledges on which it was easy to trip. Other panels were separated by chasms in which one might twist an ankle. It was by far the worst track I have ever seen in my life. The enclosed soccer field was also riddled with holes and burrows, in which unknown small creatures lived out their mysterious existences. As nightfall approached, the soccer players—mostly high-school students—twisted their ankles with increasing frequency. "See you later, kids!" they would shout bravely to their teammates, as they hobbled off the field.

    Eric was befriended by one of the soccer players, a sixteen-year-old Uzbek boy named Shurik, who wanted to join the CIA when he grew up. One night Shurik invited us to dinner. His whole family—seven-year-old identical twin sisters, a grandfather, and a baby—were sitting on pillows at a low table in a courtyard one-quarter the size of Gulya's. The parents came out of a tiny wooden lean-to with a huge pot of *plov*, fragrant with saffron, lamb, and dried apricots. The grandfather, who took a great liking to Eric, gave him a history book in Uzbek. "You can translate it for him," he told me, proceeding to write a completely illegible inscription on the flyleaf.

When we got back to the house that night, Gulya was furious. We had been instructed not to go out after dark unless someone from the university had cleared it with her first. "You can't just walk out of here and eat with strangers!"

"But it wasn't a stranger; it was Eric's friend."

"Those kinds of friends will drug you and cut you to pieces and eat you!"

At Gulya's behest, a social worker called Matluba called me on the phone. "Don't go out after dark," Matluba said. "Your mother worries about you. She loves you very much."

Eventually we stopped trying to leave the house in the evenings. Eric played with Lila, while Gulya showed me photo albums of all the Communist prizes she had won in different countries. Another of Gulya's favorite activities was to paint my eyebrows together using henna, so I had a unibrow. "You really should pay more attention to your appearance," she told me, surveying her handiwork with satisfaction.

A few nights every week, Gulya was joined after dinner by her old school friends, women of regal bearing and vivid lipstick, who sat for hours in the courtyard listening to Tajik pop music and drinking endless vodka toasts to their beautiful friendship. At the first such gathering, I politely sat with them for half an hour, drank some vodka, and even recited a toast about how great it was that Gulya had such great friends. This proved to be a tactical error, since afterward Gulya wanted me to drink vodka and recite toasts with them every night, which was not compatible with my program of study of the great Uzbek language.

"I have to do my homework," I would say.

"You'll learn more from us than from studying those books—isn't that right, Betty?"

"And how!" agreed the one called Betty.

I sat up late every night, reading Russian translations of Old Uzbek poetry, and writing various compositions assigned as homework by Muzaffar. These compositions took literally hours to write, and I had soon used up both of the notebooks I had brought with me to Uzbekistan. The only notebooks on sale in Samarkand that summer were stapled booklets of pulpy, fibrous, grayish newsprint—a kind of paper I hadn't seen since the standardized test booklets of my early childhood. For the cover, you could choose between the following images: the Russian pop star Zemfira, a motorcycle being struck by lightning, a dew-covered rose, or three cartoon monkeys variously covering their eyes, ears, and mouth. I chose the monkeys.

Outside the stationer's that day, a slight, leathery old man was selling old Russian books, which he had laid out on a blanket under the blazing sun. For fifteen dollars, I bought an amazing fifty-thousand-word Uzbek-Russian dictionary from 1973, as well as a four-volume 1956 edition of Vladimir Dal's *Explanatory Dictionary of the Great Living Russian Language*, bound in cracked brown leather, with dusty, yellowed pages. He let me bargain for the Uzbek-Russian dictionary, but insisted on the original penciled-in price for the

Dal: "That one is special," he said. The Dal dictionary went online in 2004, but I still haven't brought myself to throw out those four volumes, which Eric carried back for me all the way from Uzbekistan, and which are now sitting in a kitchen cabinet over the stove.

I wrote a composition about Istanbul, and another one about cornbread. Searching for words in the Uzbek-Russian dictionary, trying to guess which Turkish words would exist in Uzbek and how they would be spelled, I wrote a satirical dialogue between two frogs on the subject of a water outage. Another composition was supposed to use the special vocabulary that Uzbek people use to summon or dismiss animals. (Turkish has it, too: to call a dog, you say "*hav*," and to make it go away you say "*hosht*.") I wrote a composition based on *kisht*, the word Uzbek people use to repel birds. It was written from the perspective of a farmer who found a strange bird ripping up his orange trees and singing a strange song that made him incredibly sick. The bird turned out to be a qaqnus, but the farmer didn't want a qaqnus bird ripping up his orange trees, so he told it "*kisht*," and it went away.

One afternoon, to make up for not taking me watermelon shopping, Muzaffar invited me to his English translation workshop. The workshop was taught by a wiry, manic, mosquito-like American in his thirties, with a goatee and wearing the single oldest and most tattered T-shirt I have ever seen being used as clothing. The class was collaborating on an Uzbek translation of a terrible English translation of Maupassant's "Le Petit." When the cuckolded widow erupts at the nursemaid, "*Dehors, va-t'en!*" this had been rendered into the great living English language as "Done with you!"

Nine Uzbek graduate students debated for half an hour how to translate the English phrase "Done with you!"

"But that's not an English phrase," I finally objected.

"The text we have is the text we have," the teacher replied, glancing at me a bit irritably, and I noticed dark circles under his eyes.

Starting around that time, I was plagued by a recurring nightmare about penguins. I had applied for a grant to go to Russia on a homestay, and the household I got assigned to was a family of penguins in Antarctica. "But penguins don't even have a language!" I protested. In fact, those penguins did have a language, with two branches, one epic-narrative and one lyric-folkloric. I was jerked awake by the pounding of my own heart.

In our third week of class, Dilorom and I studied Navoi's three most famous love poems: *Farhod and Shirin*, *The Seven Planets*, and *Layli and Majnun*.

"God gave love to three people," Dilorom told me. "Farhod was robbed by a king, Bahrom was unworthy, and Majnun went mad." Each of the love poems, she continued, was directed at a different, insoluble question: Why were people created? Why are all people unhappy? Why are intellectuals even unhappier than everyone else? Each night, Dilorom loaned me a volume from the ten-volume Russian translation of Alisher Navoi, published between 1968 and 1970 by the Uzbek SSR Academy of Sciences.

Farhod and Shirin is about the doomed love between a poor stonecutter and the daughter of the king of Armenia. Farhod is such a good stonecutter that he actually solves the Armenian water shortage by halving a mountain with a pick-axe, creating a sixty-kilometer canal: this was the stipulated condition for his marrying Shirin. But Shirin's father goes back on his word. Because he wants Shirin to marry not some stonecutter, but a Persian king, he sends an old woman to tell Farhod that Shirin has drunk poison and died. Farhod throws his pickaxe in the air and lets it break his head in two. After that, Shirin really does drink poison.

The first great theme of *Farhod and Shirin*, Dilorom said, was the eternal problem of social inequality, classically posed in the form of two questions: "What is to be done?" and "Who is to blame?"* The other great theme of *Farhod and Shirin* was . . . crop irrigation. Despite her Uzbek national-ism, there was a touching Soviet strain in Dilorom's approach to literature.

In *The Seven Planets*, she continued, Navoi chooses a hero at the opposite end of the social spectrum: a king named Bahrom. One day Bahrom goes hunting accompanied by his beloved, whose name is also Dilorom. He takes aim at an onager, the same preternaturally elusive wild ass whose skin, in Balzac's *Peau de chagrin*, functions as a magic talisman. Bahrom not only hits the onager, but does so in such a way that the creature's hoof is pinned to its ear. Dilorom, my teacher's namesake, is overcome by pity and bursts into tears, so Bahrom kills her. Later he is sorry. In seven castles, repre-senting the seven planets, seven travelers tell seven stories for seven nights: the last story reveals Dilorom's whereabouts.

Of Navoi's three famous love poems, Dilorom told me the most about *Layli and Majnun*: the ill-fated romance between a young boy named Qays and his schoolmate Layli, who belongs to a rival clan. Driven mad by his forbidden love, Qays trans-forms into Majnun, the Madman. His heart falls to pieces like a pomegranate. Roaming the streets and bazaars, he recites poetry about the affliction that has doomed him to a life of misery. Majnun's father swallows his family pride and asks

---

* What Is to Be Done? and *Who Is to Blame?* were influential nineteenth-century political novels by Nikolai Chernyshevsky and Alexander Herzen.

Layli's father to let the young people marry. But Layli's father doesn't want his daughter to marry a crazy person with a pomegranate heart. He replies that Majnun should be taken to the Black Stone of Kaaba, to be cured of his love. Instead, Majnun goes to Layli's tent and beats himself with stones.

When Majnun's father finally does take the unhappy boy to Kaaba, Majnun is unable to pray for the love to be removed from his heart. "You torment me with this love, but I don't say, 'liberate me from it and make me like other people.' Instead I ask for more. Whatever color you made Love to be, I want to be that color, too," he tells God. He recites a poem about the characters in Layli's name. One letter has dots over it, representing nails driven into his body; another, C-shaped letter hangs around his neck; a third letter, shaped like a mountain range, symbolizes the mountains that are sitting on his heart. Majnun lurks outside Layli's tent writing her long letters: "Take the muscles out of my body and make a leash for your little dog!" Layli is given in marriage to a rich clansman, who takes her far away. Day and night she clutches a knife, poised to kill herself if he tries to touch her.

Majnun goes into the desert, forgets human language, and acquires the language of gazelles. The gazelles are beautiful, with big sad eyes just like Layli's. Majnun paces like a drunken lion, recites *ghazals*,* wastes away. In the Arabic script, which omits vowels, *gazelle* and *ghazal* have the same spelling: the language of gazelles is thus a figure for poetic language. Dilorom told me that another homonym for *gazelle* and *ghazal* is a word meaning "eyelid"; hence a famous line from one of Navoi's *ghazals*: "I sweep the floor at your feet with my eyelashes."

---

*The *ghazal* is a short lyric form of Persian origin, consisting of rhymed couplets, usually on the subject of romantic love and religious mysticism.

In the desert, Majnun also befriends lions, monkeys, deer, snakes, foxes, and some kind of bird that sometimes carries letters for him. It is difficult not to be impressed by the richness of animal life in the Old Uzbek deserts. In one story a hero perishes by killing so many stags that their blood soaks the desert floor and awakens a swamp that swallows him up, together with his hunting entourage and his beautiful Chinese bride.

Years pass, and Layli's husband dies of a heart attack. She calls Majnun to her, but someone tells her that Majnun is sick and probably won't come. In fact he isn't especially sick, and rushes to her side, but by the time he gets there, she has died of grief. He sees her body laid out for the funeral, lies next to her, and dies.

Some Eastern scholars believe that *Romeo and Juliet* was informed by a Latin translation of *Layli and Majnun*. How else to explain all the shared features: star-crossed lovers from feuding families, heroes who make journeys into exile, poetic orations over heroines' corpses? Shakespeare scholars object that Shakespeare couldn't possibly have read *Layli and Majnun* in any language, that his sources are known to have been French and Italian—and that, as for unhappy families, star-crossed lovers, and exiled heroes, they are simply universal.

The House of Ice

In 1703, Peter the Great decided to build a new imperial capital. As the location, he chose a semi-inhabited morass on the Gulf of Finland, which not only was ruled by his enemy the king of Sweden, but was frozen solid five months of the year and subject to flooding the rest of the time. Over seven hundred thousand serfs, soldiers, convicts, and Swedish prisoners were conscripted to clear the forests, level the hills, dig canals, drain the wetlands, and drive sixteen-foot-long oaken piles into the ground. For want of shovels, the workers dug up dirt with their bare hands and carried it away in their shirts. Hundreds of thousands died of starvation, cholera, and fatigue. "I doubt one could find a battle in military history that led to the death of more soldiers than the number of laborers who died in Petersburg," wrote the historian Klyuchevsky, who characterized the city as "a big cemetery."

This cemetery, which eventually became one of the world's most beautiful cities, is presided over by the Bronze Horseman: a monument of Peter the Great astride a rearing steed, apparently about to leap off a cliff into the Neva. The monument, cast by Falconet in 1782 on the orders of Catherine the Great, was immortalized by Alexander Pushkin in "The Bronze Horseman": a poem dramatizing the great flood of

1824 as the revenge of the elements against the tsar. When Pushkin's hero, a poor clerk called Evgeny, curses the "fatal will" of him who caused a city to spring up from the sea, the Bronze Horseman leaps off his pedestal and pursues him through the streets, driving him mad.

Falconet's monument and Pushkin's poem are the two linchpins of the so-called myth of St. Petersburg. Like all myths, the myth of St. Petersburg is a selective construction. Here is something you won't find in it. In the winter of 1740, Peter the Great's niece, Anna Ioannovna, commissioned a sculpture bigger, stranger, and more immediately menacing than the Bronze Horseman: a massive ice palace, built for the wedding of two court jesters who were forced to spend their nuptial night inside. Just as Catherine's Bronze Horseman catalyzed a celebrated poem by Pushkin, so did Anna's monument inspire a literary production of its own: *The House of Ice*, a cloak-and-dagger romance by Pushkin's contemporary Ivan Lazhechnikov, in which the ice palace serves as the hub of a vast political conspiracy linking a network of historical and fictional personages, including a diminutive black secretary who periodically reads aloud from his translation of Machiavelli.

I first found out about Lazhechnikov's *House of Ice* from my classmate Luba, who read it while researching her dissertation, and instantly became convinced that she and I had to bring this work—which had apparently never been published in English—to the American people. Recalling our earlier experiences cotranslating some particularly abstruse and belligerent essays on film by Kasimir Malevich, I said something to the effect that translation jobs always made me want to jump out a window.

"But this would be nothing like last time," said Luba,

who had already identified a grant we could apply for. "You'll really like Lazhechnikov. The main character has a black secretary who follows him everywhere."

"Is the book *narrated* by the black secretary?" I asked warily. I was working at that time on a typology of "narrating sidekicks," and was interested in squires, valets, and secretaries.

"Well, maybe not exactly *narrated* by him . . ."

Early in 2006, a strange sequence of events made me realize that *The House of Ice* was after all a part of my destiny. On February 6, Luba went to UC Berkeley to give a job talk about the historical romances of Pushkin and Lazhechnikov. (She got the job.) On February 8, a life-size replica of the 1740 House of Ice was unveiled in St. Petersburg's Palace Square, directly across from the Hermitage. It was almost as if Luba's attention to Lazhechnikov's out-of-print classic had generated some kind of etheric projection. Of course, the ice palace wasn't really an etheric projection; its construction had required five hundred tons of ice and $150,000, underwritten by a city-wide initiative called White Days (designed to boost tourism in the winter off-season). For three hundred euros, you could get married in the House of Ice, and for three thousand euros you could spend your whole wedding night there, just like those unfortunate jesters.

Luba and I had to get close to it—to touch it with our own hands. I decided to pitch the story to *The New Yorker*, which had recently published my first piece of journalism: a profile of a former Thai kickboxing champion who now ran a gym in San Francisco. *The New Yorker* conceded that it might be nice to have a "Postcard from St. Petersburg" about the ice palace—but only so long as I was "already going to be in Petersburg anyway." Unversed as I was in the ways of print journalism, it took me ten minutes to figure out what they really meant: they didn't want to pay travel expenses. For neither the first nor last time in my academic career, Grisha Freidin saved the day. He helped me round up two thousand dollars in departmental funds, in exchange for which I was to write a report about the role of Lazhechnikov in the Russian cultural imagination, and also take some photographs of a house in Petersburg where Maxim Gorky had once lived. (Having copied the address wrong, I ended up taking pictures of a neighboring Yolki-Palki: one of a chain of affordable nineteenth-century-themed taverns. Finding it odd that the Russians had turned Gorky's house into a Yolki-Palki, I remember going inside afterward to eat a *pirozhok* and contemplate the vagaries of history.)

"We really appreciate your undertaking this assignment on your own steam," my editor told me on the phone. "Just remember, we don't want a travel piece. What we want is a postcard, a snapshot, with lots of wonderful details. Do you know what I mean? Like if you can get an interview with whoever made the doorknobs—little things like that."

"Interview whoever made the doorknobs," I repeated, jotting it in my notebook.

"Doorknobs are just an example. Another really wonderful thing would be if you can spend a night *inside* the ice palace. You know: 'Three a.m. I hear a dog barking.' Do you think it's a possibility that they would let you spend a night there?"

"Well . . . I think you can rent it as a honeymoon suite for three thousand euros, but first you have to get married there."

"Uh-huh." I heard my editor pause to drink something. "Well, see if you can get them to let you stay there without getting married, for a few hundred euros."

I was interested to learn that, although the magazine

wouldn't reimburse me for a normal hotel, they were willing to spend up to four hundred euros for me to spend a night in an ice palace, listening to the dogs bark.

I got to Petersburg one day before Luba, who saw me off with repeated warnings to stay clear of skinheads. Petersburg has a reputation for hate crimes, and she said the two of us, with our prominent noses, would have to try to keep a "low profile."

Copious, fine-grained snow gusted and swirled through the night skies, rattling against the windows of the taxi. I had made an online reservation, which proved to occupy one floor in an amazingly cheap hostel on the Liteyny Prospekt, a narrow, dark building. In the entrance hall, behind an apparently soundproof window, a tiny wispy-bearded old man, resembling a Dr. Seuss character, was staring intently at a very old radio. When I knocked tentatively on the glass he hurried outside, greeted me in halting but very correct English, and insisted on carrying my suitcase up the four flights of stone stairs to the hostel rooms. Behind an enormous purple upholstered door, which the old man unlocked with a huge skeleton key, lay an irregularly shaped area with sofas, armchairs, and a blaring television set. Sprawled on two of the sofas, five deeply Slavic-looking men with thick necks and shaved heads were eating tinned meat from gigantic tins and drinking beer from even more gigantic cans. Because of the way the room was arranged, the old man and I had to walk between their sofa and the television to get to the hallway. The shiny-headed Slavs, who had been laughing loudly at something, fell silent and followed us with their eyes.

Luba is going to kill me, I thought.

"Pilots, you know," the little old man whispered, setting down my suitcase at the end of a dark passage. "We get a lot of them. Nice boys." He demonstrated three times how to lock and unlock the door. "It doesn't hurt to lock your door at night and leave the key in the lock."

The room was painted pale green, and contained two collapsible steel cots, a wardrobe, a table, and two chairs. A chandelier hung from the ceiling—not from the center of the ceiling, but almost in a corner, like a sleeping bat. ("Was it my heart—a bird—that was caught in your locks that unfortunate night," as the immortal Navoi wrote, "or was it bats of some kind?") Outside the bay window, sodium lights turned everything a dull pink: the street, the steps, the eddying snow. Here and there, lone Russians in shapeless fur coats and hats rushed along the sidewalks, eyes fixed on the ground.

I thought about trying to go to bed, but I wanted to shower first, and couldn't work up my nerve to go to the communal bathrooms, which were a few feet away from the pilots and their television. I put my coat back on and headed out for a walk.

"Good evening," I said to the pilots on the way out.

"Good evening," one of them replied.

An eviscerating wind blew in from the canals. Humanoid statues glared down from every alcove and pediment; atlantes and caryatids rolled their eyes under every portico. Petersburg is a scary place. In literature, it often figures as the scene of a murder.* Furthermore, the tap water is supposed to cause

---

*Dostoevsky, who called St. Petersburg "the most abstract and premeditated city in the world," chose it as the setting for *Crime and Punishment*. In Andrei Bely's modernist novel *Petersburg*, a terrorist has to kill his own father using a time bomb concealed in an anthropomorphic sardine can known as Pepp Peppovich Pepp. In Gogol's most famous Petersburg tale, "The Overcoat," a gang of thugs steals the overcoat belonging to a miserable clerk; the clerk falls into a fever, dies, and himself becomes a ghostly thug, roaming the city and stealing overcoats.

giardiasis. Bearing this in mind, I stopped at a grocery store to buy bottled water and, taking a pointer from the pilots, a five-hundred-milliliter can of Baltika. In front of me in line were two men with unshaven, alcohol-ravaged faces. They were both buying boxes of chocolate decorated with roses and music notes.

"And a teddy bear," one of them growled at the clerk, who languidly handed him a huge, sad-looking gray plush bear. Only then did I notice the cardboard decorations and realize it was the night before International Women's Day. The two men paid for their chocolate boxes and stuffed them in their jackets. The one who had bought the bear shoved it under his arm. The last thing I saw as they went into the snow was the head of the sad-looking gray bear sticking out of the man's armpit.

When I got back to the hostel, the airmen were nowhere to be seen. I took a shower. Warm at last, I spent the rest of the evening sitting on my cot, sipping the icy beer and reading *Anna Ioannovna*: Evgeny Anisimov's definitive biography of the empress who decided to marry her jesters in a house made of ice.

Today, Russians remember Empress Anna primarily for her love of jesters, dwarfs, and Germans, all of whom enter into her biography at an early point. In 1710, when Anna was seventeen, her uncle Peter the Great arranged her marriage to Duke Friedrich Wilhelm, the German ruler of the small duchy of Courland: a strategic alliance, intended to bolster Russia's support of Courland against its big neighbors, Prussia and Poland. At the wedding banquet, the tsar cut open two pies with his dagger. A splendidly dressed dwarf jumped out of each pie and together they danced a minuet on the table. The next day, Peter treated his guests to a second wedding: that of his favorite dwarf, attended by forty-two other dwarfs from all corners of the empire. Some foreign guests saw a certain symmetry in the double wedding, one between two miniature people, the other between two pawns in the great game of European politics.

On the way back to Courland, the teenage duke died, of alcohol poisoning. On his last night in Petersburg, he had engaged—rashly, one feels—in a drinking contest with Peter the Great. To the dismay of both Anna and her in-laws, Peter forbade the young widow from returning to Russia, lest her departure disturb the European balance of power. In more than three hundred letters addressed to her family, Anna repeatedly expressed her wish to remarry but, for political reasons, her uncle kept rejecting all her suitors.

Peter died in 1725. His death was followed, five years later, by that of his last direct male descendant, fourteen-year-old Peter II. To her surprise, thirty-seven-year-old Anna found herself empress. She returned to Russia that February, accompanied by her lover of long standing, Duke Ernst Johann Biron. On the eve of their arrival, it is said, the aurora borealis dyed the Moscow skies blood-red; a great bloody sphere, as large and luminous as the moon, appeared to sink slowly into the horizon.

The new empress—"seven-foot, 280-pound Anna," in the words of one courtier—was not a reassuring presence. "When she walked among the cavaliers, she was a head taller than all of them," the courtier reported, "and was extraordinarily fat." She dined nearly every day with Biron, his hunchbacked young wife, Benigna Gotlieb von Trotha-Treyden, and the Birons' three children, the youngest of whom was rumored to actually be Anna's son. Little was known about Biron, of whom another courtier wrote in her memoirs: "He was nothing but a shoemaker—he made a pair of boots for my uncle." Anna's reign is now known as *Bironovshchina*: the era of Biron.

Above all things, Anna loved to be entertained. As empress, she had her mother's aging friends tracked down and brought to court, because they had impressed her by their volubility when she was a child. For those no longer living, or too old to travel, she demanded replacements. "Send me someone who looks like Tatiana Novokreshchenova," Anna instructed her chamberlain. "She should be about forty years old, and should be talkative, like Novokreshchenova was." One courtier wrote of her first meeting with Anna, "She seized me by the shoulder so hard that I was in pain . . . and asked: 'How fat am I? Am I as fat as Avdotya Ivanovna?'" The terrified courtier replied, "It is impossible to compare Your Majesty with her, she is twice as fat." Pleased with this answer, Anna ordered her new friend, "Speak!" and made her talk for several hours.

In her pursuit of conversation, Anna did not limit herself to the human species. She issued the following order in 1739: "It has come to our knowledge that in the window of the Petrovsky tavern in Moscow sits a starling which speaks so well that all passers-by stop to listen . . . immediately send me a starling of this sort."

Different birds afforded Anna different forms of entertainment: in two months at her summer estate Peterhof, she shot sixty-eight wild ducks from her window. Unlike other Russian rulers, she rarely used borzois or falcons, and was relatively uninterested by the strategy and tactics of the hunt, but she did love to shoot. Often, an army of beaters would drive all the animals from the Peterhof forest into a clearing, where Anna would drive up in a special carriage called the Jagdwagen, and take them out one by one. Her cartridge cases were kept coated with lard, to expedite reloading. The fauna population of the Petersburg governorate being unable to replenish itself fast enough to meet her needs, Anna issued ukases to her military staff all over the empire, who kept her supplied with Siberian wolves and Ukrainian boars. Scholars have diagnosed her with an "Amazon complex."

If there was one thing Anna loved more than conversation and hunting, it was jesters. She had inherited two jesters from Peter I, including Jan D'Acosta, a Portuguese Marrano theologian and financier who spoke ten languages, and with whom the emperor had debated the relative merits of the Old and New Testaments. Anna also exercised much conscientiousness in the recruitment of new jesters and "fools," once rejecting a proposed candidate with a note: "He isn't a fool." When considering the appointment of a certain Prince Nikita Volkonsky, Anna ordered her chamberlain to present a full report on "the life of Volkonsky" detailing, among other things, how many shirts Volkonsky owned, what kind of dogs he kept, and whether he ate cabbage stalks.

The most spectacular jester-related "entertainments" in Anna's court all involved marriage. When the jester Balakirev publicly complained that his wife wouldn't sleep with him, Anna had the Holy Synod issue a special decree for the "reinstatement of previous conjugal relations." The jester Pietro "Pedrillo" Mira—a Neapolitan violinist who, having arrived in Petersburg with a theater troupe, quarreled with his Kapellmeister and ended up a jester—was famous for having a wife as ugly as a goat; the joke escalated to the point that he received visitors in bed together with a ribbon-decked goat, beside a bassinet containing a baby goat.

The winter of 1740 was the coldest in decades. Thermometers shattered, brandy froze indoors, birds dropped from the sky like stones. One of Anna's servants, a middle-aged, hunchbacked Kalmyk woman known as Buzheninova, after the dish *buzhenina* (cold roast pork), confided to Anna: "With-out a husband, my life is like a hard frost." The empress de-cided to arrange a marriage between Buzheninova and Prince Mikhail Golitsyn, a real prince who had been convicted of apostasy for marrying an Italian commoner and converting to Catholicism. Anna, having heard rumors of his "unusual stupidity," commuted his sentence and dubbed him Prince Kvasnik, the imperial cupbearer of kvass. (She also dissolved his marriage and confiscated his son; the young Italian wife disappeared some years later in the Secret Chancellery.) Kvasnik's other official duties included sitting on a nest of eggs in a reception room while clucking like a chicken.

Anna's charismatic cabinet minister, Artemy Volynsky— the protagonist of Lazhechnikov's novel—decided to make this wedding the culminating point of a mass holiday, which would simultaneously honor Anna's name day, the anniver-sary of her accession to the throne, Shrovetide week, and the ratification of the Treaty of Belgrade between Russia and the Ottomans. The wedding of a Kalmyk and a Catholic convert, representing Russia's "total victory over all infidels," was to take place in a magnificent, specially constructed ice palace.

On the day of the festivities, the bride and groom made their entrance in an iron cage on the back of a real elephant, followed by a three-hundred-person "ethnographic parade" of bridal couples from all over the empire. As Lazhechnikov describes it, the procession was led by Ostyaks riding on deer, "followed by Novgorodians on a pair of goats, Ukrai-nians on bulls, Petersburg Finns on donkeys, a Tatar with his Tataress, mounted on well-fed pigs, to demonstrate the conquering of both nature and custom. Then there were red-haired Finns on miniature horses, Kamchadals riding dogs, Kalmyks on camels, Belorussians with hair matted as thick as felt, Komi who in honorableness could rival the Germans,

[and] Jaroslavians, who attained the highest place in this human exhibition with their stature, their beauty, and the elegance of their finery."

Kvasnik and Buzheninova were transferred from their cage to the House of Ice, where armed sentries forced them to remain until morning. The newlyweds spent hours running around and dancing, trying to stay warm. (In Lazhechnikov's account, they also turned somersaults, beat each other, banged on the walls, begged the guards to release them, cursed their fate, and broke everything that could be broken.) They were found the next morning on the ice bed, close to death. Anna provoked much laughter among the courtiers by inquiring into the "sweetness" of the wedding night.

Because of the great job he did with the festival, the cabinet minister briefly remained in the empress's good graces—until his valet turned over some compromising papers to his rival, Biron. The minister was convicted of treason. That June, an executioner cut off first his tongue, then his hand, and lastly his head. In September, Anna began complaining of abdominal pains. She died in October, probably of kidney failure. In November, the Biron family was banished to Siberia. The House of Ice—elephant, pocket watches, and all—had melted in late March; only some large pieces of the walls were salvaged to use for refrigeration in the Imperial Palace.

As for Kvasnik and Buzheninova, they continued to live together as husband and wife, and even had two sons. I was happy that things had ended relatively well for them. My last waking thought consisted of a dim sense of identification with these two jesters, whose experiences in the court of Anna Ioannovna reminded me in certain ways of my own experiences working for *The New Yorker*.

. . .

The New York Public Library has an original edition of Georg Wolfgang Krafft's 1741 *Description et représentation exacte de la maison de glace*, complete with drawings and architectural plans. Krafft, a German-born physicist at the Russian Academy of Sciences, engineered some of the palace's technical components, including several cannons made of ice—loaded with real gunpowder, they fired ice cannonballs a distance of sixty paces—and a giant hollow ice elephant, mounted by an ice soldier in Persian dress. The elephant's trunk, connected by pipes to the Admiralty Canal, spouted water twenty-four feet in the air. At night the water was replaced by flaming oil. The elephant could trumpet in a highly realistic fashion, thanks to a man sitting inside, blowing into a trumpet.

The six-meter-tall building, designed by the Italian-trained architect and city planner Peter Eropkin, was erected directly on the frozen Neva. Blocks of ice were "cemented" with water, immediately fusing together, so that the finished structure appeared to have been cut from a single piece of transparent bluish stone. With the exception of a few real playing cards frozen to an ice table, everything in the palace was made of ice, some of it dyed to resemble other materials. The bedroom was equipped with a dressing table, "mirror," canopy bed, pillows, blankets, slippers, and nightcaps. On shelves and tables stood cups, saucers, plates, cutlery, wineglasses, figurines, and even transparent pocket watches and table clocks, with dyed cogs and gears. At night, ice candles in ice candlesticks and ice logs in an ice fireplace were doused with oil and illuminated. They flared briefly, but didn't melt. Next to the palace, a tiny log cabin made of ice housed a working Russian *banya*, where Buzheninova and Kvasnik took a prenuptial steam bath.

From Krafft's description, I already had a good idea of

what the ice palace would look like. Nonetheless, the real thing looked simultaneously larger and smaller than I had expected, and there was something comical about the visual fact of its existence, sitting so matter-of-factly on the embankment, with its balustrade and pilastered façade. Dense, baroque, translucent, it resembled the ghost of a municipal building.

Krafft's ice elephant had been replicated, but it didn't contain a trumpeter or flaming gasoline. Instead, determined-looking children were clambering up a staircase built into its back, sitting approximately where the Persian soldier used to sit, and coasting down the trunk, which had been converted into a slide.

The organizers' offices were in a trailer in the back. Photocopies of Krafft's engravings were taped to the wall. The heater was broken, and everyone was wearing heavy coats. One of the directors, Valery Gromov, took me on a tour of the palace. I was proud of myself for remembering to ask who had made the doorknobs. Gromov stared at me. "What doorknobs?" he asked.

All the interior walls and furnishings were either transparent or, where the surface of the ice had melted and refrozen, a milky blue. The only exceptions were, in the first room, three playing cards and a copy of the St. Petersburg phone book, encased in ice. (The publisher was a corporate sponsor.) The contents of the second room, Gromov explained, had been "improvised on a matrimonial theme," since Krafft hadn't provided a drawing. A cupid stood in the window— perhaps an allusion to the 1740 parade, which included a page dressed as a "weeping cupid," grieved by the unsightliness of the bridal pair. What appeared to be a Renaissance marble angel had been sculpted from snow, as had two albatross-size songbirds perched atop two hearts. In the corner hulked a massive snow wedding cake, and staring impassively at the cake was a life-size, bluish Anna Ioannovna, shimmering on her throne like some kind of hologram.

In a third room was the cataclysmic bed, its canopy resembling a frozen waterfall. A pair of ice slippers lay on an ice cushion on the floor. I sat briefly on the bed. It was, as expected, hard and cold. "Can this be Hymen's altar?" Lazhechnikov had demanded rhetorically, of its prototype. "Wherever they sat, whatever they touched—everything was made from ice."

Gromov said that he took a very critical view of Lazhechnikov. "His book is a work of art, and ours is a work of history. All these things really happened. Only not with dwarfs; with real people." He was alluding to a popular misconception that Kvasnik and Buzheninova were themselves dwarfs: the ice palace has gone down in history as a kind of dollhouse for Amazon Anna's human toys.

From the bedchamber we passed to the bathhouse. Two teenagers were sliding around, grabbing at the walls. "The floor turned out somehow slippery," Gromov observed, as one teenager, clutching the doorjamb, managed to haul himself outside.

At a nearby café afterward, we met Gromov's partner, Svetlana Mikheyeva, who was wearing a cardigan with a pink fur collar, and who immediately ordered two glasses of cognac. She and I drank to International Women's Day. Gromov only drank bright red multivitamin tea, of which Mikheyeva had ordered two large pots. Over a serious lunch, also ordered by Mikheyeva, the two directors told me about their dream to reestablish Petersburg as "the birthplace of ice sculpture."

Gromov, a former army management official, and Mikheyeva, a former doctor and health care manager, had conceived of this dream during an international management training program in Tokyo in 1999, where they ended up stuck in a broken elevator with the chairman of the Association of Russian Snow, Ice, and Sand Sculptors. When I asked Mikheyeva what had motivated her career change from medicine to ice sculpture, she said it wasn't such a big jump: "Ice is a natural material, it has a natural relationship to human health. So does sand." She talked about the new trend in cryosaunas, and about Chinese sand therapy: "The whole body is covered in sand, which combines heat, massage, and magnetism. We also do a lot of work with sand. In the winter, ice; in the summer, sand." The previous June, the two main sculptors of the House of Ice had built a six-meter sand Gulliver in Komarovo.

When I asked whether I could spend a night in the House of Ice, they informed me that, in the absence of any consumer interest, the wedding-night package had been canceled, and the palace wasn't equipped for overnight stays.

"Could I do it anyway?" I asked doubtfully.

"Elif, you would freeze," Mikheyeva said. "This is not California."

Luba arrived that evening. We were so excited! "There are some people who look like skinheads," I told her, "but they're actually pilots." Luba was more interested by the hostel staff, which included, in addition to the tiny old man with the wispy beard, a solidly built middle-aged man with only one arm.

"The older one speaks really good English," Luba mused. "I think he might be Jewish. But the one-armed one I don't think is Jewish . . . Elishka, there is a very large beer can outside our window." After a moment's perplexity, I recognized this can as last night's Baltika.

"I drank half of it, and then I put the rest there, in case

I needed it later," I explained. We were dissolved in laughter when a knock sounded at the door: it was the tiny man with the Dr. Seuss beard, holding two prepackaged ice cream cones. "Two young women, traveling alone," he said. "I thought somebody should congratulate you on Women's Day."

"He's definitely Jewish," Luba said, after he left. The ice cream, notwithstanding its appearance of having spent the last twenty-five years driving around Russia in a truck, was surprisingly delicious.

The ice palace had no clear purpose, but many unclear purposes. It was a torture device, a science experiment, an ethnographic museum, a work of art. It was a suspended disaster, a flood momentarily checked, a haunted house, a distorted fairy tale, with its transparent coffin, parodic prince, and dwarfs. The ice palace represents the prison house of marriage, the vanity of human endeavor, the dialectic of empire and subject. Laden with endless meanings, like an object in a dream, the House of Ice appears in poems about dreams. It is believed to have inspired the "sunny pleasure-dome with caves of ice" in Coleridge's "Kubla Khan." Thomas Moore, the nineteenth-century satirist, wrote of a dream ball in the House of Ice, hosted by Tsar Alexander I and attended by the entire Holy Alliance. When the castle and its occupants start to melt, "some word, like 'Constitution'—long / Congealed in frosty silence," drips from the tongue of Prussia's king.

As for the reconstruction, it generated an even more diverse and frenetic field of responses. I exchanged several e-mails with the editor in chief of *Orthodox St. Petersburg*, who viewed the event as a sinister rehabilitation of the tradition of "jesters' weddings": a "conscious mockery of the Holy

Mystery of matrimony" devised by "the Protestant Peter I."
(Peter wasn't actually a Protestant, but Slavophiles sometimes
call him one as an insult.) The editor particularly objected to
the wedding celebrations scheduled for Valentine's Day—a
day "commemorating a Catholic saint"—and to the coincidence of the scheduled opening day, February 6, with the
name day of St. Xenia of Petersburg.

"Why is St. Patrick's Day so widely celebrated in Moscow," he demanded, "when nobody in Scotland knows a
thing about Blessed Xenia of St. Petersburg?" The next day,
I received a follow-up e-mail: "St. Patrick was by birth Irish,
not Scottish. I beg your pardon."*

Believed to have been born in 1730, Xenia was widowed
at twenty-six, went mad from grief, gave all her belongings
to the poor, dressed in her husband's clothes, forgot her own
name, called herself Andrei Fyodorovich after her husband,
and became known as a "holy fool" and a clairvoyant. From
a public relations perspective, Anna Ioannovna couldn't have
come up against a worse saint: of two young widows, one
renounces worldly things and becomes the patron saint of
marriage, while the other entertains all Europe with her
extravagant matrimonial farces.

The next morning, Luba and I spent some time in the palace,
interviewing visitors. A middle-aged woman called Tamara
Malinovskaya, wearing the largest fur coat I have ever seen,
told us it was her fourth visit. "I can't tear myself away," she
said, gazing around with wide, startled-looking eyes.

---

*In fact, St. Patrick was born in Kilpatrick, Scotland, in the year 387. His father
belonged to a high-ranking Roman family, and his mother was a relative of St. Mar-
tin of Tours. Patrick was kidnapped in his sixteenth year by Irish marauders, who
sold him into slavery to a chieftain and druidical high priest in present-day County
Antrim.

"Does it make you think of Lazhechnikov?"

"Hmm . . . of course one has read Lazhechnikov, and found it very interesting," Malinovskaya said thoughtfully. "But I can't honestly say I think about it very often."

We also met a *blokadnik* (a survivor of the 1941 Leningrad Blockade) called Valery Dunayev, unseasonably dressed in a light beige jacket, with a huge camera around his neck.

"I'm an amateur photographer," he said, leaning toward us, releasing a wave of vodka fumes. It was his second visit to the palace. He had already developed the pictures from his first visit, which he invited us to look at in his apartment.

"Um, you're very kind," I said. "Does being here make you think of Lazhechnikov?"

Dunayev tipped his head backward, then reached out to steady himself against an end table made of ice. "It makes me think of many things, many things . . ."

In the next days, we rushed around Petersburg, pursuing two sets of contacts: historians and social scientists, acquaintances of Grisha Freidin, and people over seventy-five years old, acquaintances of Luba, who is very popular with the older generations.

One thing members of both these groups had in common was that they had nothing to say about the House of Ice. Not one of them had been inside: the academics because they weren't interested, and the old people because they were afraid of falling down. "I saw it for thirty seconds," a professor of political theory told us. "I passed it in a taxi." He knew of the ice palace primarily from *Word and Deed*, a 1970s pulp novel about the reign of Anna Ioannovna. (*Word and Deed* characterizes the petroleum-spewing elephant fountain as "the world's first oil pipeline," and Anna's cabinet minister as a cruel man but a visionary, "the *first* researcher" of Caucasian petroleum.)

"Why should I read Lazhechnikov?" the political scientist

asked. "He's a second-rate novelist. Do you read second-rate political theorists? Have you read James Harrington? No? He was the main republican of the English Revolution!"

A sociology professor, who had passed by the House of Ice while jogging, informed us that absolutely nobody went inside except tourists and children. We mentioned that we had been inside and had seen many adult Petersburgers. He was unimpressed. "They were already *there*," he observed. "Your sampling group was too specific."

Even Evgeny Anisimov, the world's foremost scholar of Anna Ioannovna, hadn't been to the palace: the idea "somehow wasn't interesting," because the ice hadn't been dyed to produce the original trompe l'oeil effect: "It was immediately apparent that it was a house of ice, and not a deception."

At the Hermitage, an art historian told us it wasn't worth visiting the palace because it was too small. Six meters had been big in 1740, but now there was a different proportional standard. "My colleague in Moscow called me and said, 'How could you *not* go?' And I just said: 'What am I—a dwarf?' "

Luba had gotten us a second interview in the Hermitage, with a septuagenarian restorer of eighteenth-century clocks: his workshop overlooked the ice palace, so he had witnessed its entire construction. Every surface in the workshop was crammed with small and medium-size clocks in varying stages of disassembly. Grandfather clocks lined the walls, doors ajar, like recently evacuated coffins. On peg boards hung clock keys of every size and shape, and round white clock faces with surprised expressions.

"Of course I watched them build it, of course," said the clockmaker, gazing out the window with startlingly clear blue eyes. "It was bitter cold, but those young guys worked all day long. For the first two weeks there were lines over a kilometer—like an ant colony! Now the ice is cloudy, but before the first snow, it was perfectly transparent. When the sun set, it sparkled, sparkled . . ." But he was reluctant to venture any claims regarding the cultural significance of the reconstruction. "Read Lazhechnikov," he kept saying. "He explains everything. They did everything just the way he describes." When pressed, he admitted there was one difference between the original and the replica: the roof. "They reinforced it with wood and plastic, so it wouldn't fall on our heads. But what of it—roofs fall everywhere, we're used to it." He proceeded to show us a partially dismantled musical clock that had once belonged to Catherine the Great, and even took us on a private tour of the eighteenth-century wing of the Hermitage. Never had I dreamed that the world contained so many snuffboxes, dinner services, military orders, portable liturgical sets, and officers' uniforms. Luba, an eighteenth-centuryist, viewed these artifacts with interest, but I soon felt the full weight of historical boredom on my soul. When I left the museum, she was gazing with a kind of rapt criticalness at the upholstery of an armchair embroidered in 1790 by pupils from the Smolny School for Aristocratic Young Ladies.

I spent the rest of the afternoon on a walking tour of Petersburg bookstores, gauging Lazhechnikov's current status in the cultural imagination by the iron law of the marketplace. Of the first eight bookstores I visited, zero carried *The House of Ice*. I found myself in a "bookstore-café" in a poorly lit basement, where a disaffected-looking young woman sold me a cup of unusually vile coffee. The only other patrons were a group of ravers with bloodshot eyes, sitting at a linoleum table. They didn't seem to be enjoying their coffee any more than I was. A dark corridor, its floor lined with cardboard, led to three bookshops: used, new, and jurisprudence-related. The used-book shop was the only establishment I visited all day whose proprietor remembered ever having carried Lazhechnikov. "Long, long ago," he said elegiacally, gazing in the distance, as if about to recite a saga.

That evening, Luba and I took a bus to an outlying residential neighborhood to visit the eighty-four-year-old literary translator Mira Abramovna Shereshevskaya.

Shereshevskaya, who had prepared an entire dinner, with egg salad, black bread, and *rassolnik* (a soup made with pickles and brine), was outraged to hear about all the professors who hadn't been inside the ice palace. "Such a beautiful thing, in their own backyards!" she said. "I would have loved to see it. But you know, with my hip, I don't leave the house anymore."

The conversation turned to Henry James—Shereshevskaya had been among his first Russian translators. When I mentioned my fondness for *The Portrait of a Lady*, she pulled a green leather volume from a shelf: her own translation. Politely I opened the book. Suddenly there it was, that first golden afternoon when Isabel arrives at the manor house and captures everyone's heart, including the tiny dog's.

"It's beautiful," I said. "It's exactly right."

"Do you really think so?" She smiled, almost childishly pleased. "I would give you a copy, but it's my only one. This, however, is my present for you." She handed me a Soviet children's edition of Lazhechnikov's *House of Ice*, with elephants on the cover. To my relief it was unabridged and all my favorite parts were still there, including the insinuated dwarf sex, and the Gypsy woman who throws molten metal on her own face so she won't be recognized as the mother of the beautiful princess.

Shereshevskaya died of cancer in the fall of 2007, a year

and a half after our meeting. Suddenly it seemed that they were all drifting away, the women of the prewar generation. My grandmother in Ankara died earlier that same year. Nathalie Babel, having correctly surmised that Pirozhkova would outlive her, had passed in 2005. Women of another century, they disappeared, like the Queen of Spades, taking with them all the things that only they could tell us.

To this day, nobody really knows precisely why Anna's ministers decided to hold the jesters' wedding in an ice palace. Lazhechnikov imagined a scene in which Biron's henchmen torture a Ukrainian informer by pouring water on his head during a severe frost: the resulting "human ice statue," catching Anna Ioannovna's eye, gives her the idea for the wedding décor. Another possibility is that Buzheninova's naïve complaint to Anna—"Without a husband, my life is like a hard frost"—inspired the ironic staging of marriage itself literally within a hard frost.

Luba suggested that we might uncover the missing link in the Kunstkamera: Peter's chamber of curiosities, most famous as the home of Frederik Ruysch's anatomical collection, which the tsar purchased from the Dutch scientist in 1717. In addition to ethnographic materials and war trophies, the Kunstkamera had once also contained "living exhibits," including a dwarf called Foma, whose hands and feet resembled the claws of a crab, as well as a hermaphroditic blacksmith called Yakov. Anna Ioannovna had spent hours in the Kunstkamera, contemplating the life-size wax replica of her uncle, as well as the stuffed corpses of Peter's favorite dog and the horse he had ridden at Poltava. Upstairs, in the astronomical observatory, Krafft used to amuse her by setting things on fire with a burning lens of German manufacture.

If each monstrous spectacle staged by Anna was actually the grotesque doubling of an only slightly less monstrous spectacle staged by Peter the Great, perhaps Kunstkamera was the primal scene of the House of Ice.

In the Kunstkamera, Luba and I were immediately struck by the skeleton of Peter's favorite giant and bodyguard, Nikolai Bourgeois. Peter, himself a tall man, loved giants. Having noticed Bourgeois at a fair in Calais, he paid a handsome sum to the giant's mother—who was, oddly, a dwarf—to release her son into his service. The employment contract stipulated that, upon the death of Bourgeois, his body would belong to the tsar. When the day came, the giant was skinned in the name of science. The skin subsequently burned in a fire and, though the skeleton survived, the skull mysteriously vanished. (The one there now is a replacement.) But Luba and I saw his cantaloupe-size heart, the original, sitting in a glass case.

The technique of preserving hearts was introduced to the Russian Academy by Ruysch, whose anatomic subjects are the gem of Peter's collection. One jar contains a child's severed forearm: rosy, doll-like, and draped in a white tasseled sleeve, the fringe suspended in the still fluid like some kind of anemone. Another jar displays a child's severed head, its pale, detailed face set in a tortoiselike expression of wisdom and repose, even as the back of the skull has been removed to reveal the delicately traced mass of the brain. Two semifused Siamese fetuses float over the brilliant red drapery of their own placenta; on the lid of their jar is a still life composed of dried corals and sea horses.

To his contemporaries, Ruysch was best known for his still lifes and dioramas, which used skeletons and anatomical tissue to illustrate the baroque topoi of *vanitas mundi* and *memento mori*. They didn't last as well as the embalmed subjects—none have survived to the present day—but catalogues describe skeletons weeping into handkerchiefs made of brain tissue, with worms made of intestines encircling their legs. Geological backdrops were made of gall- and kidney stones; trees and bushes, of wax-injected blood vessels. In one diorama, a child's skeleton, using a bow made of a dried artery to play on a violin made from an osteomyelitic sequestrum, was surmounted by the Latin legend: "Ah fate, ah bitter fate!"

Peter, however, was less interested in the dioramas than in Ruysch's advances in teratology: the study of monsters. Inspired by Ruysch's work, Peter issued several ukases prohibiting the killing of deformed children and animals; "all monsters," dead or alive, were to be sent to his collection, with the idea of simultaneously promoting the study of biological form and combating the popular belief that birth defects were caused by the devil. Treasures began to pour in: a two-mouthed sheep from Vyborg, an eight-legged lamb from Tobolsk, "strange dog-faced mice," infants with missing and extra limbs, Siamese twins, a baby with "eyes under its nose and hands under its neck."

For Peter, the teratological cabinet represented a redemption of Russia's backwardness, darkness, and malformation. Preserved in jars using the latest European techniques, deformities were transformed into data, enlisted in the great humanist project of the arts and sciences. The glimmer of a similar intention seemed to hover over the House of Ice, with its transparency, its juxtaposition of ethnicities and monstrosities, of Russian imperialism and Germanic science—but the meaning was dimmer, murkier, obscured by the material excesses of the allegory itself.

As the ice palace was "benightmared" by the Kunstkamera, so was Anna's ethnographic bridal parade a dreamlike distortion of the famous parade staged by Peter after the battle of Poltava. In Peter's parade, Russian soldiers bearing trophies

from the Swedish campaign marched alongside a whole typology of captured Swedes: officers, halberdiers, bodyguards,
artillerymen, members of the royal household ("the Gentlemen of the Bedchamber, the Master of Horses and his assis-
tants, the royal pharmacy attended by doctors and surgeons,
the king's cabinet, the king's 'secret secretary,' and the king's
entire kitchen, complete with chefs"). Also present was a
weird, jesterlike character called Wimeni, a gift to Peter from
the king of Poland. Wimeni claimed—spuriously, it turned
out—to be a French nobleman, whose fits of temporary insan-
ity were attributable to a long internment in the Bastille.
Dubbed by Peter "King of Samoyeds," Wimeni participated
in the parade from a supine position on a sled drawn by rein-
deer, attended by twenty fur-clad Samoyed tribesmen on
twenty more sleds.

Despite its bizarre excesses, Peter's parade had a clear
symbolic meaning: to manifest the total conquest of Sweden.
The "King of Samoyeds" was easily decipherable as a parodic
replacement for King Charles XII, who had fled to Ottoman
Moldavia. A similar logic of replacement accounted for the
roles played by Charles's secretary, pharmacist, and chefs.
Peter was using the "problem of the person" to his advantage:
the person might have escaped, but everything that constituted him was on display.

When Anna restaged the parade, everything became confused. Her parade was supposed to somehow commemorate
the Treaty of Belgrade, but the Ottomans were replaced by
Kvasnik and Buzheninova who had, in their capacity as an
apostate and a Kalmyk, only a very tenuous connection to the
Turkic menace. Anna also had a "King of Samoyeds": after
Wimeni's death, that title had passed to the Portuguese jester
D'Acosta, who appeared in the bridal procession wearing an
authentic Samoyed costume from the Academy of Sciences.

By 2006, who could say what was being resurrected, and why? Watching news footage of the opening festivities, my attention was drawn to a middle-aged woman in a silver gown and tiara, wandering inexplicably among the bridal couples and fashion models (there was a runway show for fur coats). Leading a gorgeous Samoyed dog on a leash, she looked as utterly lost as the meaning of the King of Samoyeds.

The most elaborate literary treatment of Anna Ioannovna's ice palace occurs in "The Task," by the eighteenth-century British poet William Cowper. Cowper, best remembered as the author of the hymn "God Moves in a Mysterious Way," was literally driven mad in 1763 by his anxiety over the entrance examination for a Clerkship of Journals in the House of Lords. After three suicide attempts, he wound up in an asylum where he began writing poetry. His most famous poem from this period is called "Hatred and vengeance, my eternal portion." "The Task" was commissioned in 1783 by Cowper's friend the Lady Austen, who, presumably trying to steer him to more neutral topics, asked him to write a blank-verse poem about "this sofa." Cowper complied "and, having much leisure . . . brought forth at length, instead of the trifle which he at first intended . . . a Volume!"

As Thomas Mann's short story about Davos became *The Magic Mountain*, so did Cowper's trifle about the sofa expand from its comic Virgilian incipit—"I sing the sofa"—into a six-canto book-length poem, taking the evolution of the sofa and the concept of leisure as a point of departure for musings on country walks, London, newspapers, gardening, thieves, laborers, domestic life, animals, and retirement. (Could the same book be writen in reverse: an anatomy of types of activity and leisure, which gradually turns into a meditation upon the sofa? Did Proust already write it?) The dominant themes in this poem are the superiority of retirement to action, and of nature to artifice. The ice palace, introduced by means of an unfavorable comparison to a frozen waterfall on the Ouse, turns out to represent the transitory nature of human achievements—an ephemeral dollhouse for miniature skeletons, a *vanitas mundi* in the style of Ruysch.

The strange thing about Cowper's description of the ice palace, a structure whose fundamental existence he deplores, is the beauty of the language:

> *Imperial mistress of the fur-clad Russ . . . no forest*
>   *fell*
> *When thou wouldst build; no quarry sent its stores*
> *To enrich thy walls: but thou didst hew the floods,*
> *And make thy marble of the glassy wave.*
> *In such a palace Aristæus found*
> *Cyrene, when he bore the plaintive tale*
> *Of his lost bees to her maternal ear:*
> *In such a palace Poetry might place*
> *The armory of Winter; where his troops,*
> *The gloomy clouds, find weapons, arrowy sleet,*
> *Skin-piercing volley, blossom-bruising hail,*
> *And snow, that often blinds the traveler's course,*
> *And wraps him in an unexpected tomb.*
> *Silently as a dream the fabric rose . . .*

What is such a beautiful description of an ice palace doing in a poem that denounces ice palaces in favor of frozen waterfalls? Why does Cowper turn the poem against itself, canceling out some of its loveliest lines?

I first became attentive to this kind of literary move in graduate school, when I began to recognize it in many of my favorite novels. I learned that it has a long history in the conversion narrative, going all the way back to St. Augustine. In the first half of his *Confessions*, Augustine recounts the adventures of his youth: competing in rhetoric contests, going to the theater, pursuing his desire "to love and be loved." In the second half, he not only denounces these adventures as hollow and vain—he also denounces narrative itself, shifting in the last four books to the non-narrative mode of biblical exegesis, interspersed with philosophical musings on the nature of memory and time.

What is the relationship between the two halves of the *Confessions*? You could call it a contradiction, but I prefer to think of it as a balance—a kind of credit and debit. Augustine racks up a debit by writing the almost protonovelistic story of a frivolous young man in Carthage—then balances it in the last four books, which are the exact opposite of the protonovelistic story of a frivolous young man in Carthage.

Cowper, likewise, racks up a debit with his lyric-aesthetic description of the ice palace—but earns the corresponding credit by claiming that frozen waterfalls are more beautiful, and that really poets should only write sermons.* (The fifth and final book of "The Task" actually *is* a sermon, on the nature of the Christian life.)

A similar mechanism may be observed in certain novels. Tolstoy writes a marvelous, gripping, seven-book-long novel about an adulterous romance—then throws Anna under a train and writes book 8, in which Vronsky leaves for Serbia to fight the Turks (the novel is absorbed into history) and

---

*An analogous balance of art and sermon also characterizes Ruysch's dioramas. The decadent miniature landscapes, made of human lung tissue and kidney stones, are redeemed by their subjugation to self-canceling sermons about the vanity of human endeavor. Pointing at their own impermanence, the dioramas simultaneously condemn and justify themselves.

Levin returns to his estate to find God (the novel is absorbed into spiritual meditation). Analogously, Thomas Mann spends a thousand pages in the decadent hothouse of the Magic Mountain—then balances his account when Castorp, woken from his spiritual stupor by World War I, leaves the sanatorium to serve on the front. Facing a likely death in the trenches, Castorp falls to his knees, "face and hands raised toward a heaven darkened by sulfurous fumes, but no longer the grotto ceiling in a sinful mountain of delight."

"The grotto ceiling in a sinful mountain of delight": isn't that just what the jesters saw above them when they lay on the bed of ice? Anna's palace is the monstrous crystallization of the anxiety that made authors from Cowper to Tolstoy to Mann cancel out their most captivating pages: the anxiety of literature, that most solitary and time-consuming of arts, as irremediably vain, useless, and immoral. The ice palace is like the first half of a conversion narrative, with no second half. Anna herself resembles one of Thomas Mann's "problem children"— the scion of a vitiated dynasty, corrupted by puppet shows, sensual love, and dimly grasped notions of zoology—and she never grows up. Spellbound in her Magic Mountain, she never recovers. She dies up there, attended by jesters and medics.

The negative fantasy of literature embodied by the House of Ice reaches its most terrible pitch in the fate of the court poet and classicist Vasily Trediakovsky: one of the most famous personages from Anna Ioannovna's reign.

The day before the wedding, Anna's cabinet minister commissioned Trediakovsky to write a matrimonial ode to be read at the ethnographic procession. Before Trediakovsky had time to complete the work, the minister summoned the poet to his chambers and, for reasons lost to posterity, *beat him unconscious with a stick.* Thrown in jail for the night,

Trediakovsky finished his ode anyway, and even read it in person at the wedding the next day, wearing an Italian carnival mask to hide his injuries. Despite this tremendous display of professionalism, in which all writers may take pride, he was returned to his cell afterward and subjected to another near-fatal beating. Reaching home the next day, more dead than alive, his first act was to draw up a will, bequeathing his library to the Academy of Sciences.

Had Trediakovsky died of his injuries, he would have become a tragic figure. Instead, he lived another twenty-five years, a subject of constant mockery. His very propensity for receiving physical abuse became a popular comic premise; as Pushkin himself put it, "It often happened that Trediakovsky got beaten up." Lazhechnikov's Trediakovsky brags about an audience during which Anna Ioannovna "deigned to rise from her seat, came up to me, and from her generous hand granted me the most benevolent box on the ear."

Trediakovsky was said to have written exactly one hundred books, each boring enough to induce seizures. "On the song 'Farewell, My Dear,' I composed a critique in twelve volumes *in folio*," remarks a character based on Trediakovsky in a 1750 comedy. Trediakovsky plus the ice palace: could there be any more vivid illustration of the pathos of graphomania? "It was considered extremely funny that Trediakovsky had to translate thirteen volumes of Rollin's *Histoire ancienne* and three volumes of his *Histoire romaine* twice, because the first translation was consumed in the fire that occurred in his house in 1747," observes the scholar Irina Reyfman, who wrote an entire book about the mania for making fun of Trediakovsky. Trediakovsky was also famous for his hatred of his almost equally boring rival, the scholar and versifier Mikhail Lomonosov. Lomonosov was incorrectly credited with some of Trediakovsky's literary accomplishments, including the development of the Russian hexameter. Reyfman's thesis is that,

in the "creation-myth" of Russian letters, Lomonosov played
the role of the founder-hero, while Trediakovsky played that
hero's "foolish twin" or "dumb demonic double."

In retrospect, however, the beating of Trediakovsky acquired
a tragic and prophetic cast. To quote the twentieth-century poet
Khodasevich: "On that 'masquerade' night, when Volynsky
beat Trediakovsky, began the history of Russian literature . . .
the history of the destruction of Russian writers." The Russian
state has always oppressed its writers: Tsar Nikolai I was Pushkin's personal censor. In 1940 Stalin, notwithstanding his busy
schedule, signed Babel's death sentence with his own hand.

The brutalization of writers was no longer funny. Meanwhile, as Foucault has observed, the institution of author-
ship is largely dependent on the author's liability to state
punishment. It's true that Russia subjected its writers to an
unusual degree of state control; consequently, it's also true
that nowhere in the world has literature been taken more
seriously. Mayakovsky wasn't really joking in 1925 when he
compared poetry to industrial production:

> I want the Gosplan to sweat in debate,
> assigning me goals a year ahead,
> and for Stalin to deliver his Politburo
> reports about the production of verse
> as he would about pig iron and the smelting of steel.
> ". . . in the Union of Republics the understanding of
>   verse
> now tops the prewar norm . . ."

Mayakovsky could never have retired to the country to
write poetry about raising cucumbers. He could never have
identified virtue with the sofa. He needed literature to be a
form of action or work, just like fighting in a war or building
a railroad. And once he started to worry that his own poems

were merely aesthetic, the mere products of leisure, it wasn't the kind of problem that could be solved simply by writing a poem about the uselessness of poetry. "I'd rather compose romances for you," he wrote, early in 1930, "But I have subdued myself, setting my heel / on the throat of my own song." This poem, "At the Top of My Voice," was unfinished when Mayakovsky shot himself that April.

The reconstruction of the House of Ice was slated for destruction on a Friday, but since the cold weather was holding up, the organizers announced they would leave it standing over the weekend. On Sunday morning, I decided to stop by one last time, to take photographs. But when I turned the corner on Nevsky Prospekt, all that remained was a pile of broken ice. A small crowd had gathered, and I heard echoes of a raven-like sound. "*Zrya! Zrya!*" they were saying: "What a waste!"

A small bearded man in a long overcoat and a fur hat stood next to me, shaking his head.

"When did they tear it down?" I asked him.

"Who knows? Late at night, when nobody saw. What a waste. What a shame."

"It was a historical reconstruction, right?" I asked, hoping at least to ascertain the contours of the ice palace in his cultural imagination.

"Of course," the bearded man said. "It was all historical. It was all made from plans, from original documents. There was an empress, you see. I'm not an expert—I forget her name. Alexandra Fyodorovna, something like that. She built the palace."

"Why?"

"Well, for a joke! For fun! Tsars had to enjoy themselves, too. And what a beauty it was." He sighed. "There were thousands of people here, such a line, you couldn't get close.

They had cannons that shot real cannonballs, and it was all made out of ice. I saw it on television. It's just shameful what they've done. A shame."

"They deceived us," said a woman nearby. She had Asian features, wore a snow-white ski suit, and spoke very precisely. "They promised that they would leave the palace standing until tonight. I bring my daughter to Palace Square for her art class every Sunday morning—we came an hour early, just to see it one last time. It's hurtful, even." Her daughter, about seven years old and missing several teeth, had joined some children who were clambering on the ice boulders, resembling, in their padded snowsuits, tiny astronauts. I remembered Krafft's *Description*. He had written that, for its beauty and rareness, the ice palace was "well worthy of being transported to Saturn and of taking its place there, as among the stars."

The next day, I met Gromov and Mikheyeva for the last time in the lobby of the Grand Hotel Europe. They strode through the metal detector with the dynamism of a figure-skating duo. I asked why they hadn't left the palace standing through the weekend. They exchanged glances. "It's complicated," Gromov said.

"We tried to reach you," Mikheyeva said. "We didn't know until the last minute."

When I told her about the disappointed citizens I had seen, Mikheyeva averted her eyes. "We didn't go there the entire day. We knew everyone would be angry at us, so we went to Vyborg."

"Why didn't you just leave it up?" I asked.

"Well, you know, an ice palace is so beautiful at first. Then the sun shines, and it melts, slowly, slowly—it's depressing. We wanted to end on a positive note."

Leaving the hotel, I stopped by the Palace Square to take another look at the heap of ice, but it had already vanished.

Summer in Samarkand (conclusion)

The housecleaning at Gulya's house was attended to every few days by Delia, a cheerful and attractive woman in her forties with fair skin, dimples, and dark hair. Bent double, she swept the entire courtyard and all the steps using a little whisk broom with no handle. Why didn't she have a normal broom? Probably the same reason Old Uzbek has one hundred different words for crying. Delia spoke perfect Russian, which seemed strange for a cleaning lady; the mystery was explained when it turned out she was one of Gulya's old high-school friends. "I help her out," Gulya said of her practice of hiring a school friend to clean her house.

I learned many interesting things from Delia: for example, that she and Gulya had both married alcoholics, but Delia's alcoholic had taken all her money, whereas Gulya had managed her alcoholic well and taken all *his* money.

"But Gulya told us that her husband was in California, studying to be a yogi."

"California? No, he lives just two streets away from here; I saw him last week." Delia thought a moment. "Maybe he was in a *bar* called 'California'?"

Her version of the story was supported, some five weeks into our stay, by the reappearance of the missing yogi. Shiny-headed, with muscular shoulders and a paunch, Sharif indeed projected the impression of someone who had never lived in California, which he thought shared a border with New York. He did, however, frequently try to make us listen to some cassettes of a Swedish yogi choir that he said could induce trances.

Sharif's dominant conversational mode consisted of repeating the same sentence over and over, for inconceivably long periods of time. One afternoon, when Eric and I were sitting in the courtyard drinking tea, Sharif came out with a stale *lepyoshka* and proceeded to tell us *at least thirty times* that Uzbeks love to tear up *lepyoshka*, put it in their tea, and call it "duck soup."

"Have some of our Uzbek 'duck soup.' We love 'duck soup' here. This 'duck soup' is the best kind of soup—filling, inexpensive, and, above all, delicious. Uzbek people love to eat delicious 'duck soup.' We call it 'duck soup' when we put *lepyoshka* in tea." Desperate to make him stop, I ate an entire bowl of the tea-soaked bread. It didn't work. "You ate our 'duck soup,' eh? So you love our 'duck soup,' do you?" He himself didn't eat any "duck soup."

Another statement Sharif liked to repeat was that Satan wasn't outside us, in the world, but within us. "You think Satan is out there" (pointing in the bushes); "but Satan is every-where—above all, inside us!" (pointing at his stomach).

"What's wrong with his stomach?" Eric asked.

"He thinks Satan lives there," I told him.

"Tell him!" Sharif urged me. "Tell your husband! Satan is everywhere!"

"He wants me to tell you that Satan is everywhere, including his stomach."

Eric narrowed his eyes, assessing Sharif's stomach.

One day when I got back from class, the neighborhood water had been turned off. Sharif was sitting shirtless in a plastic chair in the courtyard. He started to explain to me that Uzbeks can live without electricity or fire, but they can't live without water, because water is an essential need for Uzbek people. At that point, the gate creaked open and Eric edged in sideways, lugging three enormous jugs of water.

"Do you see what we have to do in Uzbekistan?" Sharif demanded, pointing at Eric, who had carried the water all the way from the fountain in front of Dynamo stadium. "We have to carry water because sometimes our water doesn't come to our house, and we can't live without it. We can live without electricity or fire, but we Uzbeks cannot live without water, which is necessary for the human organism." The water dependence of the Uzbek human organism, like most subjects, eventually led Sharif back to the problem of Satan's whereabouts. "Not somewhere out there—but inside every one of us!" he shouted, pointing at his stomach, just as Eric came out of the kitchen. "What's the matter?" Eric asked, drying his hands. "Satan in his stomach again?"

In literature class, Dilorom was teaching me about the second greatest Old Uzbek writer: Timur's great-great-great-grandson, Emperor Zaxiriddin Muhammad Bobur, founder of the Mughal dynasty.* At age twelve, I learned, Bobur had been caught up in a feudal war. He fell into a chasm with dovecotes. Bobur had an ignorant cousin, a soldier, who wasted all his time on revenge killings and on staging fights between

---

*Zahiruddin Muhammad Babur, as he is known to Western scholarship, lived from 1483 to 1530. The *Baburnama* is the first—and was for a long time the only—autobiography in Islamic literature, and is one of the longest prose narratives ever written in Chaghatay Turkish. To this day, no one knows what motivated Babur to keep a written record of his life. He hadn't finished it when he died—the narrative breaks off mid-sentence in 1529.

chicken and sheep. At fifteen, Bobur conquered Samarkand and again made it the capital of an empire. During the blockade, Bobur's army ate dogs, donkeys, and boiled trees. Bobur is the author of the *Boburnoma*, or "Book of Bobur," which recounts his conquests of Kabul and Delhi, his learned conversations with the Indian aristocracy, and the planting of many gardens.

A martyr to his own imperial vision, Bobur suffered all his life from a disease known as *gemoroi*. "That sounds like 'hemorrhoids' in Russian," I remember thinking.

"Do you know what *gemoroi* is?" Dilorom asked.

"I'm not sure," I said.

A sad smile hovered around the corners of her mouth. "Every one of us does two things. We do them every day in the bathroom . . . *Ey, Xudo!*" she called to the ceiling. "Hey, God! Forgive me for mentioning these words in front of respected Elif!" Dilorom went on to describe a certain affliction of the large intestine that caused great difficulties in one of the two things we do every day in the bathroom, involving swelling and pain and the passing of hard particles through the anus. In short, the Timurids, as passionate horsemen, suffered chronic hemorrhoids. Luckily, such was the refinement of their culture that they had a special grain that, when cooked with fat, water, and sugar, made a special porridge; when you ate it, you never had to defecate. "Oh, if I could taste it even once!" Dilorom exclaimed.

Bobur, a lover of poetry, once wrote a letter to Alisher Navoi, who wrote back. Bobur wrote another letter. Then Navoi died. "How will one survive the next hour?" Bobur shouted. After Navoi's death, a big black snake started thrashing violently. Bobur slit the snake open from mouth to tail. The snake died, and another snake came out. Bobur slit open the second snake, and out came a rat. While crossing the Himalayas, Bobur dipped his head seventy times in a hole cut in the ice. Then he swam forty laps across the Ganges, despite the undertow, despite the snowdrifts piled higher than his head.

In India, Bobur and his ten thousand soldiers defeated one hundred thousand Indian soldiers and one thousand elephants. To defeat the elephants, they used nails. Nehru wrote about Bobur and liked him, even though he had killed so many Indians, and their elephants. Bobur seized all of northern India, but gallantly installed the rajah's mother in a castle with servants. The mother bribed Bobur's cook, so that every day Bobur ate poisoned bread. He got sick, and so did his son. Bobur prayed to God that he would die instead of his son.

"This was a marked contrast from Ivan the Terrible," Dilorom observed.

Bobur outlived his son by three days. During this time, he ate only the purest birds, boiled for two hours into a soup. His hemorrhoids miraculously vanished, but then he died.

Dilorom loaned me a book of Bobur's quatrains in Russian translation.

> *I'm no martyr to miserliness, I'm no prisoner of*
>   *silver.*
> *I don't think that "domestic good" is a great good.*
> *Don't say that Bobur failed to complete his journey:*
> *I've only stopped for a moment—it's time I set out*
>   *again.*

> *In separation, Bobur grew sick and weak,*
> *From his melancholy Bobur became old and gray-*
>   *haired.*
> *Bobur sent you a present of a bitter wild orange,*
> *So even you can see how yellow Bobur has become.*

Her braided hair is a noose, into which I have
    flown.
Confused, strung up by the feet, and blinded—oh,
    woe!
Poor, poor Bobur: in affairs of the heart,
No matter what you do, you always trip up.

Poor, poor Bobur! I read these verses to Eric, who said that Bobur was like me: "He tells you about his problems, but he doesn't actually want you to solve them; he just wants you to express sympathy." We thought it was clever of Bobur to supply his interlocutor with the right response, and adapted this technique for our own use.

"No problem, Bobur, of course we can go get some ice cream!" Eric would say, and then I knew it was time to take him out for ice cream.

"Good work, Bobur! You're doing a great job learning the Uzbek language and the associated literary tradition!" I told Eric when I came back from the university covered with dust, and then he knew just what to say.

Sometimes Dilorom talked to me about the natural sciences, just as if they were aspects of Old Uzbek literature. Human nature, she told me, is composed of four elements: water, soil, air, and fire. This fact was long known in the East while Europe was still foundering in damp ignorance. Later, Europeans stole the Eastern theories and used them to found the medical sciences. The god Shamol blew the dirt around and animated the humans, who were vainly looking through the dirt for something of value. The material trace left by this process is the human thumbprint, a sign of God and a unique marker of identity, as testified by the seventy-fifth surah of the

Koran: "Does man think that We shall never put his bones together again? Indeed, We have the power to restore to perfect order the very tips of his fingers." Europe didn't know anything about fingerprints until the nineteenth century.

Dilorom also told me that every human being has worms in his or her small intestines. "Even me and you, *qizim*," she said, looking at me sympathetically. The worms are tiny parasites, and it isn't possible to get rid of them completely, but you can at least stop them from multiplying, using clay. This property of clay was known to the East already in the seventh century. Because soil is an element of the human organism, clay naturally combats many diseases, especially those of the spinal cord—including incurable hemorrhoids. In the Koran it is written: if you clean yourself with clay after going to the bathroom, and then wash it off, you'll never get hemorrhoids.

Ninety-seven percent of the soil's elements are found in the human body, and these minerals are transmitted via the soil to various fruits and vegetables. The reason the plum is the same shape as the human heart, the reason the Uzbek word for "plum" (*o'rik*) is very close to the word for "heart" (*yurak*) is that the plum contains minerals beneficial for the heart. *O'rik* is also close to *sariq*, which means "gold": among all fruits, plums contain the highest levels of elemental gold. In the human body, gold and silver are found only in the hair. All this is proof of God's conscious creation.

Muzaffar, who also sometimes talked to me about science, had a more skeptical worldview. He wasn't sure if God had created things consciously or not. "I'm an empiricist," he explained, adding that Uzbeks generally believed only what they had seen themselves. For example, the Americans said they had sent a man to the moon. The Russians said those pictures were staged, and the "weightless" American flag was nothing but a wooden board. "We Uzbeks don't get into these ideological debates," Muzaffar explained. "We keep an open mind. We don't know if there was a man on the moon, or if there wasn't a man on the moon. We weren't there."

On the weekends, Eric and I went sightseeing, a dutiful trudge from tomb to tomb. We spent hours in the necropolis called Shah-i-Zinda, or Tomb of the Living King, climbing up and down stone staircases, turning blind corners, finding ourselves in domed cubes or octagonal cells. The name "Living King" denoted one of Mohammed's first cousins, who had allegedly been introduced into the premises through a well by the prophet Elijah, and still lived there, in an underground palace.

At the ancient site of Maracanda, the Sogdian capital that fell to Alexander in 329 B.C., we visited the tomb of the prophet Daniel: a long, windowless building resembling a warehouse, with a row of shallow domes set in the roof. An old man asked if we wanted to know why the tomb was twenty meters long. "Do you think Daniel was a giant?" he demanded. "Daniel was no giant; he was a regular man! Only, his leg grows three centimeters every year! A sign of saintliness!" At a rate of three centimeters a year, I reflected, Daniel's leg would have outgrown the tomb hundreds of years ago. I glanced uneasily around the countryside. How far would it have reached by now?

French archaeologists had built a museum on the site of the old city, displaying four walls of Sogdian frescoes. In these gorgeous panoramas, courtiers riding camels were preceded by rows of sacred swans; a huntsman riding an elephant was being attacked by a leopard as a princess in Chinese dress floated past in a gondola. Islamic iconoclasts had scratched out some of the human figures' eyes, leaving blank gray circles that produced a zombielike effect. The room was torrid, damp, shadowy. A humidostat, an air purifier, and a cooling unit hulked against one wall, all unplugged. An antiquated chart registered daily temperatures around 45°C. A typed report on a clipboard, dated two years before, testified to *"une accélération alarmante d'une dégradation rapide et irrémédiable, due principalement à l'absence d'isolation thermique et hydrometrique."*

One Sunday, in the company of Eric's friend Shurik, we made a day trip to Shahrisabz, the city of Timur's birth. Timur had also, at one point, planned to be buried there. As England is a network of locations where Queen Elizabeth once slept, so is Uzbekistan a network of locations where Timur once wished to be buried. In Shahrisabz—Persian for "Green City," although in Turkish it sounds more like "City of Vegetables"—Timur even built a gigantic dynastic crypt, upon the death at age twenty of his son Jahangir. The crypt is crowned by a conical dome of obscurely organic, beehivelike appearance. Nearby stand the ruins of Timur's summer palace, of which nothing remains but a colossal vaulted entranceway whose geometrically patterned tiles spell a sad message: "If you challenge our power—look at our buildings!" The rest of the palace had been destroyed in the sixteenth century by the original nomadic Uzbek tribes— the ones who were always destroying the Timurids' stuff. Stark, vertical, unearthly, the walls shimmered in the hot afternoon.

Walking back to the bus stop, we crossed a concrete footbridge where two old men in skullcaps were sitting on crates. One of them jumped up and announced that we had to buy admission tickets. This was a common occurrence in touristic cities: old men would appear from nowhere and make you buy tickets with "Historical Site" printed on them.

"Keep your tickets, uncle," Shurik said. "We don't want to see any historical site."

"But you already saw the historical site. The whole city is a historical site!"

Shurik, who had been looking more and more beleaguered as the afternoon wore on, looked around incredulously. "I don't see any historical site—just some broken walls."

"Of course they're broken—they're six hundred years old! What do you *expect* a historical site to look like?"

"Like the Registan in Samarkand," Shurik said promptly. "It's not broken, and you can look at it for free."

I hurriedly gave the old man the money for three tickets. "A very interesting city," I said.

"But I didn't think it was interesting," Shurik objected.

The old man glowered at him for a minute, then shrugged his shoulders. "What does a donkey understand about fruit compote!" he grumbled, handing me back one of the bills.

The Registan, of which Samarkand residents were understandably proud, was a complex of elephantine university halls arranged around a vast stone plaza, with the luminous and inhuman proportions of a de Chirico landscape. When you leaned back and strained your eyes to take in the whole plaza, you saw that all the buildings were slightly skewed in different directions. The most famous building is the Shir-Dor (Lion-Bearing) Madrasa, decorated with orange-and-black-striped creatures with gaping alligator mouths; huge, white, clocklike human faces are embedded in their backs. The artist responsible for these lions was reportedly executed for violating the Islamic ban on . . . representational art.

The first of the Registan's buildings was constructed in the fifteenth century by Timur's grandson Ulughbek, the "Astronomer King," whose observatory lay two kilometers

northeast of the city center. All that now remained of the former three-story circular edifice was an eleven-meter length
of rail enclosed by two high marble parapets, resembling a
sinister roller coaster: the arc of the enormous sextant that
Ulughbek used to compile a catalogue of 1,018 stars. The
last chapter of the catalogue was about horoscopes, which
Ulughbek approached scientifically, attempting to correlate
different historical events with the stars under which they
had unfolded. The Astronomer King also composed tables
for using an approximate time of birth to calculate the precise moment of conception, "the place of the Moon of birth
in the moment of ejaculation," and the length of gestation, all
of which played vital roles in human fate.

Because of his belief that science would outlive religion,
Ulughbek had many enemies among the dervishes. In 1447,
when Ulughbek succeeded his father as king, a secret Sufic
court ordered his assassination—and appointed the astronomer's eldest son to help carry it out. (As legend has it, Ulughbek had already seen in the stars that his son would murder
him, and had accordingly banished him from the kingdom . . .
thereby driving him into the arms of the dervishes.) One copy
of the famous star catalogue was saved. The observatory was
razed, its location forgotten. Four hundred years later, a Russian archaeologist named Vyatkin made it his mission to find
it. He succeeded in 1908, and is now buried in the observatory's garden.

Gur-i-Amir, the mausoleum containing Ulughbek's own
tomb as well as that of Timur, was unearthed by Soviet
archaeologists in Samarkand on June 21, 1941. At last, scientists were able to confirm that the legs of Timur the Lame
really were two different lengths, and that Ulughbek had
been interred in the vestments of an Islamic martyr. Timur's
tomb was covered by the world's largest recorded slab of dark
green jade, reportedly seized by Ulughbek for this purpose

from a Chinese temple, and inscribed with the ominous legend "When I rise, the world will tremble." Less than twenty-four hours after Soviet archaeologists opened the tomb, Hitler invaded Russia.

Inside Gur-i-Amir, sunshine filters through high grated windows onto tasteful beige marble; coffin-shaped cenotaphs are discreetly distributed like furniture in a waiting room. The idea of spending eternity there is terrifying.

A few days after visiting Gur-i-Amir, we went to the old Soviet department store in the Russian part of the city to buy Eric some pants. The atmosphere was uncannily familiar. Scattered through the dim interior were cenotaph-like glass cases displaying the lifeless appurtenances of capitalist existence: cutlery, radios, vitamins. On the walls, all the way up to the shadowy ceilings, hung polyester suits, dresses, and handbags. Eric pointed at the pants he wanted, and a boy fished them down with a long pole. The pants, made of a shiny greenish-brown denimlike fabric, looked very peculiar.

At the department store I bought a tiny electric fan, which I brought to class the next day. When I set it on the table and plugged it in, Dilorom turned it so it was facing me directly.

"Let's put it in the middle," I suggested, turning it toward her.

"As you like, *qizim*," Dilorom said.

After twenty minutes, I became aware of a wave of heat radiating toward me. I touched the fan; it was burning hot.

"Yes, *qizim*," Dilorom said dolefully. "I didn't want to disappoint you, but I feared that this fan might become warm."

· · ·

Dilorom and I were studying the lesser Old Uzbek scholar-poets. Most of them were either madmen or saints. There was the scholar Harun al-Rashid, who either pretended to go mad or actually went mad. He knew that there was such a thing as shoes, but had forgotten what they were. He had been hired as a slave to watch somebody's shoes, but lost them. Finally, he himself made a pair of shoes, which he completed two months before his own execution.

In the sixteenth century there lived a religious fanatic called Mashrab, which means "wine-drinker." In fact Mashrab didn't drink at all . . . except for the Wine of Love. Mashrab got his name when his pregnant mother went to the market, stole two grapes, and ate them. The baby in her womb kicked and shouted, "Give back the price of two grapes, otherwise I'll leave this house!" Because grapes had such a strong effect on his temperament, scholars named the unborn child Mashrab. Even in adulthood Mashrab was concerned about injustice. He was constantly giving away his clothes to poor people. As a result, he often walked around naked. He was in love with God, and at age three could tell by looking at a man's shoes whether he would go to heaven or hell. Mashrab single-handedly fought society by defecating on the king's throne—right there in front of the odalisques. He refused to eat anything gained through labor. At difficult times he would spin with a nail between his toes with one arm in the air, until he achieved ecstasy and lost consciousness.

A great sultan wanted Mashrab to marry his daughter. Mashrab put his hand on the bride's belly and heard voices saying, "Father—food—water." He explained to the sultan that he was unable to support a baby, and left. On the way home he fell asleep and dreamed that his mother was rubbing his feet. When he woke up, a lion was licking his feet. This continued for three or four hours.

Mashrab loved owls because they live in deserted places. He had an owl who was his constant companion.

"Give me one thousand houses," the sultan once commanded this owl.

"One thousand houses? I'll give you two thousand houses," the owl replied. "In our country the people leave their houses because they are hungry. So go take their houses." Only Mashrab's owl had the courage to speak candidly to the sultan about the current economic situation.

The sultan convicted Mashrab of fomenting social unrest and sentenced him to hanging. Three days after the execution, a merchant came to town in a caravan. "Why are you all in mourning?" the merchant asked the townspeople.

"Because Mashrab has been hanged."

"No, no, I just saw him," the merchant said. "He's walking on the street, singing, wearing no clothes." Mashrab had become a saint, and saints can be in several places at the same time.

A certain sixteenth-century saint once read that Mohammed had a broken tooth. A stone had broken it. To become like Mohammed, the saint took a stone and knocked out his own tooth. Then he felt good . . . until he began to worry that he had knocked out the wrong one. Months of study and contemplation did not reveal to him the location of Mohammed's missing tooth. Just to be safe, the saint knocked out his remaining thirty-one teeth. Things weren't easy after that— especially eating and speaking. "Maybe I was wrong to knock out all my own teeth," the saint sometimes thought. But one day toward the end of his life, Mohammed came to him in a dream. "I died a long time ago," Mohammed explained, "but that was my ghost, giving you training."

Posterity has handed us a book of seven hundred lives of saints, and all of them achieved sainthood in the same way:

through love and work. Saints never lie. They can travel from Samarkand to Tashkent in ten minutes.

"Tell me, *qizim*, how long did it take you to get here to Samarkand from the airport in Tashkent?" Dilorom asked.

"Four or five hours," I said.

"And how did you travel—by bus, by car?"

"By car."

"Well, saints can travel this distance in ten minutes . . . without a bus *or* a car."

There are a total of seventy-eight flaws and two hundred virtues in the human character. Everyone has three cardinal flaws that they must battle throughout their lives. The most difficult flaws to overcome are sloth and guile. Saints have not only to conquer their flaws, but to master all two hundred of the human virtues, such as talking to animals and ghosts and exchanging ideas with vegetable life.

Some saints can cure diseases by prayer. One particular saint who had this ability himself suffered from hemorrhoids. "Why don't you cure yourself?" someone asked him.

"Because it improves my character," he replied.

A very holy pilgrim who lived in Mecca for thirty years didn't defecate once the whole time, because it would have been sacrilege.

One saintly virtue is the ability to recognize thieves. A saint was once sitting by a window, reading a book, when a thief crept up outside the window and started unwinding the saint's turban. "I see you want to steal my turban," the saint said, not looking up from his book. "But, in fact, it's so old and torn you won't get anything for it at the market. Why not just leave it on my head?"

The astonished thief paused. But the saint wasn't looking at him—to all appearances he was still deeply absorbed in his book. So the thief went back to unwinding the turban. The

saint, still not raising his eyes from his book, grabbed on to
one end of the turban while the thief pulled on the other. For
a long time, the saint held fast and the robber tugged. Finally,
the saint said, "OK, take the turban." The robber took the
turban and left . . . but the saint quietly followed him.

The patron saint of Khiva was named Pahlavon Mahmud,
or "Wrestler Mahmud." He was such a great wrestler that he
ran out of opponents and had to go to India to wrestle the
rajahs. Dilorom gave me one of his poems to read. I was able
to decipher only one stanza:

> On the streets, with nothing:
> the fourth one is still little; he hasn't left his family
>   for the street.
> The family juts out like the branches of a fruit tree;
> those who pass by will take advantage.

Saints alone are free from the tyranny of human desires,
which follow a precise timetable. From birth to age five,
Dilorom told me, we desire affection and petting. From age
five to puberty, we desire candy and sweets. From puberty to
age twenty-five, we desire sex. Until age forty-five, our desires
turn toward children. After age sixty, we desire quietude and
remembrance. It is only from age forty-five to sixty that we
desire fruits of the intellect. "In intellectual terms, age forty-
five to sixty is the cream on the milk." Dilorom looked down
at her hands on the table, smiling faintly. "Soon I will be
forty-five," she said, raising her eyes. "I'm hoping to finish
writing my book."

"Today, we're going to talk about love," Muzaffar announced.
"OK," I said.

"Love is a difficult condition . . ."

Muzaffar had fallen in love once, with a Bulgarian girl whom he met in Heidelberg, where he had been studying Kant. They had spent every minute together. He told her that if she loved him, she would quit smoking. She said that love and smoking were completely unrelated.

"We came from two different worlds," Muzaffar concluded.

Muzaffar still dreamed of finishing his doctorate abroad, in Germany or the United States. For one of my Uzbek compositions, I decided to explain how to apply to the comp lit and philosophy departments at Stanford, stressing the importance of the personal statement and plan of study. It took three late nights to write; I submitted it in installments.

"This is interesting," Muzaffar said cautiously, crossing out all the wrong verb tenses in pencil.

A few days later, Muzaffar came to class looking unusually pale, with shadows under his eyes. "I have had a funny adventure," he informed me. After dinner the previous night, his parents had piled the entire family into the car and told Muzaffar to start driving. They said they were going to get some medicine for his father: an obvious falsehood, since the pharmacy had been closed for hours. They gave directions, and he drove, passing the closed pharmacy. They ended up on a dark residential street, near the house of some people his parents knew.

"Are we visiting the Buranovs?" Muzaffar asked.

"No," they said. "Just park the car . . . not here under the lamp; better under that tree . . ."

It turned out that Muzaffar's parents had once asked him what he thought of the Buranovs' daughter, to which he had replied, "How do I know what to think? I've never seen her." Muzaffar himself had no recollection of this exchange, but now he found himself in a parked car on her street, where the entire family proceeded to sit for hours, awaiting a chance for him to form an opinion of the Buranov girl.

"I was really frightened. What if she came outside and saw us—my entire family sitting outside her house in a dark car? She would think we were criminals. Once I thought I heard her coming and my heart was pounding, but it was only a cat. I think it was very funny for my sisters. We sat in the car for two hours, and during this time my sisters made fun of me."

"So did you finally see her?"

"No—we have to go back! On Thursday!"

We both started laughing, but after a moment Muzaffar became serious again. "My parents think I've been a student long enough," he said. "I think they want to say, to the student Muzaffar, 'Done with you!'"

It is impossible for women to be saints. On the other hand, Dilorom said, women may occasionally attain saintly qualities. Dilorom had both theoretical and empirical knowledge of such occurrences.

As a student in the 1970s, Dilorom was at the top of her class in scientific communism, scientific atheism, and Marxist-Leninism. She and her classmates had never read the Koran, the Bible, or the Talmud, which they had been told were full of empty superstitions. One day, one of her classmates asked the professor of scientific atheism, "If these books are just full of empty superstitions, why are we discouraged from reading them? As a scientist, you should want us to read them, so we will see for ourselves how empty and superstitious they are."

"Who's discouraging you?" the professor said, shrugging. "If you're so curious, go ahead and take a whiff of the Opium of the People."

Infused by the spirit of science, Dilorom and her class-mates went to the library, filled out the necessary forms, and were given the Koran and the Bible. (The university library had one copy of each.) "We read parts of them," Dilorom said, "but we lacked context. There was no commentary in those books. None of it made sense."

I nodded. I was familiar with this phenomenon.

"We decided our professor was right: these books were full of superstition and nonsense. This is how scientific com-munism robbed us of our own enlightenment."

In January 1992, Dilorom experienced a renewed curios-ity about religion. She went back to the library and checked out the Talmud, the Bible, and the Koran, this time in editions with commentaries. She read each book all the way through, one after another, looking up everything she didn't under-stand. She read nonstop for three months, during which she briefly acquired saintly powers.

Dilorom first became aware of her ability to communicate with animals on a bitterly cold and snowy night, when she had missed the morning garbage pickup and had to wait for the second pickup at ten at night. So she sat up reading the Talmud, waiting for the garbage truck. Silence descended upon the house. Her husband was away, and their five-year-old son, Boburbek, usually asleep at that hour, was sitting on the floor drawing a picture of the sun. He looked so happy that Dilorom decided to let him stay up. Soon it was nearly ten, and Boburbek still wasn't sleepy, so she took his hand and they went out together to take out the garbage. They walked and walked through the snow, until they reached the Dumpster. (Why did the garbage have to be personally delivered to the Dumpster at the moment the truck arrived? I don't know, but Old Uzbek does have one hundred different words for crying.) Standing near the Dump-ster, alone in the snow, was a black dog the size of a lion.

"Are you afraid, my son?" Dilorom asked Boburbek.

"Yes," he said.

"So am I," Dilorom said.

Then an amazing thing happened. Instead of barking or running up to them, the dog calmly turned around and *walked away from the Dumpster*, to the other side of the street, where it sat down and regarded Dilorom and Boburbek—as if waiting for them to throw out their garbage, which they did. Only when they turned and began to walk homeward did the dog get up and resume its original position.

"The dog understood us," Dilorom explained, "and I understood him. He was telling us: 'I know you're afraid, but don't worry. I mean you no harm. See, I'll sit here out of the way, until you're ready to go back home.'"

A few months later, in that first long, hot summer of Uzbek independence, Dilorom had a second saintly experience. She and her sister Shirin were in a suburb near Urgut, attending a conference on religious literature. Every hour, the participants left the sweltering conference room and went outside to the drinking fountain, which tapped into a natural spring; according to local legend, those who were pure of heart could see Mecca in its waters. One member of the party, a sixty-year-old man named Musherref who was descended from a *shayx*, decided to look into the water. Everyone was sure that he would be able to see Mecca. But he didn't see anything. Dilorom was so surprised that she leaned over and took a look—of course she didn't see anything, either. But suddenly her sister, Shirin, gripped her arm, staring into the water. "*Mana mana mana*, look look look!—don't you see the pillars?"

Dilorom realized that Shirin must have seen the two minarets that rise up behind the Kaaba. "God should forgive me, because I was so surprised!" she explained. "I love Shirin very much, but she is so small and thin and lighthearted . . . how should I say it? She doesn't think about problems of the soul. But I understood that she must in fact be exceedingly pure of heart."

I had once briefly met Shirin, who worked in a psychology lab at the university. She was indeed very slight and young-looking, with a pixie haircut, jeans, and an appearance of struggling to hold back uncontrollable laughter.

"*Ey, Xudo!*" Dilorom had said to the sky. "Hey, God! Forgive me for having misjudged Shirin! I will work harder to help you make my heart pure enough to see Mecca."

But Shirin had said, "Big sister, I know you'll be able to see it. *Mana*, here"—and lo, Dilorom saw the two minarets! This was one of the happiest moments of her life. She drew a picture of the minarets in my notebook, above the name of the suburb where the fountain was located: Chorchinor.

Dilorom wanted very much to bring me to Chorchinor. "I want to know if you'll see Mecca," she said, smiling faintly. "I think you will."

"Hmm, I hope so," I said, secretly wondering which would be worst: to pretend to see Mecca, to admit that I didn't see it . . . or actually to see it. I was tremendously relieved when it turned out that, because of construction, the Urgut bus route was suspended all summer.

When I got home that afternoon, Gulya was waiting for me at the gate. "Emma, you can't have lunch yet—you have to go back to the university. It's very important. It's about your bill. Inom will drive you."

"My bill?" I knew for a fact that ACTR had already cashed the seven-thousand-dollar check that covered my body bag. "I'll talk to them about it tomorrow," I told her. But Inom had opened the door of his newly washed Opel, and Gulya was shrieking, "Emma, Emma, get in the car!"

I got in the car. Inom drove me to the university, where

the social worker called Matluba—the one who had forbidden me to leave Gulya's house at night—announced that I had overpaid my bill. The seven thousand dollars had been distributed among all the proper parties, and one hundred dollars were left over.

"It's a lot of money—*your* money," she said. "You can decide what to do with it. You can give it to Vice-Rector Safarov, as thanks for using the university facilities, or to Gulya, who has been your host for all this time . . ."

Matluba said that Vice-Rector Safarov had already received one thousand dollars from my tuition, and she thought it was enough. But Gulya had received only two thousand dollars for our room and board. "Maybe you should give the money to her," Matluba suggested.

"What about Muzaffar and Dilorom?" I asked.

"They have already been paid. They received one hundred and fifty dollars."

I stared at her. "Do you mean fifteen hundred?"

Matluba smiled pityingly. "Fifteen hundred? What for? You didn't stay at their house. You met them in Safarov's department."

In other words, as payment for meeting with me one on one, ten hours a week, for two months, Muzaffar and Dilorom had received seventy-five dollars each. I asked for the hundred dollars to be divided between them.

"You really don't want to give this money to Gulya? Did she do something to offend you?"

Matluba eventually drove me back to Gulya's house, in a Daewoo hatchback. The two women sat awhile talking in the kitchen. I couldn't hear what they were saying.

In the evenings, Eric and I watched a lot of television: Bollywood movies, Russian variety shows, Kazakh war epics,

Uzbek music videos. One video showed an overwrought young man in a car singing a ballad while purposefully parking the car in a bush. "Why did he park his car in that bush?" you wondered. Then you saw the singer lying on the ground with blood coming out of his nose, amid the flashing lights of ambulances, and you realized that he was supposed to have crashed his car into a tree and died.

The World Cup was still going on—incredibly, the same contest we had seen on televisions in California and Frankfurt. Against all expectations, the Turkish team had advanced to the semifinals. The match against Brazil aired on the Uzbek national channel, in a dubbed Russian telecast. I was dismayed, even hurt, to see that all the Uzbek people were rooting for Brazil. "Show me the Brazilian girl who came here to learn about your national literature," I remember thinking.

As the Brazilian soccer team defeated the team of my ancestral homeland 1–0, as people in the streets of Samarkand shouted, "Ronaldo! Ronaldinho!" I became aware of a deep flaw in my understanding of the world and human knowledge. I had previously thought of knowledge as a network of connections that somehow preserved and safeguarded the memory of what they were connecting. But of course it was only *people* who remembered things; words and ideas themselves had no memory. The Uzbek language truly was related to both Turkish and Russian, by either genetic origin or secondary contact . . . but that didn't make it a reconciliation between the two. When you studied Uzbek, you weren't learning a history or a story; all you were learning was a collection of words. And the larger implication was that no geographic location, no foreign language, no preexisting entity at all would ever reconcile "who" you were with "what" you were, or where you came from with what you liked.

The Uzbek soccer fans' lack of identification with the Turkish national team was what finally made me see that Uzbekistan wasn't a middle point on some continuum between Turkishness and Russianness. Uzbekistan was more like a worse-off Turkey, with an even more depressing national literature. Even I, who was always making fun of Orhan Pamuk, could see that if Pamuk were somehow magically ceded over to the Uzbeks, they would have cause for a national holiday.

Toward the end of our stay, Gulya's husband, Sharif, started confiscating our furniture, item by item. One day a chair would go missing; the next day, another chair or the nightstand. In their place, he left us cassettes of the trance-inducing Swedish yogis. Soon all we could do in the evenings was sit on the floor where the chairs used to be and look at the square where the television used to be, taking turns listening to the Swedish choir on my Walkman. Turkey won the third-place match versus Korea, but I'm not sure it was even shown on Uzbek TV.

Like a dying star, the summer in Samarkand swelled and grew more luminous toward its end. More and stranger melons appeared at the market. The classroom where Dilorom and I met was being repainted. We moved to a room with no windowpanes, the air filled with the gentle gurgling of pigeons, the surfaces splattered with guano. Some mornings we found pigeons standing on the table, gray and rose-colored with geological-looking markings, looking around importantly with their beady academicians' eyes. "*Kisht*—out you go," Dilorom would say. Looking offended, they would grudgingly hop away.

In that last week, Dilorom told me about the colonial period of Uzbek literature. The tale began with Peter the so-called Great who, noticing that the English had colonies in India, decided that Russia had to have colonies in Central Asia. Peter availed himself of a book on governance and military strategy written by the Timurids: "That's how our own grandfathers' writings sold us to slavery."

In those days Russian *muzhiks* bathed once a year in the Volga, without even taking off their shirts. Central Asians steamed themselves daily in marble bathhouses. So who should have been colonizing whom? Dilorom told me about the time in 1868 when the tsar relocated an entire Cossack village to Surkondaryo. "Now it's yours," the tsar told the illiterate Cossacks, who were good for nothing but digging up mud and spoiling the riverbeds.

The Russians were very different from the English, who had sent to India not *muzhiks* but aristocrats. "Things would have gone better for us if we had been colonized by the English," Dilorom said. It was one of their *idées reçues*; they all thought of India as their missed fate—even little Shurik, when he came over to borrow my Oxford pocket Russian-English dictionary, which he said was the best dictionary he had ever seen in his life, and I believed him. "If we had been colonized by the British, I would already speak English," he said apologetically.

At the time of the Russian incursion, there were two groups of Uzbek writers: the aristocrats, who loved beautiful women, nature, and kings; and the democrats, who loved mud and head colds. Some Central Asian intellectuals were taken in by the promises of socialism and progress, and by the appearance of lycées, trains, theaters. The poet Furqat (1859–1909) wrote poems called "Piano," "Hermitage," "Gymnasium," "Science," and "Suvorov."

Dilorom gave me a photocopy of Furqat's ode to the Tashkent Exposition of 1890.

She said that the poem was actually critiquing the artificiality of the concept of exposition, since the Uzbeks had had beautiful things, bazaars, and the Silk Road for thousands of years. The Russians, evidently not sensing this critique, had applauded Furqat and invited him to a banquet—where Furqat expressed his Eastern courtesy by declaiming some extemporaneous verses to one of his hosts' wives. The Russians banished him to China, where he eventually died.

Furqat had a friend named Muqimiy, who wrote in every genre: lyric, satiric, and comic verse, and *ghazals* composed in folk language. Muqimiy spent fifteen or twenty-five years studying in the madrasa. There was supposed to be a banquet for his graduation, but it never took place, because his parents had died. Muqimiy had no capital and no craft. Somehow he became a calligrapher and got married, but was unable to integrate himself with the conditions of life. He abandoned his wife and never remarried, though he always remained in love. In Dilorom's opinion he was never happy. He began to help his friends by writing legal requests to judges, in verse. These verses were so delightful that they smoothed the procedural way. In his middle age, Muqimiy revitalized the Uzbek epistolary and travel genres. "I went from village to village," he wrote. "In this one the women bathe naked and the men all watch; in that one the dogs bark all night, a woman sings me a song worse than a donkey's braying, and meanwhile three boys are catching a noisy bird . . ."

G'afur G'ulom, the "Uzbek Maxim Gorky," wrote anecdotes, prose, journalism, and narrative poems, and was known all over the Soviet Union, even in Ukraine and Moldova. He received an Order of Lenin and could produce a poem "at any moment." He carried his problem inside him. Like his country, he appeared to be free but wasn't. He wept at home, in solitude: "The words I want to say are left in my heart."

G'ulom's best friend, Abdulla Qahhor, was the son of a

woodworker specializing in the production of hammer handles. Qahhor wrote in the style of Chekhov, but at a one-thousand-times higher level. The authorities would print one tiny book by him every year and say it was all he wrote, to deceive people. In fact, he was always writing, writing. Because so much writing is bad for the health, Qahhor suffered from diabetes and heart attacks. He died in a Moscow hospital in 1966, but actually the hospital was a jail where Communists practiced the mass hypnosis of society.

In Qahhor's most famous story, "Pomegranate," a woman craves pomegranates. A man comes in with a cloth bundle. He stands in the doorway for a moment, then drops the bundle with a thud. Pomegranates roll out. "Where did you get them?" asks the woman. The man stares at her, wordless, trembling.

Then the past caught up with the present, and we reached the literary-historical landmark I had been waiting for: the emergence of an indigenous novel form. Abdulla Qodiriy's *Past Days*, considered to be the first Uzbek novel, was serialized in the magazine *Inqilob* in 1922–25. The action is set in Tashkent and Fergana in 1847–60, years of infighting among the khanates of Turkestan, who formed various volatile alliances with and against Russia. The hero of the novel is a young man from a Tashkent merchant family dealing in shoes and housewares. He goes to Fergana, falls in love, gets married, but is denounced by a rival as a spy. Years later he is released from prison, and his mother forces him to take a second wife, who poisons the first wife out of jealousy because the first wife bore him a son. The boy goes to Fergana to live with his mother's parents, and the father goes to war and dies. Qodiriy wrote a second historical novel, *The Scorpion from the Pulpit*, set during 1865–75, the last decade of the reign of the last khan of Kokand. Qodiriy called the khan the last representative of feudalism, oppressor of the farmer and small-craftsman classes. Compatible with Soviet ideology as these views may sound, Qodiriy was executed during the Great Purges.

On our last afternoon in Samarkand, Eric and I went to the park to meet the janitor Habib, the towering, light-haired youth who had befriended me at the university and insisted on taking my husband and me to the amusement park with his wife and seven-year-old daughter. But when we got to the park, there was no wife or daughter—just Habib. We invited him on the Ferris wheel, and then he invited us on a ride where we sat in a rotating swing suspended by chains from the rim of an enormous disk that simultaneously spun and tilted on an axis. The mechanism was jerky and irregular, accelerating and stopping, and seemed to run on forever. Overcome by nausea, I held my breath, willing myself to lose consciousness, but it didn't work.

"Did you like it?" Habib asked in Uzbek, when we got off. (As a young working-class Uzbek, he didn't speak Russian.) "Shall we do it again? No? Good." Habib looked relieved. "It made me really sick. Some things you want to do more than once. But with this particular thing, once was enough."

We began to walk back to the university. Habib asked how old I was. "Twenty-four? You're only two years younger than my wife, and you don't have any children! I thought you were seventeen or eighteen! Are you sure you're twenty-four? . . . I have to have some words with your husband. Don't worry, I won't say anything bad. I'll just explain to him, as one married man to another, what he has to do." Suddenly bethinking himself, Habib lowered his voice. "Does he know what he has to do? And when he has to do it?"

"Well, I think so . . ."

"I'll talk to him anyway," he decided. "You wait here and look at the flowers."

We had reached the garden in front of the nine-story building, where rows of waist-high, thick-stemmed, wild-looking plants had sprung up seemingly overnight, from the dusty earth: flowering thistles, foxgloves, and gigantic flat purple asters the size of soup plates.

"But he won't understand you," I told Habib. "He doesn't speak Uzbek."

"He'll understand enough." Habib pulled Eric aside and started explaining something to him, gesticulating earnestly. Eric put his right hand over his heart and looked very polite. After a few minutes of conversation, Habib clapped Eric on the shoulder and they walked back to me. "He understood, right?" Habib said, shaking Eric's shoulder. Eric nodded. (He hadn't understood anything.)

"Now we have to get you some flowers," Habib told me. "You wait here." Squinting into the orange late-afternoon light, Habib walked to the entrance of the university, spoke a few words to the security guard, then waded into the sea of flowers and began hacking away at the stems with a penknife. "I'm choosing you some really good flowers!" he called. And when I voiced some objection: "Don't you worry—didn't you know I'm the head gardener here? Who do you think planted these flowers? Who, if not me, has a right to pick them?" He wrapped the bouquet, thick as a human leg, in a discarded newspaper and presented it to Eric. "I can't give them to her, because I'm not her husband—*you* have to give her flowers," he said to Eric, speaking slowly and loudly, as if to a deaf person.

"He says to give them to me," I said.

"That's right, my dear," Eric said, handing me the leg-size bouquet.

• • •

When we had parted from Habib, we crossed the street and walked down the leafy median to the Amir Timur Monument, to meet Muzaffar. By some sculptural economy, the Amir Timurs of Samarkand bore a strong likeness to Lenin: the bald dome, the narrowed eyes, the V-shaped eyebrows, mustache, and goatee. All these things are the signs of God's conscious creation.

We had waited ten minutes when we heard the faint pounding of footsteps. A white blob glimmered in the distance—Muzaffar's shirt, like the Cheshire cat's grin, joined now by the rest of Muzaffar.

"I'm sorry I'm late; I couldn't leave the house. My parents had a special dinner. I didn't know, because it was a surprise. But I brought you a gift." Muzaffar handed me a heavy box made of unfinished wooden slats, with a metal handle. Between the slats, you could see a plaster figurine of a kneeling bearded mullah, a turban on his head and a book in his lap. The mullah wasn't looking at the book; his eyes were staring straight ahead, transfixed by anxiety.

"It's an Uzbek whitebeard," Muzaffar explained. "You can take it to America, to help you remember Muzaffar." He asked how much longer we would be in town. Our plane, we replied, left Tashkent in three days.

"I see," Muzaffar said. "So you'll miss my wedding." At these words, I felt a jolt of physical shock. The first thing that came to my mind was a line from Chekhov: "So you won't be at my funeral?" "It happened very fast. My parents brought the girl to dinner tonight, and it's all arranged. The wedding will be very soon, in the fall. But you will already be gone. I'm sorry about this. We have very nice weddings here."

As we congratulated Muzaffar and wished him every happiness, I tried to dispel my feeling of disappointment. So he would abandon his PhD—so what? Who had ever described grad school as the summit of human happiness? Wasn't it presumptuous to assume that every smart young person in the world could reach self-fulfillment only by going to Stanford to participate in Hegel seminars? On the other hand, wasn't it hypocritical to pretend I thought that any smart young person should ever leave his studies in order to perpetuate the family-centered culture of the East?

That evening, I carefully placed the box with the worried whitebeard in my suitcase. I realized only much later that the box actually opened if you moved the handle—at the time, I thought Muzaffar's parting gift was a worried whitebeard in a sealed wooden cage.

Early the next morning, a car brought us to Tashkent: a city in which I had a special interest, since Luba had lived there until she was fifteen. I tried to call up some of her childhood stories so I could imagine them happening. All I could remember was that as a little girl she used to watch the great semiotician Yuri Lotman on TV and already knew that someday she, too, would be a literary scholar.

Tashkent, like a Russian city, had a metro, a circus, a puppet theater, paved sidewalks. In Samarkand the old men had beards and bright eyes and would often stare at you or try to educate you about something; in Tashkent the old men were fragile and ghostlike, wandering around carrying strange objects: a walking stick, a garbage bag, an accordion. I remember in particular one old man with a tray full of little plastic yogurt cups, each containing a tiny cactus plant as frail and delicate as himself.

At the Tashkent Zoo we saw a disconcerting variety of

predatory birds, and a giant demented-looking porcupine that was gnawing with big white teeth on the padlock of its enclosure. An old jailhouse, an open two-story space lined on both stories by concrete cells, had been converted into a house for small monkeys. In one cell, a skinny capuchin was mashing a boiled potato against the wall, peeling pieces off, and eating them. Next door, a tiny macaque with a deeply expressive, literate face was picking chewing gum off of its diminutive person. I remembered the scene in the Tashkent Zoo in *Cancer Ward*: the monkeys, "all looking as if they had close prison haircuts, sad, occupied with primitive joys and sorrows on their board bunks," remind the hero of all his fellow inmates.

In the Uzbek capital, I was seized by a mania to buy books—less in order to actually read them than to obtain tangible proof that they existed. In vain I scoured the city for *Past Days* and *The Language of Birds*. I made a trip to the bookstore of the Alisher Navoi museum, but all they sold were flimsy stapled booklets of lyrics. When I asked about *The Language of Birds*, the clerk said it was "in the museum." I bought a ticket and went inside. There in a glass case, bolted down in the middle of an exhibit hall, were two volumes from the same 1970 ten-volume Russian translation that Dilorom had let me borrow in the evenings.

Eventually, in a used-book store, I found an old Russian translation of the *Boburnoma*, as well as the 1947 screenplay for *Alisher Navoy*, a biopic coauthored by Viktor Shklovsky. I had never heard of this movie, which was released in 1948.

The screenplay centered on the friendship between Navoi and the sultan Huseyn, portrayed as a weak man who ultimately lets the poet down. As a youth, Navoi helps Huseyn seize power from the evil Yadygar, who cuts off the water supply, hoarding water for the aristocratic beks and destroying the farmers' livelihood. In one scene, during the military campaign against Yadygar, Navoi is shown dictating passages from *The Judgment of Two Languages* to a secretary. ("Verbs are particularly well developed in our language," he says at one point, perhaps alluding to the hundred different verbs for weeping.) As far as Shklovsky was concerned, a writer was always a writer, even in a time of war. In his memoirs, he recounts a near-death experience he had while working on a Red Army demolition squad: "My arms were flung back; I was lifted, seared and turned head over heels . . . I hardly had time for a fleeting thought about my book *Plot as a Stylistic Phenomenon*. Who would write it now?"

In the screenplay, courtiers reproach Navoi for occupying himself with philology in a time of battle. Navoi counters that the point of the battle is to unite the people, and that the people will be united only when their language provides a material shape for their thought. "Writers who come from the people have an obligation to channel their talents and capabilities toward the people's language," Navoi says, describing his own civic sacrifice, as a poet. "It's quite possible that nobody loves Persian words and works as much as I do . . . But one must speak in one's own language."

A Venetian ambassador turns up, hoping to broker an alliance against the Ottomans; he likens Navoi's *Judgment of Two Languages* to Dante's *De vulgari eloquentia*. Meanwhile, Navoi uses Ulughbek's astronomy to refute his astrology, arguing that his charts prove the invariance of the stars—their essential disconnectedness from ever-changing human destinies.

The central drama of literary creation in *Navoy* surrounds *Farhod and Shirin*, which Shklovsky, like Dilorom, presents as a tale of social inequality and crop irrigation. As he composes his verses about Farhod's civic accomplishments, Navoi vows to replicate them as historical fact: to build a canal solving the kingdom's irrigation problems. But before he has time to finish the canal, Navoi falls victim to the plot of court intriguers, and ends up exiled far away. In the poet's absence, Huseyn falls into dissipation, drinking vats of kumiss and wine, and betting on sheep fights. The canal is finally built, but all the water is given over to the aristocrats. Navoi returns from exile accompanied by a Sancho Panza figure, a baker who is also a poet: "I sing the glory of lepyoshka . . . I write of the love of yeast for flour . . ." The quixotic pair rides out among the people, Navoi on a white horse and the baker on a gray donkey, and Navoi recites a poem:

> I wrote verses about Farhod,
> About the mountain-dweller who split the stony
>   crags
> In order to channel a great canal,
> About how man may achieve anything,
> When he is governed by ideas.

The baker answers with his own verses:

> Do not censure the honey cookie, O pure lepyoshka,
> Because its dough will not be kneaded with your
>   yeast . . .

Our plane left Tashkent at four in the morning. We were somber, tense, excited. Eric was practicing something he called his "Damn You Breakdance." In the airport we marveled at the illuminated FIRE EXIT signs, which showed a white stick figure fleeing for safety. *Good luck to you once you escape the burning airport, little man.*

As the plane lifted off, the sky was just beginning to turn from black to deep blue. A few car headlights inched along deserted roads, grew smaller, dimmed, and disappeared. Six hours and thousands of miles later, we descended through leaden clouds. Square green fields unfurled beneath the hoarfrosted windows, like a huge chessboard, punctuated here and there by tiny square farmhouses. We skimmed closer and closer to the earth, almost grazing Frankfurt itself, the birthplace of critical theory and interdisciplinary materialism, with its silvery river, old churches, and the black glassy obelisk where they hold the book fair.

If I didn't resist the circumstances that pushed me to Uzbekistan that summer, it was because I believed that out-of-the-way places and literatures are never wasted on writers. And yet, I didn't write about Samarkand—not for a long time. Consequently, I didn't think about it much, either. Like a Christmas ornament without a Christmas tree, there was nowhere to put it.

I found myself recalling this anomalous episode from my past only several years later, when I was reading "Onegin's Journey," the excised chapter of Pushkin's *Eugene Onegin*, intended to bridge the three years that pass between chapters 7 and 8, during which Tatyana transforms into a Moscow grande dame, while Onegin wanders around Russia and the Caucasus, trying to forget that he just killed a man. Nobody knows exactly what Pushkin wrote in the first draft of "Onegin's Journey," since he burned the manuscript, publishing only some fragments which appeared, in later editions of *Onegin*, as a footnote or appendix *after* chapter 8. Pushkin is known to have rewritten these fragments in 1829, just after completing his own "journey to Arzrum." On that journey, Pushkin returned to the lands he first visited at age twenty-one, when he wrote *Prisoner of the Caucasus*. Everything was different now: "Whatever feelings I harbored then—no longer exist. They all either passed or changed." Pushkin turned thirty on that second trip.

I began to understand why it had been so difficult to write about my summer in Samarkand which, despite all the appurtenances of a new beginning, an exotic adventure, had actually been the end of something. It had been the kind of strange appendix that doesn't make sense until later, out of order—as the surviving fragments of the "Journey" appear in *Eugene Onegin* only as a footnote following the final chapter.

When I came back from Samarkand, I almost entirely lost the ability to read poetry. It was like a language I didn't speak anymore. What I used to enjoy in poetry was precisely the feeling of only half understanding—a feeling that is intensified, as Tolstoy once observed, when the poetry is written in a foreign language:

> Without entering into the meaning of each phrase you continue to read and, from the few words that are comprehensible to you, a completely different meaning arises in your mind—unclear, cloudy, and not in accord with the original phrasing, but all the more beautiful and poetic. For a long time, the Caucasus was for me this poem in a foreign language; once I deciphered its true meaning, there were many cases in which I missed the poem I had invented, and many cases in which I believed the real poem was better than the imaginary one.

After Samarkand, the beauty of cloudy, poetical meanings conjured out of associations and half-grasped words— the beauty of things that don't appear on the page—somehow lost its charm for me. From that point on I was interested only in huge novels. I started researching a dissertation on the hugeness of novels, the way they devour time and material. And although I suppose it's just coincidence that Tolstoy compared the subjective charms of half-understood poetry to the Caucasus in particular, nonetheless, I was finished with them, too—with the Caucasus, the Russian East, and the literatures of the peripheries.

School started again, the endless cycle of seminars and coffee, coffee and seminars. Luba had spent the summer researching the life of the princess Dashkova in St. Petersburg; Matej had been in Berlin doing some kind of topographical study of Walter Benjamin. Those were cities with archives, university presses, libraries—cities where students went to learn from books, not from "life." And they were right, those students: I had seen life, and it hadn't added up to anything. For a while it was a departmental joke that I had spent two months in Samarkand intensely studying Timurid love poetry, but soon everyone forgot about it, including me. I was busy teaching first-year Russian and reading Balzac. I spent more and more time on campus, returning to the Mountain View apartment only to sleep. In the winter, shortly after New Year's, I moved out. Samarkand was the last trip that Eric and I took together.

Muzaffar and I still e-mail each other sometimes. He and his wife moved out of his parents' house last year—a difficult and controversial decision. At the present time, he works as an office manager and has two children: a little boy, Komron, and a baby girl, Komila. Sometimes he travels to Kazakhstan, near the Uzbek border, where he does translation work at a village clinic run by Americans.

For a few years, Dilorom and I exchanged letters and gifts. "Respected Elif *qizim*! I was not at all surprised to receive your letter—because I was expecting it," Dilorom wrote in a card enclosed with a hardcover 1992 edition of *Past Days*, the novel I had looked for all over Tashkent. I think she hoped I would translate it into English, but I never even made it past page two. I dreamed about that book, not about its contents but about the physical book, its black cloth cover embossed with red wallpaper-like arabesques, indicative of the bourgeois character of historical realism. In my dreams, the cover was imprinted with "performative" blurbs ascribed to old school Anglophone literary critics:

"Kicking this book will cause pages nineteen and twenty to stick together. (In the paperback edition, the stuck pages will be fourteen and fifteen.)"
—F. R. Leavis

Northrop Frye has stated that, when addressed in the form of a proper Arab gentleman, the book will clap itself over the nose of the reader's worst enemy and remain there until the enemy has touched something that once touched a camel.

I would wake filled with relief, understanding that I didn't actually have to read the book, that the book didn't work that way (by being read), but rather by being kicked, or addressed in the form of a proper Arab gentleman, either of which was much less time-consuming than poring through the densely typed pages, looking up every other word in the dictionary. And although I am reluctant to say that what ended in Samarkand *was my youth*, nonetheless, this copy of *Past Days* brought home to me, with a kind of material immediateness, the truth of human mortality.

The Possessed

Within hours of my arrival in Florence to research a magazine article about a Dante marathon, I found myself standing outside the apartment on the Via Guicciardini where Dostoevsky spent nine miserable months ravaged by debt and epilepsy. The building faces the Palazzo Pitti and is surmounted by a plaque:

IN QUESTI PRESSI
FRA IL 1868 E IL 1869
FEDOR MIHAILOVIC DOSTOEVSKIJ
COMPÌ IL ROMANZO "L'IDIOTA."

Until recently, I had no particular interest in Florence, and had no idea that Dostoevsky had finished *The Idiot* there. Moreover, in the eternal debate of "Tolstoy or Dostoevsky?" I have always been in the Tolstoy camp. But fate brought me to Dante's city at the precise moment when I was obsessed by Dostoevsky's *Demons*, the novel whose hero, Nikolai Stavrogin, is considered to be the diabolical double of *The Idiot*'s Prince Myshkin, and the early notes for which were composed right there in Florence.

. . .

In my free time from researching the drama of Florence's centuries-long repentance for having exiled their greatest poet in 1302, I raced through *The Miraculous Years*, the fourth volume of Joseph Frank's five-volume life of Dostoevsky.

I learned that forty-six-year-old Dostoevsky had gone abroad shortly after his marriage in 1867 to Anna Snitkina, the twenty-one-year-old stenographer who had helped him meet the deadline for *The Gambler*. The couple left Russia partly because Dostoevsky believed that the European climate was better for his epilepsy, and partly to escape the creditors, relatives, and hangers-on who were making Anna's home life a misery. Ironically, considering the text that brought them together, Dostoevsky was seized anew in Dresden by his pathological obsession with roulette. He made a three-day trip to the famous casino of Homburg, which in fact dragged on for ten days, during which he lost not only all his money but also his watch, so that afterward, he and his wife never knew what time it was.

When the newlyweds decided to move to Switzerland that summer, Dostoevsky was unable to resist the lure of a stop in Baden-Baden. In between epileptic fits, he lost most of Anna's jewelry and managed to cement a lifelong animus against long-time Baden resident Ivan Turgenev. The contretemps was precipitated by a chance meeting with Ivan Goncharov, author of *Oblomov*, who told Dostoevsky that Turgenev had seen him on the street but had decided not to say anything, "knowing how gamblers do not like to be spoken to." Because he happened at that time to owe Turgenev fifty rubles, Dostoevsky couldn't be seen to be avoiding him (which he was). At their subsequent meeting, Turgenev said such terrible things about Russia that Dostoevsky finally suggested he buy a telescope. "What for?" Turgenev asked. Dostoevsky said the telescope would help Turgenev see Russia better, so he would know what he was talking about. Turgenev became "horribly angry." Dostoevsky had taken up his hat and was preparing to leave when he "somehow, absolutely without intention," ended up disburdening himself of everything that had "accumulated in [his] soul about the Germans in three months." Nothing good, it turned out, had accumulated in his soul about the Germans, whom Turgenev, by contrast, admired deeply. The two writers parted, vowing never again to set eyes upon one another.

The Dostoevskys were by this point desperate to leave Baden-Baden, but Fyodor Mikhailovich had gambled away the necessary funds. Finally Anna's mother sent them a money order. On the day of their departure for Geneva, Dostoevsky was unable to restrain himself and lost fifty francs and a pair of Anna's earrings at roulette. One of Anna's rings had to be pawned. An hour and a half before their train was scheduled to leave, Dostoevsky rushed back to the casino and lost twenty more francs.

The next year, in Switzerland, Dostoevsky worked on *The Idiot*, and Anna gave birth to a little girl. Three-month-old Sonya died of pneumonia that spring. The devastated parents resumed their travels, crossing the Alps to Italy late that summer and eventually settling in Florence. "In my opinion," wrote Dostoevsky in a letter to his niece, "it is worse than deportation to Siberia. I'm speaking seriously and without exaggeration . . . If here in Florence one finds such a sun and sky, and if there are *marvels of art*, quite literally unheard-of and indescribable, nonetheless in Siberia, when I left the penal colony, there were other advantages, which here are lacking." Having to write "without continuous and firsthand Russian impressions" was a particular torment for Dostoevsky, who spent long hours in the Gabinetto Scientifico Letterario G. P. Vieusseux, poring over the Russian periodicals to which he was addicted.

Dostoevsky didn't have an easy time finishing *The Idiot*. "I wrote the final chapters day and night in anguish and terrible uncertainty," he reported to his niece. "I had two epileptic attacks, and I was ten days over deadline." The last installments of the novel appeared in the journal *Russian Messenger* early in 1869.

Because of a delayed payment from his publishers, Dostoevsky ran out of money that spring. He and his wife (who took to calling each other Mr. and Mrs. Micawber) left the Via Guicciardini apartment and relocated to a single room overlooking the Mercato Vecchio, later described by Dostoevsky as "a market-square with arcades and splendid granite pillars [and] . . . a municipal fountain in the form of a gigantic bronze boar from whose throat the water flowed (it is a classic masterpiece of rare beauty)."

I, too, had been struck by that fountain, which is for some reason known as *Il Porcellino*: "the piglet." It was quite jarring to come into the square for the first time and see, not the piglet one had been expecting, but a huge disaffected-looking boar. Gazing upon the Porcellino, I found myself recalling a line from Gogol's "Overcoat," in which a police officer is knocked off his feet by "an *ordinary adult piglet* which came tearing out of a private house." This sentence is sometimes cited as an example of Gogol's absurd use of language: If it's an adult, then how is it a piglet? Apparently, the same absurd use of language was made by the Florentines when naming their gigantic bronze boar fountain.

In the apartment overlooking the Porcellino, Dostoevsky and his wife caught two tarantulas. On the night of the first tarantula, Dostoevsky lay awake for hours, remembering a certain Cossack of his acquaintance who had died of a tarantula bite fifteen years earlier in Semipalatinsk. Only by repeatedly "reciting aloud Kozma Prutkov's didactic fable

'The Conductor and the Tarantula' "* did he finally calm himself enough to drift into uneasy dreams.

From Florence, the Dostoevskys returned to Dresden. Over the next twenty months, Dostoevsky wrote "The Eternal Husband" and the first section of the novel that would eventually become *Demons*.

Arguably Dostoevsky's most enigmatic novel, sprawling, ideologically overpopulated, generically ambiguous, *Demons*—formerly translated as *The Possessed*—haunts me like a prophetic dream. The title comes from the novel's epigraph: the verses Luke 8:32–36, in which demons leave the man whom they have possessed and enter a herd of swine; the swine rush down a steep bank into a lake and are drowned.

Demons is the story of certain "very strange events" unfolding in a provincial Russian town, a place "hitherto not remarkable for anything." The narrator—whose eccentric, discursive chronicle includes scenes at which he himself can't possibly have been present—is a friend of one of the key characters in the novel: an aging pedagogue, poet, and lapsed scholar named Stepan Trofimovich Verkhovensky, whose academic distinction consists of having once "managed to defend a brilliant thesis on the nearly emerged civic and Hanseatic importance of the German town of Hanau, in the period between 1413 and 1418, together with the peculiar and vague reasons why that importance never took place." Twenty-two years before the events narrated in *Demons*, Stepan Trofimovich is appointed as tutor to the only son of

---

*Kozma Prutkov was a fictitious poet-playwright-bureaucrat invented in the 1850s by Alexei Tolstoy and his cousins. The moral of "The Conductor and the Tarantula" is "Don't set out on a journey without any money" (lest you meet the same fate as the tarantula, who was kicked out of the carriage by the conductor).

Varvara Petrovna Stavrogina, a wealthy local landowner. He becomes very close with his ten-year-old pupil, frequently waking him up at night "to pour out his injured feelings in tears before him"; the two then "throw themselves into each other's embrace and weep."

A few years later, the boy is sent to the lycée in Petersburg, but Stepan Trofimovich remains at the estate. Varvara Petrovna's husband dies, and she and Stepan Trofimovich fall into a bizarre, intimately acrimonious relationship. Stepan Trofimovich regularly writes Varvara Petrovna two letters a day; Varvara Petrovna lies awake at night worrying about the latest imaginary slight to Stepan Trofimovich's "reputation as a poet, scholar, or civic figure." Although "some unbearable love for him" lies hidden in her heart, it subsists "in the midst of constant hatred, jealousy, and contempt."

Years have passed in this fashion, when "strange rumors" begin to reach the town about Varvara Petrovna's son, Nikolai Stavrogin, now a twenty-five-year-old officer in the prestigious Horse Guards. There is talk "of some savage unbridledness, of some people being run over by horses," of Stavrogin having fought two duels, killing one opponent and crippling the other. Finally, Stavrogin himself turns up in his hometown: not loutish and "reeking of vodka," as everyone has been expecting, but unspeakably elegant, irreproachably dressed, eerily handsome: "His hair was somehow too black, his light eyes were somehow too calm and clear, his complexion was somehow too delicate and white, his teeth like pearls, his lips like coral—the very image of beauty, it would seem, and at the same time repulsive, as it were. People said his face resembled a mask." All the women in town have soon lost their minds over him—"one party adored him, one party hated him to the point of blood vengeance; but both lost their minds"—and the town's dandies are utterly eclipsed. The townspeople are particularly surprised to find Stavrogin "quite well educated, and even rather knowledgeable," and "an extremely reasonable man." Then, with no warning, "the beast put[s] out its claws": one day at the club, upon over-hearing a senior member exclaim, "No, sir, they won't lead me by the nose!" Stavrogin seizes the elderly clubman by the nose and manages to pull him two or three steps across the room, nearly provoking a seizure. Stavrogin is unable to ex-plain his actions afterward, and his apology is "so casual that it amount[s] to a fresh insult." After multiple incidents of this kind, he falls sick with brain fever and goes abroad.

The real action begins in book 2, three years later. Stav-rogin returns to town, together with various other locally connected young people with whom he has been associat-ing in Europe. These include Liza, a beautiful heiress; Pyotr Verkhovensky, the estranged, nihilistic son of Stepan Trofi-movich; Marya, a crippled "holy fool"; Shatov, a freed serf and a "typical Russian soul," who is constantly rushing from one ideological extreme to another; Shatov's sister, Darya, a ward of Varvara Petrovna; and Shatov's friend Kirillov, a young engineer who is obsessed by his plan to perfect society by being the first person on planet Earth to commit a 100 percent fully willed suicide. With the exception of Kirillov, these young people were all educated by Stepan Trofimovich. Every one of them is obsessed with Stavrogin. Darya, Marya, and Liza are in love with him, while Shatov, Kirillov, and Verkhovensky accord him an obscurely central role in their tormented ideologies.

Like much of Dostoevsky's work, *Demons* consists pri-marily of scandalous revelations, punctuated by outbreaks of mass violence. It emerges that the aristocratic Stavrogin, apparently in an effort to see how far grotesqueness can be taken, has secretly married the saintly, demented cripple Marya. Stepan Trofimovich's son Pyotr turns out to hold a position of authority in a terrorist organization, the goal of which is to overtake Russia by means of secret five-person cells. Having established a cell of five townsmen, Pyotor begins plotting to propagate chaos, despair, and revolution. Book 2 concludes with a demonstration by workers from a factory just beyond the town limits, where poor conditions have led to an outbreak of Asiatic cholera. In addition to the cholera, which has affected both workers and cattle, the province has also been beset by an epidemic of robberies and fires. Pyotr exploits the burgeoning mass hysteria to convince the governor that the peaceful workers' demonstration is actually "a rebellion [threatening] to shake the foundations of the state," and seventy workers are brutally flogged.

Book 3 opens with an elaborate fête organized by the governor's wife to benefit indigent governesses. The proceedings commence with a "literary matinee," featuring a reading by a famous expatriate writer, a transparent parody of Turgenev: "It's now seven years that I have been sitting in Karlsruhe," the famous writer announces, "and when the city council decided last year to install a new drainpipe, I felt in my heart that this Karlsruhian drainpipe question was dearer and fonder to me than all the questions of my dear fatherland . . ." Pyotr and his five-man cell sabotage the fête, filling the hall with drunkards and criminals, and reading aloud a highly offensive poem about governesses. The escalating mayhem is curtailed only by the announcement of a terrible new incident of arson: the saintly cripple Marya and her alcoholic brother have been burned alive in their house.

Everyone immediately suspects Stavrogin. They all think that he wanted to get Marya out of the way so he could marry Liza, the beautiful heiress. In fact, the fire was set by an escaped convict, Fedka, who believed that he was fulfilling Stavrogin's orders. Stavrogin guessed at the convict's intentions, but did nothing to thwart them. Meanwhile, Liza, who knows that Stavrogin doesn't return her love, has slept with him anyway. Stavrogin admits to having "ruined her without loving her," but says that after all she might be his "last hope," so maybe they should run away to Switzerland together. Liza refuses. When word of the fire reaches her, she rushes in horror to the scene of the crime, where a mob has gathered. Holding her to blame for the arson—" 'They don't just kill, they also come and look!' "—the mob beats her to death.

The day after the fête, Pyotr convinces his terrorist cell that Shatov is scheming to betray them, and must be silenced at all costs. He then convinces Kirillov, who is still plotting his humanity-liberating suicide, to leave a note assuming the blame for Shatov's murder: he'll be dead anyway, so what difference can it make to him? Shatov is killed and his body dumped in a lake. Kirillov signs the fake confession and shoots himself.

In the novel's closing chapters, Stepan Trofimovich, appalled by the deeds of his son and former pupils, sets off on foot into the countryside, takes up with a woman selling gospels, checks into an inn, and falls into a raving fever. In his fever, he begs to hear the verses from Luke about "*ces cochons*," which excite him to a morbid degree. "These demons who come out of a sick man," he says, represent the accumulated "sores" and "miasmas" that have come out of Russia; the swine they have entered are none other than "us, us and them, and [Pyotr] . . . *et les autres avec lui*, and I perhaps am the first, standing at the very head; and we shall throw ourselves, the madmen and the possessed, from a rock into the sea, and we shall all drown." Having delivered himself of this idea, he dies. Varvara Petrovna has the body moved to the churchyard on her estate.

Meanwhile, back in town, one of the terrorists has confessed to his role in Shatov's murder, and all five members of the cell are arrested. (Only Pyotr escapes justice, fleeing to Petersburg.) At this time, Stavrogin writes to Darya, inviting her to accompany him to Switzerland to be his "nurse." "The fact that I'm calling you to me is a terrible baseness," he writes. "Realize, also, that I do not pity you, since I'm calling you, and do not respect you, since I'm waiting for you to come." Darya rushes to join him, but it's too late. Stavrogin has hanged himself in his mother's attic, leaving a note: "Blame no one; it was I."

That's it—that's the whole thing (minus a chapter excised by Dostoevsky's editors, in which Stavrogin confesses to having once seduced a twelve-year-old girl and driven her to suicide; opinions vary on whether the novel is better or worse without this information). You never do find out what the deal was with Stavrogin, or why everyone was so obsessed with him. The various characters simply announce their obsession, as if in passing. Kirillov, explaining his theory of the transformation of men into gods by suicide, adds enigmatically, "Remember what you've meant in my life, Stavrogin." Shatov, in the middle of an agonized rant about Slavophilism and the body of God, shouts, "Stavrogin, why am I condemned to believe in you unto ages of ages?" Even Pyotr, the puppeteer who so deftly manipulates others while remaining unmoved himself, pursues Stavrogin relentlessly, determined to draw him into his circle by either bribery or blackmail.

"But what the devil do you need me for?" Stavrogin finally asks Pyotr. "Is there some mystery in it, or what? What sort of talisman have you got me for?" Pyotr's astonishing reply is that he loves and worships Stavrogin as a worm worships the sun, and that the new era of Russia will begin only when Stavrogin has assumed the identity of the mythical "Tsarevich Ivan," who will turn out to have been "in hiding" for years, and then Pyotr and Stavrogin-Tsarevich will take over the world together, with specially trained gunmen . . .

The first time I read *Demons*, none of this made any sense to me. I was willing to accept the enigma of Stavrogin as a literary convention, but what did this human enigma have to do with the large-scale possession of an entire town by arson, robbery, cholera, and terrorist conspiracies? Furthermore, what was the point of Stepan Trofimovich—why did his life take up a third of the novel? Why was it precisely Stepan Trofimovich's pupils who were so susceptible to Stavrogin? I thought about it for a while, although not for too long. I decided that this must be what critics meant when they talked about "flawed novels."

As I later learned, many interpretations of *Demons* do rely on the notion of technical flaws. Joseph Frank, for example, theorizes that Stavrogin is a composite of two inconsistent, irreconcilable characters from earlier drafts. The first character, a young aristocrat of the 1860s, is embroiled in a *Fathers and Sons*–style ideological clash with the generation of the 1840s, but undergoes a moral regeneration, overcomes his own nihilism, and becomes a "new man"; the second is a young aristocrat in the earlier, Byronic type of Eugene Onegin, who has already undergone, or seems to have undergone, a moral regeneration, but who then, to quote Dostoevsky's notes, "suddenly blows his brains out—(Enigmatic personage, said to be mad)." Because he was working "under great pressure," Frank suggests, Dostoevsky was obliged to consolidate these two heroes in the person of Stavrogin. Stepan Trofimovich, "a Liberal Idealist of the 1840s," is thus made into "the spiritual progenitor of a Byronic type associated with the 1820s and 1830s"—a relationship that is doomed never really to make sense.

My favorite part of Frank's interpretation is that, in the attempt "to compensate for the anachronism inherent in his plot structure," Dostoevsky must represent Stavrogin as "a *contemporary* development" of the Onegin type. There is something convincing in the picture of Stavrogin as an Onegin taken one step further, an Onegin beyond Pushkin, a machine for provoking duels, incapable of returning anyone's love. It's as if Stavrogin has himself read *Eugene Onegin* and no longer has any illusions of what awaits him.

On the other hand, to say the relationship between Stavrogin and Stepan Trofimovich is anachronistic doesn't really resolve its mystery. How is Stepan Trofimovich, and not Stavrogin, supposed to be at the head of the procession of swine who are running into the sea? Frank again finds the answer in a technical flaw: namely, the removal of Stavrogin's seduction of the twelve-year-old girl, which Frank characterizes as "a great moral-philosophical experiment" in the style of Raskolnikov's murder of the pawnbroker. Dostoevsky was frantically finishing book 3 when the editors told him that the scene of Stavrogin's confession was unpublishable; he was thus "forced to mutilate the original symmetry of his plan" and to shift part of Stavrogin's moral responsibility onto Stepan Trofimovich. In other words, the real explanation for Stepan Trofimovich's enigmatic claim to being the leader of the demons is that those words were never supposed to come from Stepan Trofimovich to begin with; they originally belonged to Stavrogin, but had to be reassigned once the confession was removed.*

---

*Other critics think that Dostoevsky was himself dissatisfied with the confession. In his edition of the *Demons* notebooks, Edward Wasiolek proposes that "somewhere between his plans for the first published version and the publication of subsequent versions, Dostoevsky came to realize that 'Stavrogin's Confession' was all wrong": the Stavrogin of the confession is "still struggling and failing with the temptations of repentance and pride," whereas "the Stavrogin of the final version is beyond moral struggle, and only the possible loss of self-control threatens his glacial calm." Wasiolek also suggests that the formation of Stavrogin from the drafts of other novelistic characters represents not the contingent exigencies of deadlines and book publishing, but the necessary trial-and-error of literary creation: Dostoevsky "resists the real Stavrogin by evasions, twists, and wrong turns," so that the notebooks themselves "are in large part a record of wrong Stavrogins."

. . .

So is *Demons* really just a botched novel, an aggregation of mutilated drafts, lacking any unified meaning? It isn't. Graduate school taught me this. It taught me through both theory and practice.

The theoretical part of the revelation came from René Girard, an emeritus in the Stanford French department. In the 1960s, Girard introduced his widely influential theory of mimetic desire, formulated in opposition to the Nietzschean notion of autonomy as the key to human self-fulfillment. According to Girard, there is in fact no such thing as human autonomy or authenticity. All of the desires that direct our actions in life are learned or imitated from some Other, to whom we mistakenly ascribe the autonomy lacking in ourselves. ("Mistakenly," because the Other is also a human being, and thus doesn't actually have any more autonomy than we do.) The perceived desire of the Other confers prestige on the object, rendering it desirable. For this reason, desire is usually less about its purported object than about the Other; it is always "metaphysical," in that it is less about having, than being. The point isn't to possess the object, but to *be* the Other. (That's why so many advertisements place less emphasis on the product's virtues than on its use by some beautiful and autonomous-looking person: the consumer craves not the particular brand of vodka, but the being of the person who chose it.) Because mimetic desire is contagious, a single person is often the mediator for a number of different desiring subjects, who then enter into the ultimately violent bonds of mimetic rivalry.

In the next decades, Girard developed mimetic contagion into an anthropological theory, using it to explain historically and geographically diverse manifestations of social violence from Chukchi blood feuds to the cult of Dionysus. But he first presented mimetic theory in a book about literature. In this first book, *Deceit, Desire, and the Novel*, Girard posits mimetic desire as the fundamental content of "the Western novel." Don Quixote, it turns out, doesn't really want any of his ostensible objects (Dulcinea, Mambrino's golden helmet, etc.); what he wants is to become one with his mediator: Amadís of Gaul. It's only because his imitation of Amadís of Gaul demands a beautiful lady that he invents Dulcinea. According to an analogous delusional mechanism, Raskolnikov only thinks he wants the pawnbroker's money—in fact, he wants to be Nietzsche's Superman. Emma Bovary only thinks she wants Léon—she actually wants to be the heroine of a romance. Julien Sorel only thinks that his ambitions are directed toward beautiful women and brilliant promotions— what he really wants is to achieve some Napoleonic ideal of authentic being.

Because the mimetic desire of the novelistic hero is never directed at its true object, which is in any case unattainable, it is fundamentally masochistic, violent, and self-destructive. "Great" novels, for Girard, are those that end by exposing the illusory and pernicious quality of mimetic desire. This exposure takes place in a fever or a penal colony, through suicide or by the guillotine, in the form of a "deathbed conversion": the hero transcends his egoism and renounces the values that have driven the novel up to that point. Don Quixote falls into a fever, realizes he isn't really a knight, and dies a Christian death; Madame Bovary swallows arsenic; Raskolnikov turns himself in; Julien renounces Mathilde and submits to the guillotine. "Great novels always spring from an obsession that has been transcended," Girard writes. "The hero sees himself in the rival he loathes; he renounces the 'differences' suggested by hatred."

As suggested by the emphasis on conversion narrative, mimetic desire is a fundamentally Christian theory. Just as "the false prophets proclaim that in tomorrow's world *men will be gods for each other*," so does mimetic desire entail worshiping another human being as a god, with inevitably disastrous results. There is one and only one human who actually is a god, and that's Jesus Christ. Accordingly, it is only by taking Christ as a model for our actions that we can redeem mimetic desire as a positive force.

Although I am unconvinced that mimetic desire is the fundamental content of the novelistic form, or that humans' mimetic desires can be channeled productively only by imitating Christ, Girard's theory unquestionably explains a great deal in the work of certain novelists, particularly those such as Stendhal and Dostoevsky, who were deeply engaged with Christian thought and the practice of a Christian life.* The solution is particularly convincing in the case of *Demons*. Girard characterizes Stavrogin—whose name combines the Greek *stavros* (cross) and the Russian *rog* (horn), suggesting the Antichrist—as a test case of the ultimate mediator of desire: one who has no desires himself. "It is not clear whether he no longer desires because Others desire him or whether Others desire him because he no longer desires"; in any case, Stavrogin is trapped in a deadly cycle:

No longer having a mediator himself, he becomes a magnetic pole of desire and hatred . . . all the charac-

---

*Girard, maintaining that mimetic desire holds a universal, central importance even in the works of "non-Christian" novelists, counts Stendhal as an atheist—even though Stendhal's two greatest novels begin in a seminary (*The Red and the Black*) or end in a monastery (*The Charterhouse of Parma*). Moreover, Stendhal's personal and vehement rejection of the Catholic Church is itself a form of engagement with Christianity.

ters in *The Possessed* become his slaves . . . Kirillov, Shatov, Pyotr, and all the women in *The Possessed* succumb to Stavrogin's strange power and reveal to him in almost identical terms the part he plays in their existence. Stavrogin is their "light," they wait for him as for the "sun"; before him they feel they are "before the Almighty"; they speak to him as "to God himself."

Stavrogin, Girard continues, is "young, good-looking, rich, strong, intelligent, and noble," not because Dostoevsky "feels a secret sympathy for him," but because the test subject must "unite in his own person all the conditions for metaphysical success"—it has to be without any effort on his part that men and women alike "fall at his feet and surrender to him." Stavrogin is "rapidly reduced to the most horrible caprices," ending with suicide; this is how Dostoevsky illustrates the price of "the 'success' of the metaphysical undertaking." Because the purest culmination of mimetic desire is self-annihilation, Stavrogin's demise is accompanied by "a quasi-suicide of the collectivity": Kirillov shoots himself; Shatov, Liza, and Marya indirectly bring about their own murders; and Stepan Trofimovich self-destructs in a fit of madness.

Girard's interpretation accounts for Stavrogin's psychic emptiness, for the desperate mania of others to be near him and to co-opt him into their philosophies. It answers Stavrogin's question "What the devil do you need me for?" It explains the metaphor of demonic possession and, through the idea of mimetic contagion, the mass effect on the whole town. It also accounts finally for the role of Stepan Trofimovich in the novel: it is Stepan Trofimovich's "Russian liberalism," the valorization of self-fulfillment, the deism, freethinking, and Francophilia, that create the vacuum embodied by Stavrogin. "Stepan Trofimovich is the father of all the possessed.

He is Pyotr Verkhovensky's father; he is the spiritual father of Shatov, of [Darya], of [Liza], and especially of Stavrogin, since he taught them all," Girard writes. "Everything in *The Possessed* starts with Stepan Trofimovich and ends with Stavrogin."

The strange thing is that, during the "demonic" years of my graduate-student career, Girard himself played the role of Stepan Trofimovich: the pedagogue-father who gave birth to monsters. It wasn't just mimetic sickness that we had, my classmates and I, but the *idea* of mimetic sickness, and we had learned it from him.

When I returned to Stanford after fifteen months of trying to write a novel, the department dynamics had changed completely. There were two years' worth of new admits. Unlike the other students in Luba's and my class—an extremely efficient young man who completed a PhD on the Chinese reception of Shakespeare in just four years; a Romanian girl who briefly studied unreliable narrators before dropping out of the program and moving to Canada—they had coalesced into a community, taking classes together, reading one another's papers, going to lectures, discussing their work long into the night.

"They're so . . . enthusiastic," Luba said, not altogether approvingly, with reference to these students. She had just gotten back together with a college boyfriend and had moved off campus. My relationship with my college boyfriend was, by contrast, increasingly strained. I found myself spending less time at home or with Luba, and more time on campus with my new classmates.

The circle was polarized around Matej, a fast-talking philosophy major from Croatia, who combined Stavrogin's "masklike" beauty—narrow glinting eyes, high cheekbones, too-black hair—with a long-limbed, perfectly proportioned physical elegance, such that his body always looked at once extravagantly casual and flawlessly composed. The first time I saw him—as it happens, in an introductory meeting of Joseph Frank's Dostoevsky seminar, which neither of us ended up taking—the overall effect struck me as excessive, almost parodic. But the more time I spent around Matej, the more vividly I realized that I was for the first time in the presence of pure charisma, the real thing. It was an elemental power, like weather or electricity. Recognizing it had no effect on your physical response.

Like the related phenomenon of charm, charisma resides largely in speech. Matej, who had spent the last three years working for a radio station in Zagreb, had a deep, mesmerizing, immediately recognizable voice, as well as a rhetorical talent for provoking conflicts with one hand while smoothing them over with the other, making concessions and winning them at the same time, producing the impression on everyone involved that great, collegial, and somehow intimate progress was being made in the working out of ideas.

I knew of at least two extremely smart and attractive women who were in love with Matej. Both were dating other men, whom Matej befriended. He then behaved very flirtatiously with the women. The flirtation was cloaked in a kind of gallantry that everyone found exciting, until one day they suddenly didn't. One of the couples broke up; the boy transferred to Harvard and the girl, a formerly lively and charming person, wandered around campus like a ghost, her eyes red, talking about her cats.

Then there was my comp lit classmate Keren. She and her boyfriend, Ilan, a linguist, were inseparable from Matej. The three of them shared a car, and one summer they all lived together in Berlin. Keren and Matej were office-mates and spent a lot of time alone in each other's company, but Ilan and Matej would also sometimes go watch basketball together, without Keren. Matej, like Stavrogin, had a magnetic effect on both sexes.

It was a great mystery how Keren and Ilan managed to stay together despite Matej. I asked her about it once, in a roundabout way; she told me that she and Ilan were committed to each other for the foreseeable future, but that they both understood and accepted that each might not be the most intensely thought-about person in the other's psyche 100 percent of the time. "You know how intense things can get with the people you work with," she said.

For his first two years at Stanford, Matej had a roommate, Daniel, whom he rapidly reduced to a state of near-paralytic dependence that persisted long after they stopped living together. Daniel and Matej had been assigned to each other by the housing services, on the basis of their shared two-pack-a-day smoking habit. Daniel, a mathematician, was overweight, although not grotesquely so, and would have been a pleasant and entertaining person were it not for a kind of deep, inexplicable pathetic quality that he seemed to be at great pains to convey to others, even to the point of aggressiveness. He had a knack for attracting people even more forlorn than he, who then became his demons. One of them, a homeless guy called Bobby, eventually moved into Daniel's apartment and refused to leave; you could always find him lurking on the balcony, making insulting remarks. Daniel, meanwhile, became increasingly unable to make even the smallest decisions without first pouring out his heart to Matej, who patiently listened and then explained at great length the impossibility of his actually advising Daniel one way or another, because he, Matej, was powerless to cure Daniel's ontological sickness.

To my bemusement, after having met me only a few times with Matej, Daniel began addressing me long e-mails full of the most detailed and depressing confessions, many of them health-related. "I think I have never had sex with a woman," he wrote once. "Also, I haven't done laundry in almost a month and all my underwear is dirty." After debating for a long time how and whether to reply, I counseled him to go out and buy more underwear. Daniel wrote a full single-spaced page to thank me for this brilliant advice. He began telling me dreams he'd had about me. In these dreams I inevitably appeared as a benevolent figure, floating several feet off the ground.

Among my friends, only Luba was unaffected by Matej. "It's true there was some addictive quality about him," she said later. "I felt it, too. I remember sitting on that bench outside the library. He would start talking, and you would be unable to get up and leave. But afterward, hours had gone by, and what had he really said? It was all empty."

Was it really all empty? All of it? I still don't know. Sometimes I think it was, other times I think it wasn't. At any rate, the rest of us spent much of our time in much the way Luba described, reading until late at night in the library, periodically reconvening outside to drink coffee and smoke Matej's cigarettes. The library became the psychic center of our lives. We all dreamed about it—intense, elaborate dreams. Keren, for example, dreamed that I had filmed a "protest documentary" about the early Friday closing hours, the restriction of graduate-student loan privileges, and the overcrowding of dissertation study carrels; this mordant social critique, which I had apparently shot digitally in collaboration with Keren's high-school classmate Anat ("in reality, now a belly dancer in Tel Aviv"), had been screened in the library basement, where it actually fomented a violent revolution and resulted in the severe beating of one of the library guards.

In retrospect, the beating of the library guard probably derived from the story of Miguel, the genial three-hundred-pound guard who sat at the front desk, checking IDs and bags. Miguel stood out from among the other library workers, who fit a more or less Dostoevskian mold: a tiny old woman whose organism seemed designed to combine maximum disgruntledness with minimum body mass; a giant white-bearded Santa Claus look-alike who spent all his breaks sitting outside under an olive tree, playing a balalaika. But Matej said that Miguel had confessed to him, late one night when the library was almost empty, that he had an incurable cancer, and would be dead in four months.

This story, which restored Miguel to the Dostoevskian milieu of his workplace, nevertheless accorded with neither his robust physique nor his jovial demeanor. "If he really had cancer, why would he still be checking bags at the library?" someone asked.

"What do you expect him to do, spend his last hundred and eighty days in Disneyland?" Matej demanded.

But four months passed, six months, a year. Miguel was still checking bags, still smiling and saying "Take care, guys," like some obscure warning.

It turned out that Matej and I were both usually up past four in the morning, and I got in the habit of occasionally going back to his place after the library closed at midnight. Daniel would be in the bathtub, solving math problems; sometimes he would fall asleep, and we would hear him snoring. We sat in the living room, where Matej put away five or six bottles of beer and became more forthcoming about his past.

One night, to my incredulity, he told me that he had been celibate for the past seven years. Seven years ago, he explained, he had experienced a period of total, shattering lucidity, and fell in love with a girl who was obsessed with a Slovenian disc jockey. He had pursued the girl desperately, determined to tear her away from the DJ, regardless of whether he had to annihilate himself in the process. He got the girl, for a time, but they drove each other mad, quite literally. She ran away to Ljubljana. He followed her. She rushed to the top floor of her hotel and tried to throw herself from a window. Realizing he was on the verge of destroying both her and himself, Matej fled to Venice, holed himself up in a pension, and decided to read every book Nietzsche had ever written. In his state of lucidity, he not only understood immediately everything Nietzsche was trying to say, but also effortlessly identified where Nietzsche had made his mistakes. Matej began to write a philosophical work addressing the mistakes made by Nietzsche, but became distracted by a message being spelled to him by the keys hanging behind the desk of the pension. He spent three more weeks in Venice, obsessed by those keys, before he ran out of money and returned to Zagreb, where he was eventually diagnosed with bipolar disorder. He refused to take lithium. He said his brain was trying to convey a message to him, an important message about how he was living his life, and he had to figure it out on his own.

A few nights after this confession, when we had both drunk more than usual, Matej and I ended up in bed together. The next morning, I had never seen anyone in so black a mood, almost visibly black. It was as if I had stolen his soul.

People were usually surprised to learn that chain-smoking, hard-drinking Matej came from a seriously Catholic family. He was the eldest of eight brothers and sisters spaced out over fifteen years.

"Man, that is one long history of your dad banging your

mom!" yelled one of the weird characters who followed Matej everywhere—a Portuguese mathematician who I think had a mild form of Tourette's.

"I'm glad to hear you have an accurate grasp of the mechanism," Matej replied.

The most unexpected feature of Matej's family background was his great-uncle Pavao, who was not only a cardinal but had been archbishop of Zagreb for more than twenty years. We only half believed in the existence of Matej's ecclesiastical great-uncle—until the day he died and *The New York Times* ran an obituary remembering Pavao, aka "the Rock of Croatia," for rebuilding the Croatian Church after communism and preaching tolerance during the Balkan wars.

In his capacity as a leftist Catholic intellectual, Matej had already read Girard in college, and at Stanford he persuaded us all to take a class on French social thought taught by a Girardian with a joint appointment at the École Polytechnique. And when Girard himself came out of retirement to teach a literature class on mimetic theory, we all signed up.

We were all fascinated by Girard's theory, but it also irritated us. Matej said our resistance only testified to the strength of our romantic individualist delusions, and to the truth of mimetic theory. His Girardianism became the sign and symbol of his inaccessibility, the thing we all resented about him: the way he always came late and left early, inhabited a near-empty apartment, insisted on dining every day at exactly six fifteen at his depressing eating club. Such behavior was consistent with a Girardian mediator, with an iron-willed narcissist who "universalizes, industrializes asceticism for the sake of desire"; by acting in this way, Matej was thereby supporting his side in the ongoing argument, proving that we were all the slaves of our own egotistical desires.

After the night we spent together, Matej began avoiding

me. When I confronted him about it, he said that my obsession with him—it was true that by that time I, like everyone
else, was obsessed with him—was a sign of sickness. "I can't
cure your metaphysical lack," he told me irritably. "I can't
do anything for you. All I can do is make you miserable."
He paused and started patting his pockets, looking for his
cigarettes. "You think I'm different from you; you think I
have something you lack. But there's no difference between
us. You and I are very similar—we're exactly the same."

Matej often brought up the subject of our supposed similarity, which struck me as frankly ludicrous. What about
us was the same? He had spent his high-school years drinking coffee in basements during bomb scares, reading Max
Scheler, becoming convinced that he was a member of the
zoo commission and had to inspect the living conditions of
every elephant in Europe. He believed that the only way to be
good was to imitate Jesus, that Kant's categorical imperative
represented a dilution of the Sermon on the Mount, that suicide was immoral because human life doesn't belong to the
individual. What did it mean to say we were the same, when
all our experiences and beliefs were different?

In the final analysis, this is what was so hurtful about
Girardianism: it made love totally worthless. The curiosity
and empathy engendered by love, which I found so valuable,
were redescribed as flaws of human nature. The drive to commit generous errors, which I thought of as the only possible
egress from the prison of self-interest and inertia, was made
out to be a form of egotism. "The characters in *The Possessed* offer themselves as sacrifice, and offer to Stavrogin
everything that is most precious to them," Girard writes, and
such sacrifice is understood to be shameful, vain, the opposite of generous.

Furthermore, the entire Girardian enterprise began
to strike me as hypocritical. If Girard was right about the

human condition, the only appropriate course of action was to stop what we were doing, all of us, *right now*. If novels were really about what he said they were about, then their production should cease. All we really needed was one novel, and we would all read it and realize, like St. Augustine, that the basic premises of literary narrative—love and ambition—could bring only misery. Renouncing our desires, we would give ourselves up to spiritual contemplation. We would abandon our program of becoming scholars: what use were scholars in a world where knowledge, learning, and the concept of difference turned out to be a mirage?

The mood in our circle became increasingly strained. Keren dreamed that the Turks had taken over the world, and that she herself had been complicit: she had had a job in Jerusalem interviewing people about their fears, and now the Turks were using this information to terrorize people into submission.

Fishkin, who was also in the Girard class, dreamed that he was beating up Matej, in a fight over the Ottoman occupation of the Balkans. Fishkin hit Matej in the face, and Matej, bleeding from his nose, kept saying: "We just can't forget."

I dreamed that Matej and I were in the Rose Garden in Konya, immobilized by swarming hordes of pilgrims. Matej wanted to go inside the mausoleum of Mevlana Rumi, which filled me with inexplicable dread. I tried to discourage him, but he dodged me in the crowd. I hurried up the steps after him, but couldn't go inside—I didn't have a head scarf. I asked the custodian to lend me one of the scarves they keep there for tourists. In my haste, I posed the request in an undiplomatic way, not bothering to hide that my aim was only to get my friend, and not to pay my respects to Rumi. The custodian drew himself up. "If you really want to get in," he said, not meeting my eyes, "you have to tell me one thing: do you know the difference between the Lord our Father and the Holy Ghost?"

I said I did.

"Oh? Then you can't go in!"

"But—but I don't really know the difference. I mean, I know they're two separate parts of the trinity, but then they say the trinity is the same as the godhead . . . I hear that even for Catholics it's supposed to be a big mystery. Anyway, if I'm not allowed in," I added, "you should definitely send someone in there to get my friend, because he really *does* know the difference between the Lord our Father and the Holy Ghost."

"Not my problem," said the custodian, blocking the door. I tried to look around him, but all I could see was the tomb itself, covered with its green cloth.

Matej spent the summer in Croatia, and I managed to stop thinking about him. In fact, I ended up dating one of his best friends, Max, who had formed the deep conviction that he and I belonged together.

"I think it's an illusion," I told Max when he explained to me his views. "I can't actually cure your metaphysical lack." But I didn't have it in my heart to turn away what looked to me, and what turned out really to be, love.

Nonetheless, when school started again in September, Matej and I found ourselves living in the same on-campus single-student residence, and somehow immediately lapsed into our old habits, meeting several nights a week, staying up half the night, talking about Proust (whom we were both reading for the first time), and making sentimental declarations to each other. "But what will become of us?" I remember asking.

"You'll become a writer," he replied.

"But what about you?"

"Oh, don't you worry about me."

The idea that I had fallen prey to Matej's Onegin-like Byronism had meanwhile become a joke between us. One day as we were leaving his apartment, he picked up a scarf that Keren had forgotten there, and stuffed it in the back pocket of his jeans.

"OK, let's go," he said. I started to laugh. "What? Do I look ridiculous?"

"No—you look jaunty and Byronic!"

But then one night it happened again. We were talking about the problem of the person: "If you're stroking someone's hair, is that a sign of affection, or is that the affection itself?" We spent the night together, and I somehow even thought things might work out this time—I would just have to find some way of explaining it to Max. But the next morning, over stale English muffins, Matej informed me that he was thinking of joining a Carthusian monastery he had seen in Slovenia, where the monks grew some kind of herbs. Staring at him in disbelief, I said the first thing that came to my head: "But they take a vow of silence, and you can't be quiet for two minutes straight!"

"That's the point," he snapped. "It would be hard for me."

I threw out my half-eaten muffin and left, feeling like someone had kicked me in the stomach, like I had hit the bottom of some kind of abyss and had lost touch with everything real.

"There are strange friendships," Dostoevsky writes, with reference to Stepan Trofimovich and Varvara Petrovna in *Demons*.

"Two friends are almost ready to eat each other, they live like that all their lives, and yet they cannot part. Parting is even impossible: the friend who waxes capricious and breaks it off will be the first to fall sick and die." A marvelous passage, communicating so economically the diabolical undercurrent of certain friendships, their weird fatalism.

On the same subject, Proust writes of a moment when, "after a certain year," extremely close friends, as if by agreement, "cease to make the necessary journey or even to cross the street to see one another, cease to correspond, and know that they will communicate no more in this world." These lines occur in a passage about old age—about how death insidiously seeps into life toward the end, enveloping the still-living subject in its chrysalis. But who knows how these things really happen? Maybe death didn't separate those friends at all. Maybe they had to will themselves to stop seeing one another, precisely in order to let death in.

The last time I saw Matej was on a beautiful September afternoon in San Francisco. His eighteen-year-old brother, Luka, was visiting from Zagreb, and the three of us went to the zoo. I remember that Matej treated me with a certain extra gentleness—he had always opened my car door, but that day he also closed it after me. Luka turned out to be a younger and impossibly skinnier copy of Matej, with the same narrow, slightly squinting eyes. It was like meeting a Matej from the past, one lost to me forever. In the zoo we spent a long time watching the penguins, the varied saucer-eyed creatures of Madagascar, and the primates, Matej's favorite: "Human, all too human," he sighed before the long-faced patas monkey. Luka had never seen an anteater before, and squinted at it with almost frightening intensity. Last of all we visited the koalas. " 'Blind, helpless, and smaller than a nickel, the tiny embryo must find its way to its mother's pouch,' " I read from the educational display, and Matej and

I both started laughing at the joke before he said it: "Such is the nature of life on this earth."

Shortly after our trip to the zoo, Stanford comp lit held a departmental lunch for students and faculty. At this lunch, which I was unable to attend, Matej sat next to my adviser and told her, inaccurately and unaccountably, that I blamed her for my poor performance on the university orals exam the previous year, which I had passed, but just barely. (The exam had taken place at the height of the demonic period, during a record-setting heat wave, and I had delivered an apparently very weird talk on conspiracy theories in the nineteenth-century novel.)

To this day, I have no idea why Matej would have said such a thing to my adviser, with whom he wasn't even acquainted; that was their first conversation, and was later relayed to me independently by both Luba and my adviser. I wrote Matej a caustic e-mail. He didn't reply. A few weeks later I heard that he was dating an Israeli linguist who had been to high school with Keren; that Keren had passed her exams but had fallen into a depression and put on an improbable amount of weight; that the homeless guy, Bobby, had colonized Daniel's bedroom and was using it to run a bicycle repair shop.

We were all living in San Francisco by then. Keren and Ilan were sharing an apartment with Matej and Daniel in Noe Valley. I had moved to Twin Peaks, where winds howled all day and all night, and giant clouds rushed across the street as if in a hurry to get somewhere, occasionally revealing dramatic views of the city. The others all made fun of me for moving there—Ilan called it Wuthering Heights—but I didn't care. I barely saw any of them anyway, once I stopped talking to Matej.

That spring, Keren wrote me an e-mail announcing that she was pregnant. Several months later, she invited me to a going-away party for Matej: he was apparently moving back to Croatia for good. "I know you guys still aren't speaking, but it seems absurd not to invite you," Keren wrote. I didn't go to the party.

Nearly a year passed before I next saw Keren. She and Ilan had moved back to Stanford when the baby was born, and we met for lunch one day when I was on campus to use the library. We walked from her apartment to a French café on California Avenue, the kind of bourgeois establishment we never used to frequent. It was one of the almost oppressively perfect days that succeed one another at Stanford in the spring and fall, so uniform that they might have been manufactured on an assembly line. We sat outside at a table in the sun. Conversation turned to the subject of René Girard, who had recently been elected to the French Academy.

"Good for him, I guess," I said.

"Yeah," Keren said unenthusiastically, picking at her salad. "But part of me thinks it's grotesque and obscene, given what happened to Matej." As I was debating whether to ask what she meant, Keren's daughter, Malka, who was teething, began to make discontented noises. Keren absentmindedly stuck a finger in her mouth. As Malka was happily sucking at Keren's finger, an unknown middle-aged woman descended upon us, beaming: "What a beautiful baby! Whose is she?" Not waiting for an answer, she peered into my face: "Is she yours?"

What weird people there are in the world, I thought. Why would *Keren's* finger be in *my* baby's mouth?

Keren identified herself as the mother, which made it her turn to have her face peered into. Finally the woman walked away across the street, still beaming. Curiosity overcame my reserve: "So what's Matej doing now, anyway?" I asked.

That was when I learned that Matej had dropped out of Stanford more than a year ago. He had given up first drinking, and then smoking. He had sold or given away all his belongings, and applied to a theology program in Zagreb. Upon the conclusion of this program, he had entered a monastery on a small island in the Adriatic. Keren and Ilan had received one communication from him, an e-mail describing the scenery on the island.

"He says it's beautiful," Keren said.

I found myself thinking back to a long-ago conversation, when I had told Matej that he was a destructive element in the lives of others. He had surprised me by not objecting. "What can I do?" he had asked, and it sounded like a real question.

Now he had done something—like a novelistic hero, he had achieved a deathlike conversion, renounced narrative. There was a chapter in *Deceit, Desire, and the Novel* that explained it perfectly, a chapter on the secret affinity between the novelistic *vaniteux* and the religious ascetic. The "strange strength of soul," which enables Julien Sorel to scale such brilliant heights in his romantic and political life, Girard writes, is exactly the same as the strength called upon by the man of God to resist his worldly desires. One renounces insincerely, to get what he is renouncing, while the other renounces sincerely, to become closer to God, but the motion is identical. This kinship also links the demonic Stavrogin and the saintly Myshkin: "Like Stavrogin, Myshkin acts as a magnet for unattached desires; he fascinates all the characters in *The Idiot*," Girard writes. "We can understand why the Prince and Stavrogin have the same point of departure in the author's rough draft."

I was still in a daze when I got to the library. It was a day for surprises: sitting at the front desk, larger than life, was

Miguel, who was supposed to have died of cancer at least four years ago. "Long time no see," he said, beaming.

"It's fantastic," I stammered. When I got to the stacks I kept staring dumbly at the call numbers, unable to determine whether PG 3776.B7 came before or after PG 3776.B27. Eventually I found myself back downstairs, logged into a computer terminal, writing a pointless e-mail to Matej. I told him that I had been strongly impressed to learn that he was in a monastery, and that I wished him luck. To my amazement, a reply arrived the following day. "Dear Elif," Matej wrote,

Thank you for your kind wish. I wish for you all the things I wish for myself. I have been living at the monastery for about four months now. I joined the order of discalced Carmelites, whose full name is: the Order of Brothers of the Blessed Virgin Mary of Mount Carmel. In the monastery I'm in charge of setting the tables and cleaning the dining hall. Until a few days ago I was the substitute, but now I'm already the main mess boy. You can see that, as usual, I make quick progress . . .

The main mess boy—I shook my head in wonder. Was he Fabrizio in the charterhouse or Julien in the seminary? Would we all live to see Matej be made cardinal?

The following year, Fishkin actually tracked down the Carmelites' website and found several photographs of Matej taking his vows, together with two other novices: one looked like a twelve-year-old schoolboy, while the other, who had a shaved head and wore a heavy metal cross, resembled a repentant convict. One photograph showed a somehow obtuse-looking friar pulling the black habit over Matej's downcast head; another showed the three novices standing outside in the sunlight, Matej squinting with a familiar, irritable air.

The last photograph, however, captured Matej in an expression I had never seen before, the eyes watchful, the mouth set in a somehow childish line. It had been taken at such close range that I recognized, with a jolt, a birthmark on his neck that I had half forgotten. As a child, Matej had once told me, he used to lock himself in the bathroom, desperately searching in the mirror for differences between his face and that of his father, whom even at that time he resembled to a remarkable degree; he would invariably find the differences, and reduce himself to tears with the thought that he was certainly a prince, lost forever to the throne.

On my third day in Florence, I tore myself from Dostoevsky long enough to visit Santa Croce, to see Dante's cenotaph. The cenotaph hadn't yet been constructed in 1817, when Stendhal famously visited the basilica and was awestruck by the tombs of Alfieri, Machiavelli, Michelangelo, and Galileo: "What men! What an amazing group! And Tuscany can add to their number Dante, Boccaccio, and Petrarch . . ." Happening next upon Volterrano's frescoes of the four Sibyls, Stendhal was utterly overwhelmed:

> I was already in a sort of ecstasy, from the idea of being in Florence, close to the great men whose tombs I had seen. Absorbed in the contemplation of sublime beauty, I saw it up close—I touched it, so to speak. I reached the point where one encounters celestial sensations . . . leaving Santa Croce, I experienced palpitations . . . my spirit was exhausted, I walked in fear of falling.

In the mid-1980s, based on a decade-long study of 106 tourists admitted to the psychiatric ward at Florence's Santa

Maria Nuova hospital, Italian scientists identified a new psychopathology: *la sindrome di Stendhal*, a state triggered by beautiful works of art and characterized by "loss of hearing and the sense of color, hallucinations, euphoria, panic and the fear of going mad or even of dying." Unmarried European men between the ages of twenty-five and forty were found to be particularly susceptible. The average hospital stay was four days.

Walking over the tombs of knights and scientists, among my fellow tourists—still-recognizable humans who had been transformed into semi-robotic zombies, hypnotized by the screens of their digital cameras—I kept a close eye on the men in the unmarried, European, twenty-five-to-forty-year-old category, looking for signs of Stendhal's syndrome.

In a coincidence that Girard would appreciate, a Brazilian neurologist recently diagnosed Dostoevsky himself with Stendhal's syndrome. The diagnosis was based on both the "impressions left in the novel *The Idiot*, which was practically all written in Florence," and Anna's testimony of Dostoevsky's reaction upon seeing Holbein's *Dead Christ* in Basel the previous year. The great proto-existential novelist had spent fifteen or twenty minutes standing before the painting, riveted in place. "His agitated face had a kind of dread in it," Anna wrote, "something I had noticed more than once during the first moments of an epileptic seizure."

In *The Idiot*, Dostoevsky has Prince Myshkin encounter a reproduction of the *Dead Christ* in Rogozhin's house. Myshkin, too, is bowled over by what appears to him to be Nature itself made visible "in the form of a huge machine of the most modern construction which, dull and insensible, has clutched, crushed, and swallowed up a great priceless Being, a Being worth all nature and its laws . . ." As Joseph Frank has observed, "no greater challenge could be offered to Dostoevsky's own faith in Christ the God-Man than such a vision of a tortured and decaying human being."

The location of Dostoevsky's house in Florence was pointed out to me by an old Stanford classmate, the poet Eugene Ostashevsky, who had been living for the past two years on the Via Guicciardini: the Maison Idiot formed a permanent feature of his jogging route. Eugene and his wife, Oya, were now preparing to leave Italy for good, and, on the evening after our visit to Santa Croce, Max and I spent several hours helping them vacate their apartment. Having filled several suitcases with old clothes and shoes, we set out to carry them to a metal bin some blocks away, for donation to the Church. "An archbishop will be wearing this someday," Eugene remarked, stuffing a woman's tangerine-colored leather jacket into a plastic bag. On the streets the air was heavy and hot. Max, who had been given a suitcase with no handle, was gamely clutching it to his chest. At dinner afterward we all drank a good deal of Chianti, which, with the heat and the exertion, went straight to my head. Among my confused recollections of the evening, I remember Eugene saying that if he were to start out as a college student again, right now in 2009, he would study Islamic fundamentalism, because that was the richest and most significant cultural phenomenon in the contemporary world.

"Really?" I asked. "You mean you wouldn't do literature?"

He stared at me. "You mean you *would* do literature? Knowing what you now know?"

I thought about it. "I'm too shallow to study Islamic fundamentalism," I said. "You know . . . if it isn't a thing of beauty . . ."

"Well, it is, in its way, a thing of beauty—it has beautiful aspects." He said something about the mathematically beautiful complexity of terrorist informational networks. I found myself staring at the ceiling, at a stain that resembled a disembodied nose. ". . . like Dostoevsky," Eugene was saying then, and I tuned back in. "It's exactly the same thing."

I struggled to regrasp the subject of the conversation. "You mean like *Demons*?"

"Like *Demons*. 'If he believes, he doesn't believe that he believes, and if he doesn't believe, he doesn't believe that he doesn't believe,'" Eugene said, quoting a line spoken in the novel by Kirillov. "And not just like *Demons* . . ."

Islamic fundamentalism was the Grand Inquisitor and the Underground Man, it was what the existentialists called "awful freedom," the reinvention of irrationality by marginalized people, just in order to spite science. I tried unsuccessfully to imagine my life devoted to the study of Islamic fundamentalism. *If I cared, then I didn't care that I cared, and if I didn't care, I didn't care that I didn't care.*

As we were leaving, Eugene gave Max and me a copy of his new book, *The Life and Opinions of DJ Spinoza*. I immediately remembered DJ Spinoza, Eugene's alter ego, from my early years at Stanford, when Eugene had only recently left. I remembered a party in a very narrow apartment in San Francisco, inhabited by two Germans, one of whom wore a strange nose ring that gave him the perpetual appearance of having to blow his nose. I saw a girl actually reach over and try to wipe it off with a napkin, but it was a nose ring and therefore made of metal.

I spotted Matej at the counter, pouring a drink. "I want one, too," I said. He sloshed some gin and tonic in a plastic cup and handed it to me. We were standing in the doorway of the back stairs, drinking in silence, when an enormous, extremely drunk Russian approached us with a menacing expression. He marched directly up to Matej, as if he intended to walk right through him, stopping only when he was almost touching him with his belly.

"Do you know DJ Spinoza?" he demanded truculently.

Matej shrugged, stepping almost imperceptibly aside; he had a catlike talent, probably perfected over long years of practice, for evading potentially violent situations.

"Do you know DJ Spinoza?" the drunk man roared.

"No," Matej said sharply. "I know *Spinoza*."

From Eugene and Oya's apartment, Max and I walked back across the Arno to the sublet we had found through one of Eugene's friends—a minuscule, slope-ceilinged apartment on the top floor of an ancient building on the Via Vigna Vecchia. We collapsed into the tiny twin beds and fell asleep almost immediately. I dreamed of DJ Spinoza. In my dream, his initials stood for "Don Juan Spinoza."

At three in the morning I opened my eyes, irremediably awake, and went to the kitchen for a glass of water. The window overlooked a sea of moonlit rooftops. Behind them loomed Santa Croce like a pale luminous spaceship, its rocketlike spires thrusting into the sky. I remembered Stendhal's description of the church: "its plain carpentry roof, its unfinished façade, all of this deeply speaks to my soul. Ah! If only I could forget! . . . A monk came up to me; instead of repulsion bordering to physical horror, I found in myself a friendly feeling towards him."* Stendhal didn't care for monks, but this one was an exception: he unlocked the transept where he saw Volterrano's Sibyls.

My thoughts drifted to Chekhov's "Black Monk," the

---

*According to a note in the Pléiade edition, what Stendhal wanted to forget were "all the wrongs and misdeeds committed by the Catholic religion."

story that opens with a young scholar's arrival at the estate of his former tutor, a famous horticulturalist, on a night when frost threatens the orchards. The young scholar—his name is Kovrin, and he studies philosophy and psychology—falls in love with the horticulturalist's daughter, Tanya. They become engaged. One day, Kovrin tells Tanya a legend about a monk all in black, who appeared a thousand years ago in the deserts of Syria or Arabia. That monk projected a mirage, in the form of another monk, floating on the surface of a lake, before the eyes of a faraway fisherman. "From that mirage there was cast another mirage," Kovrin explains, "so that the image of the black monk began to be repeated endlessly from one layer of the atmosphere to another," from Africa, Spain, India, and the Arctic Circle, to Mars, to the Southern Cross.

According to this legend—Kovrin can't remember where he heard it—the mirage will return to earth exactly one thousand years from the day the monk first walked in the desert. "And it seems that the thousand years is almost up . . . we may expect the black monk any day now."

In fact, the black monk appears before Kovrin the very next day, notifying him that he, Kovrin, is a scholar of genius, one of the elect servants of the eternal truth. Kovrin realizes that he is hallucinating. "So what?" replies the monk. "You're sick because you have overworked and exhausted yourself, and that means that you have sacrificed your health to an idea, and the time is near when you will give up to it life itself." Intoxicated by his own martyrdom to mankind's brilliant future, Kovrin gives himself up entirely to his studies and to the monk's visits, which spur him to ever-greater heights of exaltation, scholarship, and irritability.

One day Tanya discovers her husband in a terrible state: he is talking to the monk, and is clearly insane. She takes him back to her father's house, where they prevent him from working, and nurse him back to health. But the black monk had been trying to tell Kovrin something, and in that something resided the entire meaning of his life. "Why, why have you cured me?" he demands, cursing Tanya.

The horticulturalist dies of grief. Kovrin receives a coveted professorship, but is unable to accept: he has begun to cough blood. As he finally expires of a tubercular hemorrhage, the black monk appears to him, whispering "that he is a genius, and that he is dying only because his weak human body has lost its balance and is no longer able to serve as a container for genius."

Among Chekhov's stories, "The Black Monk" is notable for its Gothic overtones, its clinically accurate picture of megalomania, and the number and diversity of its critical interpretations. Badgered by readers to reveal its true relevance to his soul, Chekhov explained that the story had been inspired by a dream in which he saw a black monk moving toward him through a whirlwind. Why is it that no consciously invented stories ever point beyond themselves as multifariously as dreams?

One way to interpret "The Black Monk" is as a cautionary tale about academic scholarship as a form of madness. This madness affects not just Kovrin but also the horticulturalist, whose articles on seemingly "peaceful and impersonal" subjects—intercropping, the Russian Antonovsky apple—invariably devolve into venomous invectives against other horticulturalists. The endlessly proliferating monk may be read as a figure for scholarly mimetic contagion. From a Girardian perspective it is fitting for ambition, the true "Stendhal's syndrome," to assume the form of a monk: "every element in the distorted mysticism" of mimetic rivalry has its "luminous counterpart in Christian truth."

In the black monk, one also glimpses the shadowy outline

of Fyodorov, philosopher of bodily resurrection, abolisher of death. Like the black monk, Fyodorov saw before him the whole glorious future of humankind. Freed from the shackles of mortality, men would set forth to collect the corporeal dust of past generations that had been scattered throughout the cosmos by the once omnipotent hand of death. The earth itself would be transformed into a spaceship, dislodged from its orbit and propelled into space "by either photo, thermal, or electric energy." The armies of the resurrected would colonize the universe, transforming it into a work of art.

Fyodorov, a Christian mystic, saw his project precisely in terms of an imitation of Christ. Only the mass, universal enactment of Christ's rising from the dead and ascent to heaven would finally dissipate the artificial rivalries that divide the brotherhood of man. A new classless society would arise, devoted to the shared task of "cosmic agriculture": a unity of perfect horticulturists.

Now the spaceship is poised for takeoff, the Sibyls look down from the ceiling, and the black monk shimmers briefly in the air, before dematerializing and reappearing somewhere else. Martians are transporting the ice palace to Saturn, for it to take its place among Ulughbek's 1,018 stars. They're hoping it will teach them to understand adverbs. Somewhere even further away, the beast waits in its thicket, watching the snow pile soundlessly on the hillside. Now the black monk is calling me—he says it's time to go, time to start collecting the ashes. This is the kind of work that will kill you. But I'll have you know, DJ Spinoza, that I haven't given up. If I could start over today, I would choose literature again. If the answers exist in the world or in the universe, I still think that's where we're going to find them.

WORKS CONSULTED

The following is a partial listing of secondary sources. Dates and locations refer to the editions consulted. In some cases, the year of original publication follows in parentheses.

Allworth, Edward. *The Modern Uzbeks*. Stanford, 1990.

Amancio, Edson José. "Dostoevsky and Stendhal's Syndrome," *Academia Brasileira de Neurologia*, 63 (4), 2005.

Anemone, Anthony. "The Monsters of Peter the Great: The Culture of the St. Petersburg Kunstkamera in the Eighteenth Century," *Slavic and East European Journal*, 44 (4), 2000.

Anisimov, Evgeny. *Anna Ioannovna*. Moscow, 2002.

Arendt, Hannah. *The Human Condition*. Chicago, 1998 (1958).

Bakhtin, Mikhail. *The Dialogic Imagination: Four Essays*, ed. Michael Holquist. Austin, 1982.

Bertensson, Sergei. "The History of Tolstoy's Posthumous Play," *American Slavic and East European Review*, 14 (2), 1955.

Bethea, David M., ed. *Puškin Today*. Bloomington, 1993.

Chekhov, Anton. *Chekhov's Life and Thought: Selected Letters and Commentary*, ed. Simon Karlinsky. Evanston, 1997.

Chertkov, Vladimir. *The Last Days of Leo Tolstoy*, 1911.

Critchlow, James. *Nationalism in Uzbekistan: A Soviet Republic's Road to Sovereignty*. Boulder, 1991.

Derrida, Jacques. *Acts of Literature*, ed. Derek Attridge. New York, 1992.

Dostoevsky, Fyodor. *The Notebooks for The Possessed*, ed. Edward Wasiolek. Chicago, 1968.

Eikhenbaum, Boris. *Tolstoi in the Seventies*. Ann Arbor, 1974 (1960).

Fierman, William. *Language Planning and National Development: The Uzbek Experience*. Berlin, 1992.

Foucault, Michel. *The Order of Things*. New York, 2002 (1966).

———. "What Is an Author?" in Paul Rabinow, ed., *The Foucault Reader*. New York, 1984 (1969).

Frank, Joseph. *Dostoevsky: The Miraculous Years, 1865–1871*. Princeton, 1995.

Freidin, Gregory, ed. *The Enigma of Isaac Babel: Biography, History, Context*. Stanford, 2009.

———. "Isaac Babel," in George Slade, ed., *European Writers: The Twentieth Century*. New York, 1990.

Girard, René. *Deceit, Desire, and the Novel: Self and Other in Literary Structure*. Baltimore, 1976 (1961).

———. *Violence and the Sacred*. Baltimore, 1993 (1979).

Golburt, Luba. "The Historical Novel and the Versimilitude of Attractions" (unpublished dissertation chapter). Stanford, 2006.

Goldner, Orville, and George Turner. *The Making of King Kong*. South Brunswick, 1985.

Greenleaf, Monika. *Pushkin and Romantic Fashion: Fragment, Elegy, Orient, Irony*. Stanford, 1994.

Grenoble, Lenore A. *Language Policy in the Soviet Union*. Dordrecht, 2003.

Iampolski, Mikhail, and Alexander Zholkovsky. *Бабель/ Babel*. Moscow, 1994.

Leatherbarrow, W. J. "Misreading Myshkin and Stavrogin: The Presentation of the Hero in Dostoevskii's *Idiot* and *Besy*," *Slavonic and East European Review*, 78 (1), 2000.

Mandelker, Amy. *Framing Anna Karenina*. Columbus, 1993.

Mandelstam, Nadezhda. *Hope Against Hope*. New York, 1970.

Nabokov, Vladimir. Commentary to *Eugene Onegin*. Princeton, 1964.

Pelham, Brett W., et al. "Why Susie Sells Seashells by the Seashore: Implicit Egotism and Major Life Decisions," *Journal of Personality and Social Psychology*, 85 (5), 2002.

Pirozhkova, Antonina. *At His Side: The Last Years of Isaac Babel*. South Royalton, 1996.

Pogosian, Elena. "Svad'ba shutov v Ledianom dome kak fakt ofitsial'noi kul'tury," *Toronto Slavic Quarterly*, 15, 2001.

Povartsov, Sergei. "Isaak Babel': Portret na fone Lubianki," *Voprosy literatury*, 3, 1994.

Rayfield, Donald. *Anton Chekhov*. New York, 1998.

Reyfman, Irina. *Vasilii Trediakovsky: The Fool of the "New" Russian Literature*. Stanford, 1991.

Robb, Graham. *Balzac: A Biography*. New York, 1996.

Scheler, Max. *Person and Self-Value: Three Essays*, ed. M. S. Frings. Dordrecht, 1987.

Shklovsky, Viktor. *The Knight's Move*. Normal, 2005 (1923).

———. *The Theory of Prose*. Normal, 1990 (1925).

Siddiqi, Asif A. "Imagining the Cosmos: Utopians, Mystics, and the Popular Culture of Spaceflight in Revolutionary Russia," *Osiris*, 23 (1), 2008.

Thackston, Wheeler M. Preface to *The Baburnama: Memoirs of Babur, Prince and Emperor*. New York, 2002.

Troyat, Henri. *Tolstoy.* New York, 2001 (1965).

Volkov, Solomon. *St. Petersburg: A Cultural History.* New York, 1995.

Wachtel, Andrew. "Resurrection à la Russe: Tolstoy's *The Living Corpse* as Cultural Paradigm," *PMLA*, 107 (2), 1992.

Zholkovsky, Alexander. "How a Russian Maupassant Was Made in Odessa and Yasnaya Polyana: Isaak Babel' and the Tolstoy Legacy," *Slavic Review*, 53 (33), 1994.